Anti-Electra

A UNIVOCAL BOOK

Drew Burk, Consulting Editor

Univocal Publishing was founded by Jason Wagner and Drew Burk as an independent publishing house specializing in artisanal editions and translations of texts spanning the areas of cultural theory, media archaeology, continental philosophy, aesthetics, anthropology, and more. In May 2017, Univocal ceased operations as an independent publishing house and became a series with its publishing partner the University of Minnesota Press.

Univocal authors include:

Miguel Abensour
Judith Balso
Jean Baudrillard
Philippe Beck
Simon Critchley
Fernand Deligny
Jacques Derrida
Vinciane Despret
Georges Didi-Huberman
Jean Epstein
Vilém Flusser
Barbara Glowczewski
Évelyne Grossman
Félix Guattari
David Lapoujade
François Laruelle
David Link

Sylvère Lotringer
Jean Malaurie
Michael Marder
Serge Margel
Quentin Meillassoux
Friedrich Nietzsche
Peter Pál Pelbart
Jacques Rancière
Lionel Ruffel
Michel Serres
Gilbert Simondon
Étienne Souriau
Isabelle Stengers
Eugene Thacker
Elisabeth von Samsonow
Siegfried Zielinski

A N T I

The Radical Totem of the Girl

ELECTRA

Elisabeth von Samsonow

Translated by Anita Fricek and Stephen Zepke

University of Minnesota Press
Minneapolis
London

The University of Minnesota Press gratefully acknowledges the financial assistance provided for the publication of this book by the Academy of Fine Arts Vienna.

The University of Minnesota Press acknowledges the contribution of Jason Wagner, Univocal's publisher, in making this volume possible.

Originally published in German as *Anti-Elektra: Totemismus und Schizogamie,* copyright by diaphanes, Zürich-Berlin 2007.

Published by the University of Minnesota Press
111 Third Avenue South, Suite 290
Minneapolis, MN 55401-2520
http://www.upress.umn.edu

Printed in the United States of America on acid-free paper

The University of Minnesota is an equal-opportunity educator and employer.

23 22 21 20 19   10 9 8 7 6 5 4 3 2 1

Library of Congress Cataloging-in-Publication Data
Names: von Samsonow, Elisabeth, author.
Title: Anti-Electra : the radical totem of the girl / Elisabeth von Samsonow; translated by Anita Fricek and Stephen Zepke. Other titles: Anti-Elektra. English
Description: Minneapolis : University of Minnesota Press, 2019. | Series: Univocal | "A Univocal book." | Includes bibliographical references.
Identifiers: LCCN 2018037440 (print) | ISBN 978-1-5179-0713-6 (pb)
Subjects: LCSH: Feminist theory. | Electra complex. | Girls. | Totemism. | Social psychiatry.
Classification: LCC HQ1190 .S2425 2019 (print) | DDC 305.4201–dc23
LC record available at https://lccn.loc.gov/2018037440

For Gaia

Contents

Acknowledgments | ix

Preface to the English Language Edition | xiii

Introduction | 1

1. Electra as Female "Oedipus" | 7

Positive Unrelatedness and Exogamy | 26

Constitutive Strangeness or Primary Exoticism | 46

Schizogamy | 51

Xenological Anamnesis | 58

Totemistic "Objectification" | 62

2. Radical Totemism and Automatism | 65

Theogenesis and the Twilight of Machines | 65

Totem and Xenocracy | 69

Animal Mummy and the Apparatus-Function | 73

Anthropomorphization of the Deity | 82

Apparatus or Weak Totem | 88

3. Totemism and Sculpture: Preliminaries
   to a Theory of Schizosoma | 95

   Metabolism and Therapeutic Schizosoma | *103*

   Pre-oedipality as a "Plastic Phase" | *106*

   Excursus: Plasma, Forming, Sculpture | *116*

   The Statue Delivering Oracles | *119*

   The Two-Body Doctrine | *126*

   The One and the Many | *131*

   Social Sculpture | *136*

4. The Labyrinth: General Theory
   of Schizosoma | 147

   Pasiphae's Cow | *150*

   The Satellite | *156*

5. The Four Pre-oedipal Objects | 163

   Failing Equalization and the Emergence of the Complex | *167*

   Electrification | *169*

Appendix: Solyanka State Gallery | 181

Notes | 191

Acknowledgments

NATURALLY, THIS BOOK HAS more mothers than fathers. It is dedicated to the memory of the splendidly impressive thinker Gerburg Treusch-Dieter, the pioneer and guide, who died on November 19, 2006. In October of that year we had the chance to talk about this book, and as always she listened closely and replied very constructively. I have built my theoretical construction on her shoulders in the hope of continuing her work. The last chapter on the labyrinth is dedicated to Renate Lachmann, whose mental and linguistic agility I treasure. I am obviously connected to her by an unresolved labyrinth complex, which makes her my spiritual mother and me her daughter. I lay the same chapter at the feet of my endlessly admired friend Friederike Mayröcker as a token of my affection. From her I have learned that writing is always an incomplete completion and a complete incompletion. Anti-Electra has the nimble and profound Ina Rösing in her backpack; her rare visits were like a wonder of nature and gave me back a joy for my work, opening up a future I no longer dared to think was possible inside the empire of the institution. Her understanding of the house, the most beautiful characteristic of a universal ecosophy, shone like a torch guiding my philosophical path back to earth. The book is also for my philosophical friends Arno Böhler and Susanne Granzer, the first really existing electrical couple, who immediately anticipated its contents and in their conviction of its effectiveness gave me a stage on which I could help Electra to find her voice. It is for Victor Faessel, my intelligent doctoral student who came to me from Japan through a calling over continents and who has been a decisive help. It is for Dorothea May, my housemate in Hades, whose rich and subtle experience helped me to test my ideas with my students under laboratory-like conditions. It is also for Peter Sloterdijk, who in fact has no time but who nevertheless dealt with my ideas and, through a form of positive background radiation, helped them prosper. It is for Erwin Wurm, another resident of the Dionysian fields, who shares my cheerful and productive fate of being stuck in the pre-oedipal phase. It is for Christian Rasch as well, my Dionysus, who let me see and hear the existential insecurity of men. I thank Hans Belting for overseeing my intuition that his clearly contoured, strong theses were predestined for feminine revision. Anti-Electra is for the women of the organization Frauenhetz in Vienna who twice invited me to lecture and discuss my ideas about the female child. I thank Gotthard Fellerer, Lizzy Mayrl, and all my artist and philosopher colleagues who so lightly and full of phantasy participated in the ritual animation of my statue of Electra. Finally, I have Eric Alliez, the father of my daughter, to thank, insofar as my close friendship with him over many years amounted to the erection of a post-structuralist French embassy in my house, and who gave me the idea to finally answer the Anti-Oedipus with the Anti-Electra. I thank my endlessly competent and prompt publishers Sabine Schulz and Michael Heitz, whose critical comments meant the fruit did not fall from the tree before it had ripened, and Elisabeth Schicketanz, who with great patience went through the imposition of the anarchic editing of the manuscript with me.

And I thank my students, whose questions and critical interjections made the journey through the thicket a shared adventure.

Translators' Acknowledgments

The translators would like to thank Victor Faessel, whose nearly complete earlier translation of the book was an indispensable reference for our own work, and Drew Burk, whose patience and sympathy were always appreciated.

Preface to the English Language Edition

AS THE TITLE OF THIS BOOK indicates, it was conceived of as the feminist counterpart to Gilles Deleuze and Félix Guattari's *Anti-Oedipus*. By making this resounding statement, one can immediately see how the book that follows will be inextricably snared and engaged within a much longer and rather complex history. *Anti-Electra* inscribes itself onto the intertextual planes of *Anti-Oedipus* as unfolded by Deleuze and Guattari while also maintaining a conversation with the numerous other tightly woven threads of feminist theory. It attempts to make use of and further the many endeavors that have been achieved in order to give shape to the notion of "woman," in all its mythical as well as political connotations, by sometimes even emphasizing to the extreme those aspects that make feminist theory more than a pleasant occupation. By suggesting to follow the logics of the nonmale and, by doing so, if necessary, exaggerating the anomalies entailed by the signifier "woman," I was hoping to touch upon peak moments in this field, a field populated with so many traps, dead ends, and vicious circles.

Consequently, the productive point from which to start became the one distinctive argument that formed

the common ground or structure of both feminist theory and psychoanalysis: the idea of the eccentric position
of the feminine and its latent and manifest effects. This
eccentricity—meaning a noncentered qua nonidentical or
nonnormative position—was successfully emphasized by
radical anti-Freudians such as Luce Irigaray and Christina von Braun.[1] However, in the aftermath of the early
success of these aforementioned thinkers, this eccentricity at the heart of feminist theory would find its utility and
effectiveness under the guise of quite different debates.
There is a whole field of notions engaged in the debates
on the female that repeatedly highlights its eccentric position. This eccentricity, that seems to provide the logical
as well as social, political, and technical dimensions to
the feminine, has been revised, reaffirmed, and contin-
ually reformulated over the past forty years in a process
that has turned the eccentric feminist argument first into
a question for theories on cyberspace and the cyberthe-
oretical (by Donna Haraway), then into a basis for queer
and transgender theories, as well as discussions concerning the equality of things and subjects,[2] and finally into
debates around theories of the posthuman.[3] Through this
vast staging of a theoretical *événement* that has quite quickly
belabored and reduced formally similar arguments into
one single current, this "eccentric position" must be recognized as something extremely powerful. Recently, Rosi
Braidotti has even offered additional urgent thoughts to
the constellation of eccentricity, arguing that the notion
of "sexual difference" has been subjected to such an infla-
tionary value that it has led to a paradoxical new unifor-
mity of thought.

A myriad of philosophers—"postmodern" (Lyotard),
"deconstructive" (Derrida), "microphysical" (Foucault),
"critical" (Deleuze), and still others—have first sexual-
ized the question of difference and, second, have turned

it into a generalized philosophical item.[4] The tendency to turn the feminine position into a quality, a functor, an atmosphere, a regulatory principle, can be strongly felt, and this is exactly what interests me. For even the latest essays on these topics—namely, the markedly posthumanist feminist ones, such as *The Xenofeminist Manifesto* by Laboria Cuboniks—do not seem to provide any new insights except to reaffirm this very same logical figure of (feminine) eccentricity.[5]

The feminine becoming a philosophical principle— might this mean there is a matriarchic theologization on the horizon? To me, these debates appear much more like symptoms; they are not so much elaborate, well-grounded theories than indicators all seeming to point in the same direction. What appears to be at stake here—besides simply touching upon feminism—has much more to do with a radical paradigm shift: a melting down of the well-known signifiers that have organized thought up until now. However, in light of these recent theories, it is perhaps productive to make an effort to update, contextualize, and sharpen the theoretical vectors detailed in this book. This might be beneficial in order to map the multidimensionality of the ongoing discussions and offer a diagnosis of all the symptoms within an appropriate constellation; it might also help to provide a precise contour to the specific issue this book takes as its central concern.

Contextualizing the Girl: The Energies of the Noncenter

Unlike the vast majority of feminist works, this book does not emphasize the figure of the woman but instead focuses on the figure of the girl. Feminism tends to righteously address the features and structures ascribed to the woman as *the problem* to overcome. But every woman passes through a becoming-woman—a notion coined by Deleuze and Guattari—that makes the *not-yet-woman,* the figure of becoming that is *not yet* or only indirectly involved in the social and cultural programs, quite an attractive figure for theoretical exploration. It was no coincidence that Deleuze and Guattari granted the becoming-woman, followed up by a becoming-girl, a pole position in the reorganization of subjectivity. The girl is the one endowed with all hope and future. The not-yet-woman is a potential, a promise, which is precisely why I shifted my theoretical focus to the girl. The girl is in a paradoxical position of being both much less and much more charged than a "woman," simultaneously engendering the negative commentaries on the girl and the figure's collaborative nature (as in the case of Tiqqun's book *Preliminary Materials for a Theory of the Young-Girl*)[6] as well as positive commentaries found, for example, in some existing advanced theoretical romanticisms. The girl as a concept and as a figure escaped gender trouble as long as it was kept concealed by her mother's multiply marked and domesticated body stimulating endless critique and analysis; it has bypassed the gender bias to which it does not belong. This is why "the girl" forms a theoretical ground and material ripe for providing an outline of a future world.

The (Freudian) assumption of a girl neutralized by her awareness of lack (of the penis) was still guiding the first feminist wave in the seventies. It took the girl for a deficient woman, not yet fully "mature" in terms of subjectivation, for something neutral more in the sense of a thing than a person endowed with the power for action. The girl was further thought to underlie the castration complex and be, of course, oedipalized, in this way—in full contradiction—simultaneously being doubly devalued as a not-yet-woman and a castrated being. This would form the obvious criteria for why the girl is regularly "left out" of theoretical discussions. But from our current contemporary vantage point, things are beginning to look a bit different. This "being-left-out," all these conditional modes contained in her position, is obviously charged with explosive material, and therefore the girl's position is much more than just a feature of immaturity and of a not-yet, which is why it comes back as an organizing principle of postmodern debates. Furthermore, the girl's "qualities" seemed to have productively reaffected the model of the woman and the feminine while the debates got stuck in the program of gender bias. "Girlish" eccentricity became viral through the concept Rosi Braidotti names "nomadic subjects"; it was viral (on a technical level) in Haraway's cyborgism and it is viral in what I call "epidemic subjects."[7] Via this effect, it becomes quite evident that the concept of "woman" was pushed toward its very eccentricity much less by the "dominant" figure of the male, who may have achieved this in a malign action of strategic exclusion, than by the woman's magnetic satellite or eccenter, *the girl.*

The girl bypasses the gender binary. She highlights, if not creates, the asymmetric position of the female in relation to the male. This is why the girl is a great point of departure when issues surrounding gender have to get revised, analyzed, fought, or undone. In this respect, I follow Luce Irigaray's argument that the "woman" must be considered through the "modalities" of mother and daughter, and I agree as well that a strong emphasis must be placed on the intergenerational factor as a logical prerequisite that works like a bond or (affective) link. Luce Irigaray's intuitions regarding this topic have been quite precise. Irigaray's stroke of genius was to have supposed that the fear of castration (which was considered as inevitable since castration would have always already happened in the case of the girl who does not have a penis) was more of an allegory of a lost origin than a phantasmatic or real organic defect.[8]

But unlike Irigaray, I do not place the mother in a dominant position that would, as a consequence, introduce a sort of ontological "fetalization"[9] run amok following the theological model and thereby creating a female metaphysics of the womb.[10] Irigaray proposes a highly differentiated idea of the "feminine-mother" as a (mute) substratum of space that is invisible, quoted by Elisabeth Grosz as the "spaceless ground of space and visibility."[11] If, according to my argument, the girl is (chronologically and logically) the a priori of a woman, then the girl offers not only a generational or dynastic position but a logical starting point (as a conditional, since there is no woman without girl). Beyond the age-old discussion regarding the chicken or the egg, the girl is apt to provide a starting point since the story of women begins with that of girls. But beginning with the girl does not define a true beginning; it is more of a question and means for introducing a principle that is able to reorganize the various fields of forces. The girl—and here she is called Electra—walks on stage the moment a so-called symbolic order of the girl begins to become manifest.

But the girl does not only serve as principle of that kind because of her very specific (non)position, which, by the way, labels her as definitively complicit with the boy in the guise of (Pre-)Oedipus; the girl's importance is also derived by way of the symptoms of crisis she expresses. It is her crisis that makes her interesting, in a Hölderlinian way who supposes in a beautiful line that the crisis would itself provide the means for escaping from it.[12] Unlike some other recent examples of feminist literature, I consider the position of the girl less as a motive or as an imperative for transgressing the gender binary in a trajectory toward the posthuman, object-oriented, new materialist, postgender, or, at very least, the queer and transgender model—I think that all these directives draw proper conclusions in their own right and are each rather intense and convincing. However, I prefer the analytical mode of regression or tracing back, which is why I end up with a different reading of the conflictual "not-yet" and the "in-between" of the feminine in the girl. In stark contrast to Tiqqun's facile diagnosis of the girl—and her lack of profiled (self-)definition—as a cheap prostitute and super collaborator of the turbo- or hypercapitalist regime, I consider the girl's mysterious "latency" as a hint that must be taken very seriously. I strive to seek out and uncover the reasons for this "latency" and its possible psychic, social, and political functions and uses by granting "the girl" the status of an organizing principle according to the methodology of regression and retracing. I felt compelled to scroll backward through the entire history of the concept of the girl's latency so as to carefully retrace and follow its viral ruptures, breaks, and concealments. Because would it not be fully contradictory to state the position of the girl as productively nondefined in this way and then consequently fight to grant this concept of the girl more power and a more thorough definition? How then can we deal with the fact that the girl equals the (affective, social, economic, technical) *infrastructure*? How can we think of "dominant latency" or an all-organizing infrastructure?

Not-yet, Latent, In-between, Electric, Empathic

It looks as if the girl was something to come. But my diagnosis is more radical. I consider the concept of the girl as something that is there and already fully impregnates the contemporary world: The girl is the climate, the atmosphere, the quality, the complex architecture of things. To say something like this presupposes what I have already pointed out in the paragraphs above: namely, that the term *woman* and especially the term *girl* tend to turn into abstract or philosophical principles and demand to be recognized in their proper place. The exercise to be achieved is accomplished the moment it becomes feasible to think of a symbolic order "in the name-of-the girl."

The main thesis of this book is that focusing on the Electra complex or the figure of the girl provides the framework for understanding the fundamental shift we seem to be experiencing today in some of our most common views concerning media and art. The critique and deconstruction of the Electra complex—which is what all the early feminists took as their task—reaches its goal when the Electra complex's central thesis is dispensed of: namely, love of the father and hatred of the mother. This "hatred of the mother" reread at the level of a hypothetical symbolic order of the girl would seem to have implications for social structures, technology, and ecology. What if the Electra complex and its hatred of the mother were dismantled and uncovered as being a propaganda trick? What if, on the contrary, the relationship between the girl and the mother forms the original relationship from which all acts of empathy, solidarity, and friendship stem? What if the relationship between the girl and the mother was the origin of all flows and distributions of energy, the original electric thing? There is a relationship between the mother and the girl, there is "relation," there is contact, there is a continuum. To the extent that modern and contemporary media tend to be "techniques of relations/binding/bonding," this present book shows how the girl, the girl's electric body, would play a central role in "connecting," in staying connected (with the mother, from whose continent she is never expelled, unlike the son who undergoes the incest taboo). Eccentricity as a key feature of the "girl" (as opposed to the boy's asymmetry) is nourished precisely through its very relationship to "mother," who, similar to Irigaray's conclusion, forms a plane charged with manifold codes that are spatial, metaphysical, energetic,

logical, and social. In this sense the "girl," namely Electra, represents not only the contemporary perfume in the
paradoxical function of latent dominance or infrastructure. While modern philosophy has privileged difference,
analysis, and an existential "outside" that was of course
performed at its best by Oedipus, the main argument of
this book proposes an alternative guideline along with the
trajectories designed by the girl's being-in-the-world. This
is not only a hypothesis on the quality of ambiance, of a
social structure that is organized around networks, electronic clouds, (inter)nets, and total control producing
an invisible womb, but a strong hint regarding the girl's
potentials explicated and performed by the appropriate
technical means. The girl is the origin of technique, the
concept's major reference, as the girl is the self-reflexive
body able to produce bodies. There is no technique that
would not embrace and try to copy this core in a "Frankenstein" manner.[13]

The plasticity of art or the art of plasticity emerge
along with the girl's (real, capitalist) capacity of production (bodies, human bodies). The girl, the anti-Electra,
forms the *energy* of the contemporary world: Electra's name
already evoking the spark springing from amber—in other
words, "electricity." Consequently, the main thesis of the
book presents an interpretation of contemporary technics,
arguing that today's technologies encompass Electra's gadgets and toys. Satellite-driven technologies like wireless
telephones, WLAN, and GPS echo the "pre-oedipal constellation" in which the girl specializes. Understanding the
Electra narrative is to recognize the "false" symbolic attribution of the earth system that had conditioned (Western) humanity to remain in Electra's problematic position
(hating the mother). "Sexed" bodies appear as secondary
bodies derived from the Earth's constitutive principles,
bodies that may now escape cultural rigorism.

The most important (symbolic and political) consequence of a rehabilitation of the mother–daughter relationship is therefore a change of viewpoints, a new viewpoint concerning the Earth, which is repeatedly considered
as "mother." The Electra complex, as it was programmed
by either the Greek dramatists or Freud, mirrors the damaged bond between humankind and the Earth. The rupture
between humankind and everything else that "remains" in
nature represents a gnostic problem. The symbolic order
of the girl can intervene by offering another form of access
to the Earth in the position of "mother" (or the Earth as
a bipolar electric-sexual thing) by constructing a passage
away from krypto-earth or earth-oblivion.

Radical Totemism

One way the book explores this "escape" is through the
bond between the girl and the animal that represents
"the mother" in her prehuman aspect. With the help of
"the girl," the cartography of overlapping zones between
humankind and animals, as well as between humankind
and apparatuses (as gadgets), is reconfigured through
what the book will name "radical totemism." The totemic
model is one of the main themes considered as a central
tenet in the present work, as I argue that it fits perfectly
into the symbolic order of the girl as its social theory. The
totemic object further introduces a set of differentiated
values connecting animals, gadgets, toys, subjects, and
intelligent media that must be urgently analyzed in order
to understand the communicative architecture of the contemporary world. This point welcomes the posthumanist
argument. The "radical totemism" proposed in this book
addresses the Earth as the relevant totem from which all
other totems may be derived.[14] Taking into account that the
family nucleus that was Oedipus's proper stage was built to
place the child under pressure (in order to form a glue, a

link, a catalytic bond for the fatal binary complex of the "parents"), there is a strong motive to break it open in favor of an additional constituent: namely, the nonhuman actor or totem, which consoles the child, inducing the girl to feel empathic with it, and explains how complex it is to be engaged in a becoming-human.

In order to establish a "radical totemism," we had to dig back up the archaeological evidence from early childhood and ask the neuralgic questions: How does the original relationship between the child and the mother (in the form of a landscape of affective organs) become transferred to appropriate objects? In other words, how does this relationship encounter and engage with the world?[15] Does it make sense to postulate, based on the idea of the early experience of the mother-as-landscape of organs, that the possible candidates for relationship will be found among humans as well as among nonhumans (the latter echoing and incorporating the affective memory of the "prehuman") in a way that both human and nonhuman partners stabilize erotic, empathic, and informatic activity? In parallel with the subtitle of Deleuze and Guattari's *Anti-Oedipus,* in the original German-language edition of my book I chose to provide a similar subtitle for *Anti-Electra*: "Totemism and Schizogamy." Schizogamy here refers to the marriage rule that plays a central role in the concepts that anthropology provides in terms of understanding social cohesion. The prefix "schizo" is much less dramatic than it would be in the subtitle from *Anti-Oedipus,* "schizophrenia." It serves as a reminder concerning the layered construction of relationships as an activity of transferring original evidence, meaning that the construction of relationships shifts the original scene of love for the affective landscape of organs to appropriate partners (humans and nonhumans). This process ends up in a triangulation of a very different kind creating a constellation of the lover, the loved, and the totem—the last of these echoing the primal partner or prehuman "mother" ("schizogamy"). In the end, are not those totems—apparatuses, gadgets, electronic devices—manifestations of Electra's characteristic: electricity, which equals Earth's epiphany? The model of schizogamy rooted in early activity of building relationships can be seen as a key for the symbolic order of the girl. In my view, the many impressive attempts, for example by OOO theoreticians and posthumanism, claiming equality among all beings can be read as symptoms of a transformation in the direction of the "symbolic girl." In this sense, the anti-Electra gives way to a thought bridging feminist, posthumanist, and new materialist perspectives by suggesting another symbolic order. It is precisely these recent developments in affirming another possible symbolic order that have led me to propose a new subtitle for the English-language edition of *Anti-Electra*: "The Radical Totem of the Girl."

The Symbolic Order of the Girl and the Schizosoma

Dare to imagine such a thing as the symbolic order of the girl. What might this be? How may things such as latency, eccentricity, and the nonoedipalized attached to the figure of the girl ever appear at the level of the symbolic? From my viewpoint, I would claim that anti-Electra works as an operator for the transformation of the symbolic order. But, is not the "girlish" just the antithesis of everything that qualifies for that? As I said, the girl equals the infrastructure that is differentiated from superstructure. In the age of electronic networks, subliminal patterns, nanotechnologies, and transterrestrial architectures of interaction, the given symbolic order ("the name of the father") is deficient, as its official-myth-producing, imperative, top-down gestures conceal those things that actually drive the whole machinery (the "soft" ware). The symbolic order of the girl is therefore "public relations" on all levels—i.e., the going-public of the infra-things (instead of the supra-things), the politics of infinite conditionalities, and the plane of liminality and of the full recognition of the primacy or primordial presence of life. The psychic and vital impetus or impacts (unconsciously) grounding, pervading, or animating the world are the domain of the symbolic girl. This is why the symbolic girl, in a first step, is a conspiracy theorist: Because conspiracy works as a guideline or preparatory means for infrastructural awareness. As the girl is empathic with the imaginary child, she is the prophet as well as the spy of life, connected to life through her body-producing body, which puts her in a schizosomatic position. Schizosoma is the body shared by the many, the populated earth as a system manifested by infinite bodies arranged in an infinitely expanded schizosomatic cosmic concerto. The schizosomatic pole of subjectivation is provided by the girl who forms the original or intimate binomial body (the mother–daughter schizosoma). This is exactly why the girl must be understood as symbolic: Because she works as a philosophical principle reorganizing the vectors and functors of the fields of power, energy, and intelligence. Unlike within the framework of the given symbolic order ("the name of the father"), it is impossible to shape a structure like theology under the premise of the girl. So what will the principles of this new order look like? This is why Bruno Latour was besieged with great difficulties in striving to posit a non- or posttheological interpretation of Gaia and the Earth in his recent lectures—namely, what does a nontheological goddess look like? What is the relationship between the "people of the Earth" and this nontheological goddess?[16] The symbolic order of the girl provides access to this posthuman macroconstellation without disposing of the necessary potentials of subjectivation.

Introduction

ELECTRA IS "THE RADIANT SUN." *Electron* describes pale gold (a special alloy of silver and gold), as well as amber and amber coral.[1] Whereas the technical and scientific career of the *electron* took off and became the conceptual and energetic center of an electrified and electronic world,[2] the woman named after this abundant brilliance, after that spark emitted from the bright stone, a daughter of the Atreides, was trapped inside a strange story. For about one hundred years, so since the invention of the Oedipus complex, Electra has been Oedipus's female counterpart (even if Freud did not mean for this to happen and did not grant women the right to have their own complex that would mark their sexuality).[3] Electra is the mannequin on which Oedipus hangs like a coat. Her "name, 'amber,' suggests the paternal cult of the Hyperborean Apollo,"[4] and from then on she is destined to demonstrate what it means to hate the mother and love the father. But the phantasy goes wrong if one now imagines a father bewitching the daughter, a father who perhaps succumbs to her youthful charm, to her irresistible *petites fesses,* and who lifts the daughter over the incest barrier and into his bed. In the end—according to the Greek logic of tragedy by which one violation of divine law produces another—this will lead to the murder of the mother (who had proba- bly reproached the young girl appropriately). The attrac- tion between older or aging men and young women (it is quite commonplace for men today to lead two lives one after the other, by marrying females from two successive generations, while women are left with only *one* life or *one* so-called erotic career—and usually a short one)[5] could well be underpinned and interpreted psychoanalytically by a mythologem reporting something similar. But in the Greek versions of Electra there is no father in love with his daughter. Agamemnon's desire to sacrifice his daughter Iphigenia to attain success in war is not characterized by such softness. What this means, however, is that one has to read from the impassioned perspective of the daugh- ter whose love—and here we are already caught up in the middle of the onstage action—only really ignites when her father is dead. When she finally becomes aware of whom she loves, her father is not lying in the incest bed with her but in his grave. What is going on? Why is Electra not *permitted*? Why is it that Electra should be the Oedipus of femininity? There are many open questions here, and it is high time to add a second ending to the one Gilles Deleuze and Félix Guattari gave to the oedipal delirium of mama– papa–child in their *Anti-Oedipus,* an ending in which the Electra complex implodes through its precise and compre- hensive analysis. This second ending cannot simply be a philological exegesis of the drama, nor an unfurling of the Greek understanding of the fatal genus, species, or tribe, nor a psychoanalytical debate that energetically attempts to rearrange the mama–papa–child triangle. The analysis will have to connect parallel but widely separated threads of history and memory—no easy task—and will have to pil- lage the archives, imaginarium and iconography of cults and religions, as well as the hyper- and subtexts of cultural

history, art history, and the history of religion. First, this
will remind us of a form of identification of the female
child that has been almost entirely erased or omitted in
theory, and second, it will refute, or at least structurally
extend, the family drama of mama–papa–child in order to
evade the disastrous role given to Electra and the collective
phantasies attached to her. In this sense, I unhesitatingly
affirm Félix Guattari's thesis that the oedipal triangle is
too small a frame for the contemporary psyche, and along
with others I share the belief that this triangle was already,
in the twentieth century, too narrow to produce an adequate analysis. But this is still not sufficient as a criterion
for psychic mechanisms and, in particular, the genesis of
gender identity. Guattari does not fix the psyche in the
triangle but immediately has it jump into a square, where
surprisingly the four terms marking out this extensive
landscape are not—as one might think—papa–mama–boy-
girl but the machinic phylum, the flux of libido and capital, the immaterial symbolic constellations, and the territory. Optimally, the oedipal triangle mutates through this
square into a vector that puts the square's terms into relation. Guattari interlaces the history of contingent identity,
or singularity, with the histories and systems of transpersonal signs, traffic, goods, places, and their meanings.[6]
This undertaking—a demonstration of how Marxist schizo-
analysis implodes the triangle—encourages our own investigation of Electra to break new exploratory ground, to
make Electra's relationship to mama and papa visible, and
to examine its circumstances in a way that Freudian analysis does not allow. Necessarily connected to this insight is
another: that analytic principles often obscure the problem they pretend to solve. Consequently, our new insights
may not be the final word, but they will have at least shifted
the meridian along which the discussion of the theme of
the mama–papa–child most persistently oscillated and so

reveal more clearly than ever before the true contingency of the Freudian position.

The field on which the tragic figure of Electra emerges is surrounded by a thicket of rampantly mythologizing and psychologizing interpretations that we can cut through with multipurpose tools—carefully selected *tools* that are modern as well as archaic. In order to envision this figure within the complexity of her world, and to finally establish her inherent rights, a succession of beings, persons, and media will have to be explored whose deep connection with the realm of the girl have thus far not been apparent.

For a start, *totemism* offers a new structure that will be used to lift the veil covering the symbolic horizon of the girl. Totemism reveals the significance of the relationship to the animal, which for the girl is the equivalent of the relationship to the mother thematized in the Oedipus complex, and elucidates its erotic, social, and political explosiveness. After this, we will scan those valencies of the girl's imaginary that are relevant to the foundation of technology, including modern technology, within the context of media theory's analysis of the meaning of otherness in the human relationship to animals. This would imply that the girl, whose neutrality prevents her from advancing onto the level of the signifier, operates instead as a matrix of contemporary aspects of cultural and technical "business." But insofar as the suppression of the girl coincides structurally and temporally with the founding of the Greek *polis,* our investigation must first explore her older cultural layers. In order to determine the specific orientation of a society and culture that places its highest symbolic value in the girl, we will start from the strong femininity implied by the principle of a body–body relation (*schizosoma*). In this relationship, the institutionalized bond between mother and daughter is understood positively because it is not, in contrast to the mother–son relationship described in the Oedipus complex, incestuous and subject to prohibition.

The concept of *schizosoma* will illuminate the empire of the plastic arts [*Plastischen*], a realm that is not understood here as an academic artistic discipline but rather as a form of experience and as a productive technology. The plastic arts belong to the girl as the phantasm characterizing her drive and are connected to her power of "making humans" as well as to her becoming. Besides the fabrication of cult images and dolls, the phantasmatic work of "making humans" also includes the production of mummies and shows that when the girl puts her potency to work symbolically, birth and death coincide. The common equation—or rather pairing—of death and the girl will make a theoretical excursion into the underworld inevitable, where we will journey into the hypogeum, into the place of the unborn, into the labyrinth. While the connection between mother and son in the Oedipus complex is treated as prior, and as a nonprohibited relationship, the figure of the girl in the Electra complex remains somehow blurred, like a shadow standing in the shadow of the father. Electra functions as "spare parts" for her already sacrificed older sister Iphigenia; she is always already a potential candidate for sacrifice, addicted to the king of sacrifice. This girl waiting to be sacrificed is locked up in a labyrinth, and the specific constructions of body and space found in the analysis of the plastic arts will have to be reviewed in relation to it. The girl in the underworld is archetypically Kore or Persephone, but Electra is another example. A disturbed relationship with the mother is a necessary consequence of the girl being appointed as a sacrificial victim. Significantly, the Electra complex has remained blurry, *almost a complex,* the result of her vague status as the sacrificial victim in an act that is always impending (not a *devenir fiancée* but a *devenir sacrifée*[7]). In contrast to this, we propose a *strong girl* who is destined to be queen (as a successor of Clytemnestra, despite everything): the *anti–Electra.* That is to say, on the large scale of globalism, an Electra complex would mean that the hatred of the mother is directed against the Earth. A system that includes the sacrifice of the girl inevitably involves an all too dominant mother who is then subjected to general aggression. What is at stake here is the *justification of the Earth itself,* as the schizosoma the girl forms with the mother (a binomial of corporeality) is itself marked by injury and imbalance, deranged by the rage of Demeter who searches for the sacrificed daughter (and who hides her guilt under a veil of mourning). But if the girl returns, if she could end the story of her shadowy existence, how would the schizomatic relationship of humans with the huge body of the Earth (whom they call *Mother*) take shape? Would the Earth be a "Mother" at all if the girl was put back in her proper place, ending her disfiguration and displacement? Ariadne, the daughter of Pasiphae, was the one who returned from the labyrinth. She had the red thread. Is she anti-Electra?

1

Electra as Female "Oedipus"

ELECTRA'S SUITABILITY AS A FEMALE Oedipus is uncertain
from the outset, not because Freud did not want a female
Oedipus, a tragic *Oedipette,* but because he wanted to let the
woman gently slide into an eternal penis envy (as the form
of the female unconscious), thus distinguishing Electra's
symbolic acts from those of Oedipus.[1] Freud saw women
as being morally immature and incompetent in their relationships and thus incapable of achieving consciousness
and tragic greatness.[2] But it is *precisely* Electra who casts
doubt on this view, the figure in whom systemic female
inferiority was supposedly incarnated in an exemplary
fashion. Instead, this young woman observes and comments on proceedings like an *embedded journalist,* one who is
absolutely and profoundly knowledgeable. While the tragic
hero Oedipus would be unthinkable as a virtual lover who
only phantasizes about embracing his mother, the incestuous *act* is only attributed to Electra as a phantasy, as a hallucination. Is this distinction separating the girl and the
young hero a "phase difference" between the love of the
man and the love of the woman?[3] But one could counter
that Oedipus did not want incest and that he did not know
that it was *his mother* with whom he was involved. Electra's

7

hallucination takes possession of him in reverse, and he ends up in a *physical* connection with the *not-mother* (as he believes). Electra, however, has a *nonphysical* connection with the *real* father. The result is that Oedipus acted without thinking and only then arrived at knowledge, whereas with Electra it is exactly the opposite: She thinks and knows but does not act. What Electra *cannot actualize* is her love for the father—an almighty bastard, a merciless killer, a battle-hardened warrior who sacrificed his daughter Iphigenia to the goddess for a favorable military wind. According to Jean Giraudoux, who rearranged the Greek material into a twentieth-century play, Electra only lay in her father's arms a single time, as she reports when she rushes to meet him upon his return home:

> From my cheek against his cheek I learnt of the heat of my father. Sometimes in the summer, the whole world is as hot as my father. It makes me faint. And I embraced him with these arms. I thought that I could take the measure of my love, but it became the measure of my vengeance. Then he was free, he mounted his horse again, more alive, more luminous! And Electra's attack was completed. I ran to the palace in order to see him again, but I wasn't running towards him, but towards you, his murderers.[4]

She is just waking up, she has just warmed herself on her father. She wants more of him, to see him again— and already he is dead. Her "action" is not as real, not as bombastic, as that of Oedipus. Oedipus kills his father, unknowingly but with his own hand, just as he unknowingly sleeps with his mother, but unlike Electra does so in a real and direct sense. Thus, one can insist that the suitability of the stories as analytical *narratives* depends on Oedipus and Electra acting in a bracketed or restricted way, partly active but also partly qualified and restricted: He does not know what he does and she does not do what she knows. There is an equivalence here inasmuch as they both amount to the same thing. Both withdraw their accountability, he in knowing and she in doing, a withdrawal that speaks the code of a collective phantasm. What is therefore tragic in the tragedy is what did not remain in the realm of phantasy, that terrible form of ontological excess that was not satisfied with simply remaining within the realm of internal images but wanted to penetrate or plunge into the real world. Like some kind of homicidal fantasy, something Melanie Klein tells us innocent babies regularly experience, and which in this case leads to murder—the murder of Oedipus's father, King Laius, or of Electra's mother, Clytemnestra. We shudder to think that such acts arise so easily from this abyss of irresponsibility, just as the audience shudders in recognition as the figures of the drama rush headlong to ruin along their paths of partial amnesia.

But what happens if Electra is neither incestuous nor its murderous opposite? Who actually kills her mother Clytemnestra now? As we saw, Electra is just a hanger-on who leaves the grand gesture, the heroic monstrosity to others. While Antigone chooses love and is content with it, Electra is all hate, mother-hate, but not enough to act. Even here—and the irony of this remark is irresistible—she is all woman. She prioritizes the man. She hisses into the ear of her brother, Orestes, until he is convinced that he has to murder his mother's lover Aegisthus, the unlawful king who occupies *his throne* and then his mother. In Hofmannsthal's text, Electra says to him:

> Then you will do it! You will do it alone?
> O you poor child.[5]

And he makes an effort to answer:

> I will do the deed,
> And I will do it quickly.

And then:

> ELECTRA: The deed is like a bed
> On which the soul reposes, like a bed
> Of balsam, where the soul can take its rest,
> The soul that is a wound, that is a blight,
> a-running and a burning!
>   . . .
> ELECTRA: Blessed alone is he that does his deed,
> Blessed is he who touches him, and digs
> The axe up out of the earth for him, and holds
> The torch for him, and opens the door wide.[6]

Hofmannsthal unmistakably constructs this scene as an unholy doublet to the Sermon on the Mount, although it is not the unshakable sufferer or the naive flower who is blessed but the perpetrator ("he who is coming to do his deed"). Electra adds that the assistant is also blessed, the one who passes the instrument and holds the door open. We should note that in Hofmannsthal's version, the great tension at the moment when Orestes enters the chamber of Clytemnestra causes Electra to "forget" to hand Orestes the hidden weapon, the very ax by which Agamemnon was murdered.

> ELECTRA: I have not given him the axe!
> They have gone in, and I have not given him the axe.
> There are no gods in heaven![7]

Her blessedness is gone. She is not even a good assistant in this shameful act, and it remains open as to how Orestes actually does the deed.

In Hofmannsthal, an overwhelmed Electra simply drops dead at the end of the play while Chrysothemis screams out for her brother; the last words of the play being "Orestes! Orestes!"[8]

Why has nobody ever come up with the idea to construct and popularize an Orestes complex? An Orestes complex that adds something specific to the Oedipus complex— namely, a model for the sublime hate of the stepfather that reflects back onto the now totally unavailable mother? Would not an Orestes complex lend itself wonderfully to a psychoanalytic commentary on the difficult child of divorced parents, so common today? The heir to the throne is exiled and his father, abandoned by the floating libido of the mother, has to be liquidated so that queens, such as Clytemnestra, can take consorts. After Clytemnestra and her lover Aegisthus have eliminated Agamemnon, her lawful husband and king, it is not only Electra's rage that heats up but that of the heir, and the son now becomes really dangerous. In contrast to Electra's motives, which are clearly impregnated by phantasy (she appears to compete with the mother in a rivalry between sexual power and the powerlessness of virginity), for Orestes there is more at stake. The flux of libido is complemented, or rather calculated by a flux of capital, by the power and honor upon which it is based. The line of succession is clearly conceived as patrilinear, in open contradiction to the strong figure of the mother. Clytemnestra appears as a powerful queen, covered in jewels, making her inferiority not entirely credible. She is a stay-at-home queen, war-damaged like Penelope, although she maliciously assaults Agamemnon rather than valiantly returning her husband's rights to him upon his return. How is it possible that the queen, as if it were nothing, is allowed to take a new husband while the legitimate king is still at war? What gives her such fabulous rights? Why does not Clytemnestra have to *automatically* abdicate in favor of Orestes when Agamemnon does not return, or die the moment when Orestes comes back? It is clear that the banishment of Orestes and the order to kill his father, a classic motif in heroic narratives, has to be discussed in relation to automatic inheritance. Nevertheless, one cannot get rid of the impression that the mighty mother, authorized to find a new husband, is the true anomaly of the story. Does she make a secret pact with the sacrificer, sacrificing the sacrificer so as to ensure that Electra remains without rank, place, or inheritance, nothing more than scum, refuse, garbage? Orestes's return appears not just as a vengeful homecoming but as the return of the *lawful* heir who is flattered by Electra and acts like a profiteer benefiting from nepotism. The Oresteia celebrates the young man who violates the mother's right and therefore truly deserves to be called his father's son. He is the only one who appears to act in the name of public interest, as everyone else seems driven by private obsessions and guided by individual resentment. How dare Clytemnestra inform us that Agamemnon has not been an agreeable husband? Is it appropriate for queens to so violently express their private opinions of their high-ranking husbands? Where is what Freud described as the kingship taboo, which stipulates that a dignitary has to conduct himself as if he were his state in miniature? The heroes who attempt to sail into their harbors after a long absence (Odysseus and Agamemnon) seem more like visitors honoring the territorial principles of place: drifters, groups of men who finally observe their long-postponed appointment with the chthonic goddess, the natural guardian of home, life, territory, children, and earth.

Clytemnestra is not only Helen's sister, on whose account the Trojan War was fought, but also the type of woman who had rights and, most of all, the distinct self-consciousness this implied. Could we assume that beyond oedipal and electral triangulations there is a collision of different understandings of the law, oppositions that can be construed as the origin of the polis—male versus female inheritance, territorial versus political power—and that entangle their subjects in even more far-reaching formations? At the very least there is something wrong here.

Orestes, the true heir to the throne and the only legitimate successor of his father, keeps close tabs on Aegisthus, the new king and Clytemnestra's lover (a difficult figure: unpleasant, somewhat pale, and even rendered by some authors as sympathetically naive). Clytemnestra resorts to the well-known, but usually unsuccessful, tactic of banishing the son to prevent his feared (anticipated) revenge. In truth, it is always banishment that prepares the avenger's return. One day Orestes comes home to the palace—changed, older, or in any case matured and sporting a beard. Like Oedipus he returns incognito. No tragedian would think to stage Electra leaving her gardener's hut to visit her mother in the palace as a recognition drama. The ones no longer recognized are always men. Electra (in Hofmannsthal she is the crazy pet of the palace, cowering in the corner, severely disturbed, or, we could say, damaged by her milieu) is not banished but merely married off to a farmer (or a gardener in Giraudoux). When Orestes returns, his prompter Electra stands next to him at the crucial moment in order to drive out his wobbly courage. Orestes has human, conciliatory, and filial doubts about assaulting the mother's flesh. Shortly before the decisive blow, as he dimly remembers a previous comfort, his determination begins to falter. Clytemnestra does not clench her fists in self-defense and, in fact, does something even more disarming than offering her throat; she bares her breast.

Wait, my son—no respect for this, my child?
The breast you held, drowsing away the hours,
soft gums tugging the milk that made you grow?[9]

The bewildered Orestes asks his faithful friend Pylades:

What will I do, Pylades?—I dread to kill my mother![10]

And Pylades, keeping to the plan, and not wanting his heroic friend to miss this opportunity to achieve the most tremendous act of his life, answers:

What of the future? What of the Prophet God Apollo,
the Delphic voice, the faith and oaths we swear?
Make all mankind your enemy not the gods.[11]

Only then is Orestes convinced, telling his friend:

O you win me over—good advice.[12]

Naturally, Electra is overjoyed that her mother is going to get her comeuppance, but the one who actually carries out the deed and who has to live with the consequences— Aeschylus unfolds this in fine psychological detail—is Orestes. After the act it is *he* who sees the Eumenides rise from the blood-soaked ground:

[ORESTES] look—like Gorgons,
shrouded in black, their heads wreathed,
swarming serpents!
—cannot stay, I must move on.
  . . .
[CHORUS LEADER] The blood's still wet on your hands.
It puts a kind of frenzy in you.[13]

In the continuation of the story in Aeschylus's *Eumenides*, Electra entirely disappears from the stage and it is the murderous son who talks to the shade of his mother. Orestes

alone is guilty, and the instigator has fallen into insignif-
icance. The Eumenides are not interested in her and this
should make us think. In the cosmic ledger Electra is not
considered worth haunting, she is too lightweight. The
bailiffs come by but want nothing of her.[14] As a result,
those who argue that the Electra complex is a uniquely
female complex underived from a male one must retouch
the image of Electra and paint her deed in more glow-
ing colors. Hendrika C. Halberstadt-Freud, for example, writes: "Electra, however, has over a period of many
years planned the cold-blooded murder of her mother,
and carries out the act with cunning and trickery."[15] In this
way, the idea is reinforced that Electra is the equivalent
of Oedipus; Electra: mother-hater = mother-murderer.
The figure of Electra could possibly be sketched as a poly-
morphous hater, but what would be great about this hate?
Is there really something interesting about Electra apart
from her pathological condition? First, she hates herself,
then her mother (who has anything but an easy fate), and
then the mother's lover. Perhaps she even secretly hates her
brother Orestes, whom she bewitches and, in Giraudoux's
version of the play, offers the outrageous phantasy of their
parentless birth to make the mother expendable:

> I do not strangle you. . . . I do not kill you. . . . I
> caress you. I call you into life. From this fraternal mass,
> which in my confusion I had barely perceived, I form
> my brother in all his detail. Here, I formed the hand
> of my brother with its smooth, lovely thumbs. Next I
> create the breast of my brother and I breathe into it so
> that it rises and falls, and now my brother lives. Now I
> make his ear. . . . I should make it small, shouldn't I,
> with a firm edge and diaphanous like the wings of a bat?
> A last stroke and the ear is done. They've both come
> out quite the same—oh what a fine job I did on the ears!

> And now I form my brother's mouth, gently cold, and
> I nail it all, palpitating, on his face. . . . Take your life
> from me, Orestes, not from your mother![16]

Obviously a bit of Wälsung blood flows in these two. The incest barrier, if we finally want to mention it, must be securely erected not only between father and daughter but between the sister and brother who had every reason to imagine themselves as the young couple replacing the old.

But Electra, as we see in the quoted passage, wants to be intimate with her brother and goes as far as imagining—perhaps inspired by the family resemblance (they have exactly the same hair color)—that she is his creator. This phantasy may cover up something else (as is the general rule in the realm of the soul)—namely, the female inferiority complex in relation to the other sex that is expressed here as a kind of sublimated sibling rivalry. That Electra arranges herself so strongly around the dead father can also be read as meaning her fixation (i.e., her "oedipalization") cannot and will not be successful, because the attempted fixation and its object repel each other. As a result, Electra flees from the Electra complex and so falls back into what psychology describes as primary homosexuality. As Judith S. Kestenberg puts it: "There is a further correspondence where, at least in some cases, homosexuality among women means a flight from the positive Oedipus complex, resulting in a lingering father-identification. Sibling rivalry that leads to the identification with a brother and a frustrated longing for a child are frequently described as characteristics of female homosexuality."[17]

Perhaps it is too quick and convenient to see the homosexuality of the heroine as a theoretical triumph over the Electra complex. But such an interpretation, first, has the strategic advantage of introducing some movement into the solidified schizogenesis, and second, this opening introduces something like a multivalent relationality or a politics of relations that is consistent with the mythological dimension of the Electra narrative. In this interpretation, a game of open identifications is established, and the mama–papa–child cards are reshuffled. Homosexuality is privileged in our investigation because, as the analysts emphasize, it encompasses the girl's primary sexual identification with her mother. Female homosexuality is a path into the pre-oedipal world of the girl to which Electra belongs, because before the complex is forced upon her and she is betrayed by her mother, Electra is the daughter of a Great Mother and thus inhabits a world where the mother provides the primary identification. This world represents antiquity in both the history of social forms and an archeology of the psyche. The pre-oedipal comes before kingship; it designates the unrestricted sovereignty of the mother, an uterocracy.

The mother carries the symbolic order, which ensures the growing hatred toward her (as a mirror image to patriarchy). As Gerburg Treusch-Dieter argues, sacrifice becomes a crime if it no longer serves immortality and apotheosis.[18] The queen who allows killing or equips herself for killing then becomes a case for criminal investigation. The thesis that Electra's hatred may also be rooted in envy is reinforced by the fact that she, as Giraudoux writes, has been married off to the gardener. In any case, she lives in a marriage that was designed as a punishment and banishment and continuously imagines her mother amusing herself in the lap of luxury in the palace of her murdered father:

> And I! In a peasant's hut . . .
> thrust and barred from my father's home

to a scarred mountain exile
while my mother rolls in her bloody bed
and plays at love with a stranger.[19]

Electra's onerous and secondary role in which, one could
say, she hates "upward" has rarely been recognized or commented on.[20] What is instead underlined is the long period
of time she imagines the murder of Clytemnestra, and it is
this projective realization phantasy that is given as a pre-
text for the deed. The envy we are talking about, however, is not the usual penis envy inducing oedipalization.
Indeed, if Electra hates her mother because she is a powerful, sexually active woman, could this envy be a "vagina
envy" instead? How does Electra arrive at such an affect?
Could the fact that the poets of the Electras were exclusively
male have played a role?

In Hofmannsthal's version a "woman-hating" Electra
emerges, one who does not want to give birth, one who
revokes her joy in femininity, finding sexuality and motherhood equally ridiculous, and one who uses her brother
as a tool. In the context of the reception of hysteria at the
fin de siècle, Electra could almost be seen as a *role model*
for the paths, and false paths, a repressed sexuality takes
through the female psyche. One sees in the heroine—
curled up in convulsions—how unhealthy it is to want to
escape the urges of her gender in a new nonfemininity. In
this way she only succeeded in—and this is what is tragic—
"the opposite."[21] But the opposite *of what*? Masculinization (which, as we have seen, is not achieved in reality)
leads to eliminating the meaning of the feminine or, more
precisely, to the destruction of the symbolic order and its
canon of structures appropriate to feminine being. Electra
is the one who deviates from the order and does something
that is not commonly associated with women. Bizarrely,
this would mean—if, as Lacan suggests, the phantasmal

father, the public, and language is included in the symbolic order—that the attack on this order (I do not want to be a woman who is like a woman) exposes *what antecedes it,* the *imaginary.* The result, following this logic, would be that the explosion of the Great Father, and thus of the symbolic order assigning femininity to both the girl and the woman, revives an original- or primary-womanness [*Ur- oder Primär-weibchenhaftigkeit*], a kind of pure instinct of the flesh. This primary-womanness, imagined as nature in the form of a woman, equates to an instinctual drive toward merciless copulation, merciless killing, and giving birth. But was this Electra's part? Should her role be read as a masculinization at all? Is the pleasure Electra feels for the father, this incestuously tinted attraction, in fact a motivation for her imitation of the masculine, of the fatherly? Could the father actually like such a masculinized daughter—if it were even possible?

But one can push the love of structural symmetry so far that, as Silvia Kronberger does, Electra becomes the opposite, the inverse of giving birth. She suggests that Electra perceives the commoners living in the palace in direct connection with the circumstances of their coming into being.[22] A terrible haunting. The only thing she could see in children was what their parents did to create them, and she could never imagine emulating them. Even today it is better to avoid such ideas. Instead of being a birth-giver, with all its rights and curses, Electra puts an end to giving birth by entering a kind of deeply material and perverted Buddhahood. Thus Electra chooses killing, which shows that her fall back into the imaginary was not without friction, but finally has much more to do with a loss of friction, and with a revolution that backfired because it shifted the compression ratios of repression. The diagnosis points to the mother and refers to a disturbance of what is called matrilinearity. The mother–daughter relationship is

unbalanced as it stumbles over foreign bodies; these foreign bodies are the men. "Shifted compression ratios"
would mean that Electra, as the good daughter that she also
is, *shares* original womanness with the mother, and does so
in a literal sense, inasmuch as she has the most difficult
part—namely, to represent *similarity in difference*. Whereas the
mother asserts a privilege in coitus, giving birth, and killing, the daughter exclusively chooses killing—*as a phantasy*
whereby she might triumph over the range of motherly
gifts. The death of the mother annihilates her omnipotence. In the image of killing the mother that takes possession of Electra there is a powerful but unrealizable desire
to replace their unity with difference and being-apart,
whose backdrop is the archi-relation. The daughter who
wants to echo her nonrelationship to the mother, who tries
to make it clear that she wishes to break away from her lack
of consideration, can only be obsessed by extinguishing the
mother. Against bringing-into-the-world the taking-of-
life. But what should the psychotic daughter identify with
when she wards off her similarity to the mother while also
renouncing her similarity to the father?

Electra appears as anti-Clytemnestra, as an inverted
birth-machine who, as a distorted image of her mother,
presents her *mode d'emploi* as a Big Black Zero. A daughter
who appears as an inverted mother has to be understood
as her symptom, and she obviously suffers from inversion
(per-version) herself. The birth opening (vagina) of the
mother and the murder-hand of the daughter can only be
connected when birth and death are inadmissibly equated
or confused. What surprises both mother and daughter
is the devaluation of the female power of procreation
(instead of the birth opening, a Black Hole) and the sacrifice of the girl (a murder-hand laid on the daughter,
but *whose* hand?). At the moment of this inversion, the
system to which mother and daughter belonged becomes

irrelevant. The disoriented daughter suffers a psychotic attack that is described as a relapse into the imaginary, as a return journey that takes its destination in hand, like an ax. This slipping free from the original system could be an explanation for Electra's "masculinization." But with this masculinization the undertones resonating throughout the Electra complex disappear, undertones that exhilarated the sweet girl who initially was narcissistically fixated on herself, before genital panic made her fixate on the father. It rather seems that there is an imitation at stake, an assimilation that could be easily explained by the strength of the erotic connection to the respectable position of the father. The categories proposed by Deleuze and Guattari to present the *imitatio patris* are certainly more useful than those derived from the triangulation of the family: the king's public position, his power of definition, and his representation of freedom and order.

In the symmetrical scenario a certain feminization should have been Oedipus's doom. Could it be that in his case it is only as a being with strongly feminine feelings that he desires the mother? It feels like neither a structuralist nor a free asymmetric reading can lead any further. In both there is still the suspicion that manifest contents simply conceal latent ones of an identical scope: "All theory is expropriated myth, all myth expropriated memory."[23]

Underneath the symmetrical pairs of female–male, papa–mama, mother–son, and father–daughter visible in sexuality yawns the abyss. Underneath the agora of early Greek society long pipes branch out connecting individual and collective memories and containing an old story of which only the ending is still narrated. So far the abundance of failed interpretations we have examined have only worked against our declared project, so that we begin to see how these options—father in front, mother behind against mother in front, father behind/father no, mother yes against mother no, father yes, etc.—all become blurred and begin to shimmer when the gaze focusses on a distant background, on a context that is even farther away still, like the far-off blue of a mountain range beginning to show in the distance. The collision that is narrated in Electra is certainly a power struggle between mutually hostile spheres, between a male and a female realm, but it expresses a deep collective amnesia (or rather the situation by which the story reveals itself is a concealment). It is strange, however, that so little information is given about Clytemnestra's power ("Clytemnestra murdered her husband, married Aegisthus and seized power over Argos")[24] and that the daughter "spins out." Such an "amnesia" is present in every myth insofar as it consists of numerous rewritings and finally survives in postrhapsodic form as literary drama.[25] At the moment when the dramatic figure of Electra stirs the poetic reason of Aeschylus and Sophocles she is already refined and *coiffed* as a gestalt of political theater and its pedagogics. All that matters now is the increase of plausibility and the consistent support of the polis. The wind rising from the double origin of the story blows through the amphitheater and guarantees a successful catharsis.[26]

Freud admitted that he lacked the means to explain the pre-oedipal phase, but he nevertheless argued that precisely this phase could help us understand "woman."[27] In a diagram of cultural layers, this phase corresponds to the Mycenaean-Minoan "pre-Greek" age. Freud maintained that collective and individual memory had equal footing up until the mythopoetic or dramatic classical age, which leads up to that of the pre-Athenic. This age, a kind of primordial age of the soul, was left shrouded in mist, but Freud nevertheless affirmed that the mother figure played a leading role there, a Primal Mother with splendid, universal characteristics. This Mother has an omnipotence and an All-being insofar as she is the first living being to learn to "nurture" the "world" with "love." Mother and universe are the same, and her signs are the signs of heaven: the moon, the sickle of the eyelids, the sickle-shaped cut between her legs. In the first perceptual delusions of the nonspeaking soul (*infans*/child) it perceives these objects, these hieroglyphs, these thing-like signs, as saying it all.

Freud neglected to mention that the signifier of the Minoan mother is not, as well-intentioned feminists have tirelessly claimed, a phallus similar to the male's (meaning this mother represented the miracle of a noncastrated woman). Rather, her symbol is an ax, possibly a double ax, which in an imaginary operating through signs combines a tool with the moon and the female sex. The ax is the sharp half-moon, a half-moon blade, a waxing and waning moon lying opposed to each other and making a gap, a cleft, a *vulva* in fact (the from-below, the open-down-below, the introitus). The cleft is signified by the ax, the holy instrument that creates and rules over the gap.[28] The invention of the ax deserves its own written memorial, especially because it opened up possibilities for working in wood and stone and consequently was the first writing instrument to grant the ability to script an eternal permanence. This entanglement of the technical with symbolic and medial dimensions distinguishes this simple instrument and allows it to claim via this very vertical primitivism a mnemological status because it draws, or literally engraves, cultural memory. As Giordano Bruno, a Renaissance mnemotechnician, philosopher, and historian of cultural inventions, notes, "The ancients first took pains to write on the bark of trees with knives. This age was followed by one that wrote with an axe in quarried stone. This age was followed in turn by one that wrote with ink from squid on papyrus scrolls. Then came an artful age that tinted parchment with writing instruments."[29]

In *Greek Myths* Robert Graves writes: "Clytaemnestra's axe was the Cretan symbol of sovereignty, and the myth has affinities with the murder of Minos, which also took place in a bath."[30]

Following the collapse of Minoan culture after the invasion of Crete by Athenian cultural heroes (Daedalus), the power symbolically represented by the ax was erased. Never again will anyone be capable of imagining the ax as anything other than a sacrificial instrument. An extraordinarily nasty instrument. Today, if someone wants to commit an especially barbaric act of violence, he uses an ax as if compelled by a bad memory. The ax in the woods is what remains of the previously appreciated cleaver. Even if splitting—from the hair to the atom—remains the order of the day, nobody associates the profoundly common tool with a symbolic split. The relationship that was created between symbolic femininity (ax) and the queen appears in a distorted form in the murder scene, which withholds what cannot be said: that the murdered king was deified as a hero, as an immortal killed by the one who gives life, and thus *revived by her in death*.[31] From the perspective of the new ruling order only the killing, and thus the crime, has remained. As Heinsohn confirms, the sacrifice was not an original procedure but belonged to the time of the foundation of religion.[32] That means that it reveals a paranoid activity that logically also put the continuum of maternal power under fire.

When Saint Catherine appears with her wheel, or Saint Barbara with her tower, it is difficult to see in their hagiographic attributes more than a logic of symbolic signification. It sounds absurd to suggest that the consortium of saintly women, and saints in general, had continuously carried their technical objects as a subjective expression of memory, but in fact this form of significant accompanying object took its model from the older form of an animal escort.

Can it therefore be assumed, as it is in our story, that when a woman shows up with an ax she must be filled with evil thoughts, consumed by revenge, rotten with the worst promiscuity, and desperately wants to dispose of her beloved husband? May we also assume that if this figure celebrates the sacrifice of the king in solemn rites, she does so in the most hair-raising cold-bloodedness?[33] But the cold-bloodedness ascribed to Clytemnestra is not yet all of it, because the murderess—that is "the woman"—had to pay for her deed with the most heinous of punishments—namely, *castration.* The ax is not simply the instrument that initially generates the gap, or the principle of the sickle-shaped line that frames a recess, rather it is what hacked off the original phallus and left the red wound in its place. Actually, a gap. Not the shining, rising red moon, but instead the wound that allegedly lacks what is most important: a phallus. Ever since this reading has become so painfully fixed, women remain castrated. Does a cut in the crotch refer to an original punishment? Perhaps the tendency to interpret the Cretan scepter (the double ax) as an executioner's tool (a "decommissioned" sacrificial ax) comes from an impulse to deprive women of something: a legal status that hinged on sexual difference. Once revoked, this loss of status is phantasized as the loss of a sexual organ, one that could never have been lost because women never had it in the first place. Are women—without allowing any falling off in sophistication—perhaps the better men because, in contrast to men, they can never lose the penis? Actually, what kind of logic is that?

In regard to the murder of Agamemnon, Graves laconically notes: "Basically, then, this is the familiar myth of the sacred king who dies at midsummer, the goddess who betrays him, the tanist who succeeds him, the son who avenges him."[34] This explains how Clytemnestra attained her freedom and why she does not leave the stage discretely, grieving like an "ordinary" king's widow. Clytemnestra is evil only because the cultic practice she stands for will be as little appreciated by the new Greek religion as the Babylonian Astarte (later the Great Whore) was by the Jews. The mama–papa–child triangle exhausts itself fighting on two fronts, against both the Minoan and Athenian cultures and their religious principles. "Matrilinear inheritance was one of the axioms taken over from the pre-Hellenic religion. Since every king must necessarily be a foreigner, who ruled by virtue of his marriage to an heiress, royal princes learned to regard their mother as the main support of the kingdom, and matricide as an unthinkable crime. . . . they knew that the son never punished his adulterous mother, who had acted with the full authority of the goddess whom she served."[35] But when the king refuses the sacrifice, flees, or allows himself to be murdered, the sacrificial ax begins to "fall back" on the queen, whose castration causes formidable problems for her female child who now finds herself *in statu privationis* or, in other words, *without definition.*

Positive Unrelatedness and Exogamy

Is this perhaps the reason why, in Hofmannsthal, Electra hides the murder ax (and with this ax her own gender, from which, when properly affiliated with the symbolic order, so much power may be derived) and makes such a fuss about it? Had not Clytemnestra quite logically murdered Agamemnon with an ax, with that instrument that grounded her power in a constitutive sense and thus on a political and institutional level? In fact, it seems that the sacrifice of the king was also a theme in the older Cycladic and Attic religion, where the sacred king had always been betrayed by his goddess-wife, killed by his tanist, and avenged by his son.[36] It is not simply the case that the lovely lady only becomes a threat to the sacred king in the malicious patriarchal propaganda of the Athenian poets, because the sacrifice of the king is a religious demand whose fulfillment guarantees that the cycle of nature turns in its traditional manner. The imperative of the sacrifice belongs to a continuum of paranoid interpretations of ancestral catastrophes that has been described in detail by Heinsohn, drawing on Velikovsky.[37] Tellurgic cataclysms, meteor strikes, floods, and earthquakes traumatized humanity to the point that the world itself appeared as a mighty man-eater in whose wide-open mouth, like Moloch, one had to regularly throw the food that was demanded. Heinsohn explains that human sacrifice, its transformation, substitution, and overcoming are the central contents of religion.[38] Concerning the timing of the sacrifice of the king, Aeschylus indicates that mountaintop fires heralded the return of Agamemnon and announced that the ritual killing of the king, which took place at the time of the summer solstice, was imminent.[39] The solstice, the apparent reversal of the sun, was staged as the transit of the king into the underworld or another world. Inasmuch as the king was connected with the astral order, the events of the heavens were his destiny; the sun's closeness to the earth at the turning point in its annual course became the highest festival of the sun hero deified by his sacrifice.[40] The king shows himself as *energoumenos,* as a divine actor who recites an astronomical epic. To be king means becoming-general, not to "create order" but to be the *concept* of order. The queen, however, knows herself as earth-empire, as a living and originary cleft subject to a rhythm, and secures this function in a universal polyphony.

From the early Bronze Age, the woman's territorial sovereignty has been inextricably connected to the agricultural sense of the *Demeter-galaxy*: The high lady performed admissions and levies in a simulated vegetable state, she was chthonic, earthy, and subterranean, like her executives the Erinyes. She was the land and the principle of the flora and fauna that sprang from it. She was the *locostabilitas,* the real estate. To be daughter of such a woman meant being the earth-child, the secured becoming, the power of the body. How does she feel, this daughter? Will she have a dark mien like Electra and Cinderella—something especially terrifying in a child—and perhaps lie with the dogs? Never. She stands on the shoulders of the mother from whom she grew, like a strong branch from its tree. In contrast to male genealogy, which is imagined as a (descending) structure of derivation, the female line ascends, rising from the earth like a tower of girls built on the mother. What role does the father play in such an "ascendency"? How did little Electra perceive the change of men that constitutes the mythical condition for her mother's form of existence? How did she take the sacrifice of the father? Did she have a relationship at all with her father/substitute-fathers? How did she deal with the fact that the king had to step down and that the son in return had to appear in front of his successor in such an unpleasant manner? Astonishingly, there are no indications about this whatsoever. One has to clearly say that in regard to the oft-cited matrilinear inheritance to which Clytemnestra owes her royal dignity, the lack of information about the small heiresses, the daughters, is very strange. Antigone, Iphigenia, and Electra are the female members of the younger generation in the dramatic curriculum of Greece, but they are estranged from the old order by their pathological identification with the affectations of the new culture. The repression of any *real* information about the daughter, who is after all the most important figure in these folktales that trace the older religions and social orders, is certainly systematic in the dramatists discussed here. A new understanding of the old

constellation must be introduced, and if possible the original evaluation must be turned upside down. The cultural
interpretation of the husband as a foreigner who immi-
grates, and who in time marries the heiress of the territory, still wafts through both the *Iliad* and the *Oresteia.* But
instead one must turn the tables and describe the women
as the strangers who are drawn into the new social order.
Endogamy means that fathers prevail in the hereditary line,
and the basis of the older society—the mother–daughter
relationship legitimizing inheritance—is abolished. The
model of the good daughter is now embodied by Athena,
the Earth-betrayer, the one who sprang from the skull of
a man. At the scene of Athena's birth one sees what an ax
in a male head creates; when the daughter's eagerness to be
born becomes too strong, Zeus receives an ax cleft enabling
him to give birth, a vagina. No instrument in the world—as
we now know—is better suited here than the sacred ax.

Thus, what we will initially focus on is the sequence
and folding together of these two different social systems,
which symbolically nourish themselves from contradictory
phantasies of ascendance. The question of mama-papa as
psychoanalysis poses it is certainly central. But the emergence of "mama" and/or "papa" assumes a far more fundamental definition that determines their difference, which
only then proliferates in the social system. If the mother
counts as signifier, then she has the defining power and
is the origin of the differences. The appearance of the
father is of secondary importance, which is why he drops
in as a "traveling lover" and can never become more than
a weekend father. How shall we conceive of the mother
if the generative difference from which "mama–papa" is
derived depends on her? Because if one makes the mama–
papa set the founding event of the social system—as has
become common within the gender debate, transforming
it into a raging dialectical machinery (a first couple that

then becomes the principle of all transgression, recom-
bination, synthesis, etc.)—the sexes petrify into mutually
mirroring, opposed phalanxes.

The recording and structural interpretation of marriage
rules by ethnologists and anthropologists could unlock the
discussion of mama–papa that is deadlocked in reduction-
ism and combinatorics. We cannot avoid studying these
rules as a kind of protophilosophical (rather than sociological) logic, which will then achieve the status of amnesia in
psychoanalysis. The richness and complexity of marriage
and kinship rules have been translated, under the conditions of the bourgeois family, into the two-dimensionality
of civilized forms of life. The multiplicity of codes by which
individuals could identify and recognize themselves has
been dramatically reduced.

We will significantly enrich our analysis by critically
revising the difference between exogamous and endogamous marriage rules, which classify the position of the
mother or father as either related or as foreign/unrelated.
Frank Robert Vivelo laconically notes that it is important
"to remember that kinship is only *modeled* somewhat on
biology and only to a greater or lesser degree. *Kinship* is
that part of a conceptual system or a culture that deals with
notions of, or ideas about, 'relatedness'—or relationship
through birth and (more broadly) through marriage."[41]
Vivelo names kinship, descent, and residence as the essential elements constituting the social. The relationship
between parents and children forms the basic model of this
social construction, which is therefore grounded in a biology of reproduction but which is "*interpreted through culture*."[42]
Fatherhood—Vivelo stresses this—is to be understood in at
least three ways: First, there is the *Genitor,* who is the actual
biological father; second, the *Pater,* who is the sociological
father, from whom the child derives its kinship relation.
"Actually," Vivelo writes, "this person need not be a male,

or even be alive; the Nuer have 'female fathers' and 'ghost fathers.'"[43] Third, there is the Vir, who is simply a man or husband, whether father or not.

In judging the figure of Agamemnon, we will draw upon the general papa–mama–child schema and examine the circumstances by which Agamemnon coupled with Clytemnestra. What was the self-understanding that preceded him, by the power of which quality did he depart and by which does he return? What was his position in the Mycenaean household? One must ask whether he came as a foreigner or whether he visited a foreign woman. He is a foreigner if Clytemnestra's sovereignty is based on exogamous marriage rules—or is he a "relative," a cross-cousin or something similar? It must be clarified what the position of this foreigner is, if he is to be a husband and father what sort of rights he could have, and what sort of duties. Lévi-Strauss points out that exogamous marriage rules means that one must choose beyond what is considered "human": "True endogamy," he writes, "is merely the refusal to recognize the possibility of marriage beyond the limits of the human community. The definitions of this community are many and varied, depending on the philosophy of the group considered. A very great number of primitive tribes simply refer to themselves by the term for 'men' in their language, showing that in their eyes an essential characteristic of man disappears outside the limits of the group. Thus the Eskimoes of Norton Sound describe themselves exclusively as the 'excellent people,' or more exactly as the 'complete people,' and reserve the epithet 'nit' to describe neighbouring peoples."[44] Thus exogamy seems to have represented the risk, the experiment, the venture of engaging with the unknown, but through this venture one was also able to form new alliances on a disparate field of microscopic territories. Lévi-Strauss writes: "Thus, as in New Zealand and Burma, exogamy is

specified at the top of the social hierarchy, and is a function of the obligation of feudal families to maintain and
widen their alliances. The endogamy of the lower classes is
one of indifference, and not of discrimination."[45] Endogamy and exogamy typically appear in a particular mixed
form. "From this point of view," Levi-Strauss writes, "any
society is both exogamous and endogamous. Thus among
Australian aborigines the clan is exogamous, but the tribe
is endogamous, while modern American society combines
a family exogamy, which is rigid for the first degree but
flexible for the second or third degrees onwards, with a
racial endogamy, which is rigid or flexible according to the
particular State."[46] If we assume that Clytemnestra comes
from a high-ranking family obliged to marry exogamously,
then the drama takes a new twist. The alliance resulting
from the marriage with Agamemnon is a pure winner as
long as the house of Agamemnon does not come up with
its own capricious idea of a rule constituting the group. If
Agamemnon is married as a foreign king who subordinates
himself to the customs of the chthonic power, including
its paranoid obligations in securing cosmic affairs through
sacrifice, we will have to examine the dimension of feudal exchange that is always a given in such a matrimony
rather than just the simple collision of gender and politics.[47] Under the auspices of an exchange economy the
goddess would offer her husband for a new harvest, thus,
in a certain sense, sharing the man with nature, which on
the symbolic level seems acceptable. In this way the man
gains—paradoxically, precisely because of his foreignness—
the status of a first constitutive unit of value. The shares
of the high lady are valued in male units and constitute a
loan of foreign currency. What she gives is the man—the
floating capital, the liquidity—from which the fixed territory symbolically lives. The rule of exogamy comprises a
logical operation, one that only tolerates the business of

couples because a foreigner secures their equivalence, like an Archimedean point from which the entire construction hangs. What happens then, if the queen marries a "nit"? Later, we will see more clearly how creatively the proto-political agrarian society dealt with foreignness. Foreignness, or rather a new interpretation of foreignness, is the achievement of a social group still practicing an archaic rape-marriage. The intertwining of otherness and familiarity and the eroticism of attraction and repulsion thematically traverse the complexes of Electra and Oedipus. Psychoanalysis, perhaps also inspired by the ethnological and anthropological discourses current at the turn of the twentieth century, explained these figures in a compelling way through the question of incest or the incest taboo. But this central topic will also be deciphered from social, political, media theory, and economic points of view.[48] What would become of the Electra complex if one merely saw it as the mnemotechnical arrangement of the repression of an older, more primitive matriarchal culture by Athenian ideology? If one saw it, in other words, as rendering consistent the continuous humiliation of amnesia, an absence that ranges from intimate forgetfulness to the prohibition of memory and its reconstruction in the cultural sciences. "Intercourse" with the mother is not, in fact, prohibited. It is prohibited in relation to an experience and thus to a mnemotechnical date that encompasses a more primordial integration of foreignness and intimacy. Castration anxiety is related to a deeper prohibition of memory, to a weakness of memory that is constitutive for "mature" consciousness.

Indeed, when the mother appears to her child for the first time, the child has neither a concept of "mother" nor a concept of what a "human" might be. Contours are inscribed into early perception that connect its prelinguistic hieroglyphs (prior to the concept) with being pre-human. One does not yet know that there are "humans."

Small children make incredulous faces when they are described as "humans," who says they are "humans"? What precedes humans and splits them into males and females? What image does the child form and retain of what it sees, feels, senses, and tastes? What a wonderful barbarism this is where everything is monstrous, huge, and without words. Is it then also perhaps something of the "extrahuman" that one later marries, guided by the exogamy rule? We see that the stone steps leading into the cellar of the Athenian agora are covered with moss and that at the entrance to these depths great caution is necessary.

Which path leads back to the "pre-oedipal phase," to the universe of the All-mother, the primordial mother, the mother *as world,* where, when one is within her, it is not yet clear that there even is a "mother"? Freud bracketed off the continent of the pre-oedipal as a sphere without words or concepts, as a realm deprived of theory and revoked from the psychoanalytical model. One senses this continent but has always already been expelled from it, has always already had to leave it, is always already expatriated, emigrated, when one begins to think about it. For this simple reason the pre-oedipal became the great catcher of the projections of feminist psychoanalysis, which hoped that this ancestral continent could be taken (back) simply because of its feminine logos.[49] Its mythical nature easily lent itself to many interpretations: either it is projected as a Golden Age and deputizes for all lost experiences of oneness and bliss, or it serves as a golden ontological frame for the construction of a noncastrated, unpunished, and thus complete "phallic mother." But it is hard to accept this "uncastrated" mother because in *this* superdialectical position she merely stands for the loss reversed, for the *loss of the oedipal in the pre-oedipal* as seen with the nostalgic eyes of the oedipalized. Then the concept of the mother will only appear "uncastrated" from the perspective of loss (from the perspective of internalized castration), which simply looks back to a phantasm of original possession. Would it not be more likely that a memory, that which is *re-collected,* can restore the condition of noncastration—of something not-lost and not-fallen-off—as the positive condition of completeness, through the simple ability (or potency) to remember it? If anything gets lost it is not a sex organ, which is usually pretty well attached, but rather the memory of what lies in the deepest layer of memory and organizes itself there. The fear of losing the sex organ stands for the threat of memory loss, in relation to the eternally preceding (pre-oedipal) preconscious. The sexual code of amnesia conceals the fact that the origins of a person are lost in a darkness that is itself a cultural product. The "noncastrated" mother becomes someone who, under these conditions, is miraculously remembered. She appears, however, as the *Other* mother, the foreign mother.[50]

For the interpretation of the figure of Electra these questions are extraordinarily important. I have suggested that Electra's "pre-real" status should be explained by her mediocre ability to act, by her general regression into a primary womanhood. The figure of Electra in fact implies the possibility of regression, and we need only shake her a little for the pre-oedipal to fall out. Electra and her sisters are the last girls of the pre-Athenian, Cycladic, Mycenaean, or Minoan world, and it is only under severe coercion that they would take on the role of the subservient daddy's girl "Athena." In the end they remain—and this is the core of the tragedy—surface symptoms for the abdicating territorial queens. To derive a psychologically standardized father-love from the grief and despair these daughters must have felt over the public perverting of their mothers is high art, the poetry of the state. This reorientation around the father and the consequent "masculinization" of the daughters meant their becoming-woman could not be completed, and they remained in an in between state without sexual definition except as not-(yet-)woman, which in fact means: man. But what is automatically lost here is what should have officially been the generative pole of the Electra complex in the first place: being-woman (i.e., becoming-woman) with an explicit and obsessive preference for *the* man (given that love is always a phenomenon of polarization: a becoming-woman—Deleuze's *becoming-woman*—that leads to the universal *girl*). The idea of a general *devenir-femme* as the first stage in the recovery of an open existential potential is a clever attempt by Deleuze to utilize repressed otherness as a structural supermotor. It is no accident that *devenir-animal* (becoming-animal) comes next. Woman and animal form an amnesic complex, a matrimonium of regression that one must pass through on the descent into the plutonium of primary energy.[51]

The project of becoming-woman has two directions: First it moves ahead, forward into an open future, it is a virtual being that projects potentialities under unrestricted, emergent, "should be" conditions. As this type of future-project, the Electra complex has been able to gain philosophical honor and attention. However, the openness of becoming-woman is based on going *back* to a primal scene, to an unnamed but always taken for granted hardly-I and hardly-you, one celebrated in song (incanted, magically fixed in phonetic signs) by the Dada-king's name: MAMA. Significantly, Electra concentrates almost exclusively on the most interesting organs of her mother, directly imagining their function in birth and in the sexual act. As if Clytemnestra was *in truth* a general function, who just happened to be wearing the mask of Clytemnestra. Electra *overlooks* the actual Clytemnestra in order to track down the real one. One senses that Electra is psychically fixated on a mother who has very little to do with the complex personality of Clytemnestra, the woman whose atrocious tale of woe is told in myth and ancient dramas. To this mother as prehuman being, as hardly-you, Electra directs both primary love and its counterpart of unchecked primary hate, the desire to bash her, to bite her and destroy her with toxic pee and exploding poo. Why such extreme feelings? Because Clytemnestra let the king's daughter scream and did not come at once. Because for some reason she turned away from their perfect love and did something else, while little Electra screamed for the immortal milk, a bit like Melanie Klein imagines it. And because—this would be the juridical and political interpretation—in accordance with Athenian propaganda she must come to terms with the end of matrilinearity: There is nothing left to inherit. The girl who witnesses the disempowerment of her mother will fake a royal symptom of her suppression, one appearing in the Electra complex as if in a distorting mirror. When she is told, "If you knew your duty/ You might be known as Agamemnon's child,"[52] the outbreak of primary mother hate reveals the internalization of the inescapable and provides the ground for the psychological sketches of the dramatists.

The Greek dramas present the two figures of Electra and Oedipus as having limited accountability for their acts, and by doing so the bowels of the imaginary are laid open. Heroine and hero move as if in a fog, they cannot break into the clear space where motive, knowledge, and deed are one. The fascination of the dramas is precisely that the plot rests on a mountain of shared presentiments and vague recollections that send cathartic shivers down the audience's spine. Nevertheless, Oedipus always acts, and he will be punished accordingly. Oedipus is defined as a political subject, as a person with rights, as a son and husband, whereas Electra appears as though she were a member of an anarchist commune.

Although the primary emotions rage inside Electra, in

the text the murderous relationship is between Clytemnestra and *Orestes*. I say "in the text" because the way in which
Sophocles conceives the figure of Orestes means he effectively supplants Electra in the dramatic spotlight. Electra seems to be added as a mere footnote to the drama of
Orestes. The prophetic dream, in which it is foretold that
the mother must suffer sorrow because of the one she gave
birth to, does not frame Electra's self-perception—as one
would think—but Orestes's. He pompously assumes the role
of the dragon-snake by understanding, in an usurpational
oneiro-criticism, that his mother's prophetic dream was
all about him:

> ORESTES: I pray to the Earth and father's grave to bring
> that dream to life in me. I'll play the seer—
> it all fits together, watch!
> If the serpent came from the same place as I,
> and slept in the bands that swaddled me, and its jaws
> spread wide for the breast that nursed me into life
> and clots stained the milk, mother's milk,
> and she cried in fear and agony—so be it.
> As she bred this sign, this violent prodigy
> so she dies by violence. I turn serpent,
> I kill her. So the vision says.[53]

This dream is the key to understanding the Electra
story. Like an oracle it unlocks a space in which interpretations can grow. The motif of the child distorted into a
dragon is accompanied by other distortions, so that many
levels of meaning are interwoven in this scene. Above all,
one has to ask whether Orestes's overhasty "deciphering"
of this dream is actually an interpretation at all or whether
his determination to murder simply latches onto a few key-
words such as "fear (of the mother)," "milk," and "blood"
in order to make his reading into a *self-fulfilling prophecy*.

Orestes prays at his father's grave that things will go as he plans: "I wish to be the fulfiller of her dream." Could it be that for Electra, as for Oedipus, a wrongly interpreted oracle is what first complicates things? Could the oracular pronouncement be a semantic fossil, but one that Athenian propaganda denies to the one who struggles to interpret it? Is it that Electra—like Oedipus, warned by an oracle that is only fulfilled through the desire to avoid it—crashes so disastrously because Orestes takes the utterances of the oracle personally, although the oracle's words were not meant for him? Orestes's simplistic reading of the oracle is so unsophisticated, so exegetically dull, because it is too unfamiliar with the mechanisms of repression and distortion and their reversals and processes of substitution. Clytemnestra dreams a genuine snake dream that arises like a relic from the antiquity of the female soul, showing that, as much as they may differ from each other, both the Stesichorean and Aeschylus's versions are concerned with what *comes forth* and rewriting it. First a king emerges from the snake (with a bloody head), then a snake comes out of the woman and sucks from her breast. Why does Orestes believe that he could, or should, take on the powerful role of a shapeless, gigantic monster? In his extensive analysis of Clytemnestra's dream that focuses on the older Stesichorean version, George Devereux notes: "All four persons from whose body something is extracted are female, though in the Stesichorean Klytemnestra's dream the snake is male."[54] But who actually says that the snake with the bleeding head should be masculine?

Devereux proposes the following translation of the Stesichorus text: "[Klytemnestra] dreamed there came a serpent with a bloody crest, and out of it [crest] appeared a Pleisthenid king [Orestes]."[55] In this version the king comes out of the head of the snake, but is it really necessary to think the king's birth according to a patriarchal template, where the swelling red glans is the organ giving birth to a legitimate successor?[56] Devereux himself proposes a large number of arguments that are supposed to underpin the masculinity of the snake and thus its identity as the death-king Agamemnon. "The Stesichorean imagery implies that Orestes emerges from the snake's head as fully formed as Athene emerges from Zeus' skull. Now, A[eschylus] . . . affirms that only the father procreates the child. This might imply that, figuratively speaking, the father ejaculates a kind of homunculus."[57] Devereux, the author of a remarkable work on the "phallic vulva" (on Baubo, the Greek female exhibitionist), is astonishingly unburdened by doubts and never asks if perhaps the snake head in Clytemnestra's dream could also represent female genitalia.[58] Although, as he correctly states, "The snake is a chthonic creature," he nevertheless concludes that it represents the "wrathful dead," the assassinated Agamemnon killed by a wound to his head.[59] But Devereux does grasp an essential element of the literary and dramatic dream story when he writes: "One can begin with the assumption that Stesichorus invented a (dreamlike) dream for his Klytaimnestra, which then *elicited* the invention of (related) dreamlike dreams by his two great successors. The process is the same as that which can be observed when, after A narrates one of his dreams to B, the latter partly echoes A's triggering dream in a 'responding' dream of his own."[60] Thus the key problem is "worked through" by all three authors in different but nevertheless related ways.[61]

What then is the meaning of the dream of a woman, as Aeschylus tells it, of a woman who feeds a snake at her breast with blood and milk? This is clearly the nightmare of the sacrificer, who allegedly takes the shape of a dragon, as in the story of the virgin saved by Saint George in the *Legenda Aurea*. There, a knight comes along and seizes the girl from the dragon and so wins the victor's laurels. What is strange is that the dragon had earlier been quietly led out of the city by Margaret and was *harmless*. The knight in his armor, cheerfully galloping along and seeking a deed appropriate to his stature and that of his lovely equipment, indeed kills the dragon, but in the structure of the hagiographic narrative this act is in fact a slipup.[62] Margaret, patron of midwives and foremost expert of the birth space and its tunnel-like qualities, leads the dragon through the city on a red string like an obedient dog and in the manner of Neolithic goddesses who were also accompanied by animals.

In Greek mythology, snakes and the victims of snakebites are found everywhere.[63] The snake is a symbolic pictogram so universal (it is a street and transport route, a channel for energy, a rising power, a hysterical muscle, a faint scribble) that no imaginarium lacks its manifold employment. It is inevitable that Orestes finally dies by snakebite. At the beginning and the end of his life, there is a snake to help him across the threshold. This proves his original affinity with the snake, even if he manifestly denies it by murdering his mother. In his dream and in his accidental death, it is the snake who both brings and takes away life.

One begins to suspect why Orestes begs for hermeneutical assistance. Fatefully, he confides in his friend Pylades, who reminds him of the authority of the Apollonian oracle (and in doing so glosses over the fact that he also intends to settle an old score with Clytemnestra). Even for the hagiographers of the twelfth century, snake/worm/dragon was an umbrella term about which there were contradictory opinions, first of all in its great oscillation between masculine and feminine genders. In the Saint George phantasy, the saint imagines that the dragon is about to eat the woman, and so he immediately kills it. Orestes takes it a step further; he wishes to be the dragon who will kill the woman, his mother. Assuming that Clytemnestra, as we have shown, was not a wife without rights who took advantage of her husband's absence to scandalously remarry but rather a highly ranked dignitary in a protopolitical agrarian and totemistic society, then Orestes's claim of legitimacy—one not so easily acknowledged—appears in a new light.

It is, as one notices in Pylades's reference to the oracle, the Athenian-Apollonian approach that sees death in an open dragon or snake's mouth. In other words, he sees the death that the Apollonian, non-mother-loving hero brings for the dragon. Apollo's hostility toward snakes is well known. It was, after all, Apollo who chased and killed the snake Python, the Earth-snake, when it escaped into its shrine and where he then set up his own sanctuary. It is the Apollonian attitude that sees snakes as pernicious. Devereux clearly registers the chthonic origin of the snake, recognizes it as "earth-born," as a being belonging to the earth, but he does not see it in the queen, in the mistress of the land whose animals were her allies. This is surprising given that the queen's dominion is ruled "from below," and her power derives from the importance of animal alliances in territorial matters. This queen "knows" that the animals are the true lords of the earth and recognizes their "instinctual" mode of life as a higher form of knowledge. In her primordial identification as mother, she is theriomorphic, she is part of the primitive and ascending lineage of the snake.

After polishing our glasses in the collyrium of our methodological preliminaries, and with their sharply focused lenses of a nonpropagandistic iconosophy, we see a beautiful queen who has united with a snake or a dragon, or rather united a snake or a dragon's mouth with her breast. And if one leaves aside the anti-serpent *ressentiment* of the later cults, one quickly recognizes in this image the organological icon of a so-called phallic vulva

(Devereux). This vulva is distinguished by its ability to produce and is placed next to its corresponding flow-organ,
the breast, and indeed in the case of the biting snake it even
hangs from it. Thus the woman shows her snake-totem,
the theriomorphic equivalent that constitutes her quality.
As a result, the woman (here and in the interpretation of
dreams) does not have a snake-child but is *herself a snake-
daughter,* a descendant of those holy living channels from
where all living beings come. Clytemnestra's dream would
therefore be *her self*-legitimizing dream, a kind of epiphany
of the chthonic powers to which she owes her rule. In a
totemistic reading this dream would be taken for granted,
something expected from a queen, as one expects the new
Dalai Lama to recognize the objects he owned in a previous
incarnation. This dream is a kind of subtle automatism,
a general form of affirmation that has achieved the form
of a codified script, a recitative whose repetition becomes
the duty of all adepts. One could expect this from every
female owner of the Delphic tripod, down the endless
line of arch-priestesses that accurately pronounce oracles,
bringing forth the most beautiful verses of Pythian poetry
and giving precisely those hints that were the *specialty* of Delphic prophecy. Thus, Clytemnestra dreamed as the proud
owner of the snake's power, just as her predecessors had
done. Before the dream was arranged in its literary version
it was, to some extent, orally transmitted and so dreamt in
reaction to similar tales. It is the dream that confirms the
calling. Thus, Clytemnestra's dream was not an individual's neurotic panic dressed in the hieroglyphics of a stam-
mering unconscious but a set of meanings with which edu-
cated wise women, familiar with transferred symbolism,
worked. Additionally, the occurrence of blood and milk
in Aeschylus's version of the dream correctly quotes the
attributes of the phallic vulva, to keep Devereux's expression: Menstrual blood and the milky white fluid indicate

fertility. Their appearance alone obviously makes the snake female, but as we have seen this story is not about its being male or female but about the *conflict* over its gender and how this has displaced its signifiers.

The dream-script produces an automatism by which the atmosphere and expression defining the most remote sphere of the cultural situation interferes within it. Via this automatism, the organs transfer their vibration to objects and concepts, which would also suggest that mantic dreams have no individual meaning but, on the contrary, individuals become general signs within them. It is therefore possible that the delirium of attributions, dissolutions, and interpretations in the conflict over the snake, this collision of ownership claims, is expressed in the genealogical line. Each sex tries to secure its privilege through the more or less obvious snake-like form of its genitals, with familial and political consequences of the highest order. To make the snake rule over time and its order, as the Mithraic figure of Chronos encoiled by snakes illustrates, means to secure sovereignty for oneself, and not just for today and tomorrow but in the long and longest term, from the mouth to the tail of the cosmic track. The preference for the snake is therefore also explained by a desire to be the first or earliest: a prince, a princess, a principle that possesses the power of foundation. This was precisely that with which the heroic age appears to have been obsessed. The history of cultural control-organs clearly shows how a more or less fixed "organ-modus," constituted by the original tautology of an imagined natural or creative priority, takes over the task of upgrading consciousness by connecting itself to self-consciousness. To find oneself in the privileged genealogical line also means standing in the right queue [*Schlange*].[64]

But if queens now take themselves to be the daughters of snakes, what does this mean for their own interpretation of ascendance? It means that what Vivelo claimed in regard to fatherhood (that being a father occurs in at least three different ways) is also valid for motherhood. Mothers appear either as Genetrix (as biological creator), as Mater, or as Uxor.[65] The snake, or as the case may be the dragon, will fulfill the role of Mater, of the queen, with whom the daughter identifies and symbolically understands herself. The mother line thus defines itself through this first foreigner, otherwise how could a first mother be produced by a mother? The Bible attempts a counterproductive answer that uses the logical style of the Electra complex, making its first man the "mother" of the first mother, Adam as a "Genetrix" who lends the first flesh. There are representations that depict a wound like a caesarian section on Adam's breast from which Eve emerges. This wound serves as an artificial vulva, and Christ's main organ of blessing will also be of this kind. But if a female child feels the primeval layer of the identification with the mother, she will find that this mother-image does not transform into a man but anamorphically stretches into the image of a dragon, a snake, or a monster, which, like Dalí's clocks, are half upright while the other half hangs into an abyss where it loses its face and form. The production of femininity through identification with a mother is easier said than done. Femininity is grounded on the femininity from which one comes, through "motherness" [*Mutterheit*], something hypothetically captured by the animal vitality of an elongated muscle ending in a mouth that has the appearance of a snake. Where a specific and particular mother gets caught up in the endless curves of motherness, she is represented by a symbol that, as always when memory only provides bleached out images, provides a functional similarity.

Female identity produced in relation to the snake, and thus by a proto-Hegelian *passage* through an archaic *otherness,* will explicate this otherness in an arrangement of social cohesion. First, the "mother," symbolized by a venerated animal, is invoked as constituting a harmonious ascendance, and only then is the rule of exogamy formulated through a generalization of this original "furtive foreignness." Exogamy confirms that the mode in which the intimate appears is the foreign [*Fremde*]. If the experiment of matrilineal society was to set up a permanent pre-oedipal state, then this logic will not tolerate any break with the original bond with the mother, which is binding in the Electra complex. The quality of this first love enters through the exogamy rule and leads to the theriomorphic symbolization of the mother. The exogamous relationship repeats the constellation of this initial closeness, insofar as it is grounded in a "mother" who appears as other and foreign. Clytemnestra's relationships are in this way xenologically constituted and allow her husband to occupy the same systemic position that her snake-identity has. Who is desired by a woman that is not polarized by the Electra complex constituted by her mother's rejection? She desires a *nonwoman* (man?) and thereby activates that part of the mother (as an archetype of the pre-oedipal erotic relationship) that was a "nonwoman" (animal). If, as psychoanalysis never tires of claiming, the primordial relationship supplies the model for every relationship, then this is especially true for pre-oedipal mother-society. Through the formation of couples, the relationship previously established by the all-powerful child with her animal once again becomes virulent.

Constitutive Strangeness or Primary Exoticism

The imperative to seek out the strange and unknown, to seek what one does not and will not know by heart, is a particular way in which humans define themselves, namely

that of *eccentric* hominization (in contrast to the weary con-
firmation of the superiority of anthropocentrism), but
above all it also expresses the possibility of the *differentiation
of the sexes*. The animal makes the nonanimal clear in itself
and—something thus far neglected—enables the *internal* differentiation of female and male. The primary gender constellation is determined when the female joins with the
animal. This is the first difference, the first categorical
distinction. The female, insofar as she is "motherness,"
only becomes the origin and reference of both sexes when
she is grasped as both equivalent to the animal and separate from it. Aristotle's attribution of the power of procreation to men only simply begs the question of how it
is possible for women to beget or give birth to children
of both sexes.[66] The primitive classification counting boys
with men and girls with women is called into question by
this motherness from which both sexes derive. Just as the
symbolic order of the father introduces an authority that,
through a transpersonal bracketing, contains the feminine
and the masculine (right, law, name, state), the symbolic
order of the mother likewise comes from the difference
of the sexes, as well as the civility of the social, gifts, and
exchange. The symbolic order of "motherness" thereby
cultivates an opening to the nonhuman and integrates the
animal as its partner.

There is a new and increasing intellectual interest in
the human–animal difference that locates the genesis of
becoming–human in species difference. Giorgio Agamben,
for example, builds on Heidegger and Uexküll in order to
answer the question: Why has the human been separated
from the animal?[67] Agamben argues that the metaphysical
narrative of the human being as uniting an angelic soul
and an animal body poses an illusionary task that conceals
the original problem. The infrequently achieved union
of human and animal in the human is not a Herculean

task but rather the primal scene of humanity's contemporary world. Man separates from the animal in order to
be human on his own, and it remains to be seen if he can
bear the consequences. Agamben treats the human–animal
difference from different perspectives, but "the human"
remains no more and no less than "the human" for Agamben. "The animal" repeatedly appears in the shape of the
ticks that hibernate in Uexküll's laboratory for eighteen
years, but "the human" remains, up until almost the last
page, simply a species, without form, shape, or gender. On
one side, the impossibility of "humanism" is presented in
the style of the Foucauldian critique of anthropocentrism,
while on the other, "the human" is employed as a universal concept, although it also deserves criticism. Only in
the last chapters does the curtain unexpectedly lift, and
man and woman finally appear in a Titian painting.[68] The
tension rises. Agamben sees that the relationship between
human and animal shapes humanity's self-relation and
self-understanding, but his conclusion in light of the *myste-
rium coniunctionis* remains vague and postmodern, ironic. He
circles around sexuality, around what the man and woman
are actually doing, painted by the great master as lying
underneath a tree on which an animal grazes. His interpretation turns out to be pathetic. Agamben says of this
painting, which he compares to Titian's *Three Ages of Man*:

> The enigma of the sexual relationship between the man
> and the woman, which was already at the center of the
> first painting, thus receives a new and more mature
> formulation. In this mutual disenchantment from their
> secret, they enter, just as in Benjamin's aphorism, a new
> and more blessed life, one that is neither animal nor
> human. It is not nature that is reached in their fulfil-
> ment, but rather (as symbolized by the animal that tears
> up the Tree of Life and of Knowledge) a higher stage

> beyond both nature and knowledge, beyond conceal-
> ment and disconcealment. . . . In their fulfilment, the
> lovers who have lost their mystery contemplate a human
> nature rendered perfectly inoperative.[69]

The aim of the treatise is, it appears, a dialectical sub-
lation of animal and human in an "outside of being,"[70]
leaving behind the zone of being that is at once the privilege and trap of the human being. The goat stands for
this beyond-good-and-evil and demonstrates what postmodern thinking is able to do; it chews over misunderstood old things. One could also read Titian's paintings
in another way. A man and a woman together with a tree
and an animal make up paradise, which illustrates an older
Babylonian phantasy, a dark memory of a tree goddess,
the apple-girl who rules over life and who also appears as
a snake, which does not surprise us. The goat is Ishtar's
totem, mother's milk equals goat's milk, the value of the
mother is the same as the value of the goat, long before it
becomes a nanny goat.[71] Man and woman lie beneath this
therio- or phytomorphous symbol and there receive the
difficult task of life: the task of love as caprice. They should
recognize each other, but this recognition is, as Agamben
also underlines, anything but easy and divides into several
phases. First they move toward each other, then they unite,
and finally they gaze at each other intently while the devas-
tated tree of paradise looms above, into the sky.

What is this ultimate "letting-be" that Agamben has in
mind? "To articulate a zone of nonknowledge—or better,
of aknowledge (*ignoscenza*)—means in this sense not simply to let something be, but to leave something outside of
being, to render it unsavable."[72] This sounds wonderfully
conciliatory. Does it mean that "letting-be-outside-of-
being" is the erotic magic formula? Obviously this gener-
osity does not come from someone without means; rather,

it comes from someone disgusted, from a "human" who suspects that being-human in a positive sense is impossible. If being-human is to be dismantled, then retiring into uncertainty is clearly one way to bring the little wheels of proud human self-reflection to a standstill. From the point of view of the totemistic state, the slogan of letting-be sounds absurd. In the totemistic state, being-human—which comes from the animal—is the *goal*. It begins in a primordial consciousness that does not yet know there are "humans."

Totemism is the political version of a fervent becoming-human, a model for collective ascendency. The animal is the patron of this operation. One is reminded of the fact that the "human," before they became one, looked different, exotic. First they were an egg, then a budding leaf, then a kind of crocodile, and finally an awesome aquatic creature, before they fell onto dry land as a baby. Only then did they begin to grow up and finally become that which does not grow anymore: an adult. The lovers no longer know anything, they are ecstatically "held out into being," they *are* the animal.

In Titian's painting the tree of paradise appears ruined, broken in half after a lightning strike, like an ancient column in a field of ruins. This means not only that the sexual act has taken place but also that the principle of difference and the erotic imperatives connected to it now lie in ruins. One sees the man and woman are lovers, but this tells us nothing. Nevertheless, it does mean that one is far from simply "letting-be." Titian paints the tree of paradise, nibbled by the goat, as the sign of a fading memory. The snake no longer defends the tree. He paints a shrunken tree of paradise, a bit like how the wide aprons of Hungarian costumes later appear in salon-approved versions as annoyingly broad ruffles around the waist, as a beacon of oblivion. Love is dialed down to a postorgasmic tone, that of depression.

Schizogamy

We have announced a descent not into the cave of Trophonius, where a visionary intrauterine culture had created a
space for itself,[73] but into the cellar of the Athenian agora,
where the spoils of Cycladic, Mycenaean, and Minoan cultures are stored. With the tree of paradise (struck by lightning) we found ourselves on a totally different terrain.
Nevertheless, a "cellar" can also be discerned there, a level
appearing as an older sediment of a literary stratigraphy.
On this level the animal belongs essentially to the human
but in an opposite sense, one that demands a second reconciliation with the animal. That is to say, *before* (and here
we introduce the elemental BEFORE) "the human" notices
the animal, the animal—this is the totemistic thesis—has
noticed the human. The animal was there earlier, it was
already *there* when the human was not yet human. The level
of the animal is the first living and intensive identification
for a consciousness whose humanity is not yet a reflex. It is
not the case that the level of the animal designates a purely
functional line of emergence, as Schelling imagines it: a
milieu of pure nature struck by the beam of consciousness.
Consciousness despairs when it searches behind/below
for a trace of its emergence, because it is always only the
luminous part of a history that loses itself in the dark. In
its symbolic form, however, pre-oedipality offers another
solution to this. The level of emergence, the "nonground,"
is *no more unconscious* than a nanny goat is to her kid. Contrary to the common belief that once one has achieved consciousness only forgotten and inaccessible things lie in the
preconscious, totemism most certainly seeks out a rapport
with the level of emergence. The level of origin is "generic
motherness." She is not yet recognized as human, she has
no face (from inside), and is merely a stimulus-release
schema. Is this Mrs. Smith from Church Street? No, how
could it be? She is far too civilized to have ever caused such

a primordial storm of primary desire and nondesire. Who was it then? It was the animal mother who, once known so intimately, is the first intuition of being for those on their way to being human. It is no coincidence that certain origin myths strictly adhere to this *plot*. In the Roman origin myth, for example, an animal mother—the Capitoline she-wolf—suckles a pair of twins. Similarly, sometimes a male human marries a beautiful female animal who sheds her fur in the water, in the evening. This intuition, also given to the daughters of Mrs. Smith, means that there is an original *Great Stuffed Animal* from which they may derive themselves. What needs to be more deeply understood is why this intuition has a prior validity, in a symbolic sense, in groups dominated by females.

Let us assume hypothetically that the evidence for this first Great Mother Animal is communicated to both sexes, to male and female children. But if this is so, then the path of male and female sexual identification essentially diverges at a point that is of such significance that it no longer seems conspicuous: the mothers are simultaneously perceived from *inside and outside*. The woman is initially faceless (from inside), a container-you, before she turns herself "inside out" to show the newborn child her outer face. She has the improbable nature of a Möbius strip, whereas the father appears only on the outside, always showing his exterior image. He has *no* interior image. Whereas the mother is anthropomorphic in only one of her two modes, the father always appears in a male human form. The proof of anthropomorphism in regard to the mother is still pending today, whereas fathers are more than happy to stand up for their humanity, or rather for their human appearance, which is called masculinity.

In the first volume of his great *Spheres* trilogy, Peter Sloterdijk explains that humans gain their humanity in an interior, before moving out and undergoing what he calls a change of envelopes [*Hüllenwechsel*].[74] He correctly describes the contact with a warm and nourishing nearness, the placenta, as the model for a broader movement of socialization. After the change of envelopes, the mother, then the father, and then the siblings emerge from the "primordial twin." But he gives little attention to the enigma of anthropogenesis, to the *shape-shifting* the placenta undergoes on its way to becoming the extrauterine human mother. Our analysis concerns exactly this moment when the tender, primary-You changes its in-sight (inner view) for an *outer appearance*. What memories will there be of this first container-You, and in what symbolic form will it be *recovered*?[75] Which mask will one add to the living "surface" that contains the inner view?

When small boys begin to identify with the father they can build on their real father, or on figures resembling the father, even though it is through their separation from the mother that this identification provokes a permanent and deep destabilization.[76] When a father appears on the horizon, he comes as a human, but the mother never appears like a father does. To begin with, she always looks different, and indeed at first she does not look human. There are more conditions for falling into an Electra complex than for oedipalization, which only requires a power relation between three actually existing agents. The identification with the mother, however, the becoming-woman, leads down to the psychic antiquity of a prehuman Mother. If the girl imagines herself in the place of the mother, she immediately lands between two mutually enclosed modulations of the feminine. If the girl envies the mother she envies everything the mother has, and especially what she phantasizes the latter calls her own. This amounts to a situation in which, irrespective of rational objections, a great animal Mother is identified with a specific person. The lines of sexual identification separate at exactly this point, in the difference between a gaze uniting an interior and exterior view and one coming from the pure outside. The girl who looks at her mother senses that she holds something back in herself, that she has swallowed a constitutive concealment—her inner view—and that as a result she always appears as double, as a binomial of the prehuman and the human. Freud would have done better to have grounded the fear of the hole on this rather than inspiring little girls' revulsion at their inferior sex with his views of their already punished and castrated mothers (who no doubt lack a penis). The girl who attempts, irrespective of reason and "reality" and her *"fear of the hole,"* to align the great animal Mother and her concrete mother does not become aware of the lost penis but of the depth of the procreating container-You.

Now it begins to become clear in what way the animal helps in the identification of gender difference. With the help of the animal, the lines of identification can be traced in a double descent, and their feminine names now emerge: jaguar-woman, dragon-woman, toad-woman, *spider-woman,* wild buffalo, fast horse, *cat-woman,* sly vixen. We begin to understand why contemporary feminism has fought so hard against the dictate of the exterior gaze, against the male gaze that objectifies the woman.

Why are women so oversensitive about this gaze that strikes them from the outside, to the point that entire feminist libraries compose war machines against the validity of this gaze? The primordial layer, the human animal-woman and animal-Mother is absent by definition, both symbolically and politically, in any society that privileges the male gaze. Consequently, this layer is reflexively registered by women as *her deficient Being,* as insufficient beauty, insufficient intelligence, *insufficient humanity.* Women despair because of this regime of the male gaze, because its all-encompassing validity casts doubt on their complex interweaving of inner and outer perceptual certitude in which spatiality and subjectivity coincide. The daughter senses that the mother, despite being in the middle of "humanity," inexplicably believes she is stuck in the prehuman. Deep inside, girls know that if they want to hold onto their mother, then they too are not-yet-human. In a world dominated by man and the hu-man they cannot rid themselves of the suspicion that there is something wrong with them, and as time runs out in which to realize their (impossible) becoming-human-woman, they begin to panic.

In totemism, this primary relation connecting the girl to the "container-mother" is symbolized by her personification of an animal. It gives the intuition of the nourishing, caring quality of the "container-You" the form of an animal and in this can be called a feminist humanism. In feminist humanism, the part of diffuse prehumanity is identified and defined as an animal-being and integrated as an essential aspect of social structure. It becomes the Archimedean point of ascendency. In this way the animal embodies the *legacy of the mother.* The mother bequeaths the animal part that she in turn received from her mother. Totemism's specific characteristic of meeting the concerns of female identification becomes clear if we avoid calling totemistic consciousness a type of "primitivism."

One might object that the totem animal should instead be understood as the father of the tribe, as the male patron, and that it is curious that female identification should presuppose an animal "primordial father."[77] While Freud's concept of the primordial father returning as an animal has often been criticized, it is to his credit that he made totemism fruitful for psychoanalysis, even though his prioritization of the father meant that he saw the father in the totem animal. The interpretation of the totem animal as a social fact of matricentric culture is, however, only partially opposed to Freud. Insofar as we assume that the

level of emergence is personified in the animal, which is
a being capable of relationships, of nurturing and caring,
we can, rejecting Freud's interpretation, credibly call it
"mother." That goddesses are either represented as theri-
omorphs or accompanied by an animal has also, however,
been understood by feminists as meaning that the animal
is the *husband* of the goddess.[78] But the animality of the
mother and the animality of the groom do not exclude one
another; they belong together structurally according to the
principle of exogamy. This confirms, if by other means,
Freud's assumption that female identification and erotic
orientation do not simply follow a changing of object.[79]
Freud certainly registers the ambivalence that the continuity of the mother-bond evokes: "The woman's husband,
who to begin with inherited from her father, becomes after
a time her mother's heir as well."[80] Mechtild Zeul goes a
step further, arguing that the intensity and vividness of the
early mother–daughter relationship remains an integral
component of a woman's later life.[81]

The patterns built in the relationship to the primordial Mother are reactivated by an intimus who, like the
apersonal Mama, is shaped like an animal (the beauty and
the beast). The frog prince is such an intimus. The bride
vaguely remembers feeling a great intimacy in the vicinity
of animal warmth and the animal's instinctual automatism.
The concrete man, in this respect like the concrete mother,
arises from the level of vital emergence, and from a distance he is nonhuman, other, foreigner. The exogamic
model, which instructs one to seek the foreigner, is the
opposite of the popular Platonism of erotic matters, which
is designed for recognition. The primordially known is not
married but the nonrelated. The foreigner becomes the
intimate alien, the same title under which the vital sus-
tenance, the monumentally intimate Mama, had already
appeared. Here, it seems more appropriate to speak of
schizogamy (rather than exogamy) because the primor-

dial animal-Mother qua principle of imaginary and social cohesion must be split in order to produce the groom as her equivalent. In schizogamy a triangle is in fact inscribed, although it is a *pre-oedipal* one. Schizogamy explains how the woman's attachment does not change object (as Freud assumed) and that this object constancy is in fact grounded in a deeper layer that introduces a "distance" or blurring of the attachment through a mnemological difference (the "antiquity of the soul"). But schizogamy does not *enable* a "cool" or detached relationship and instead initiates *Eros as search modus.* The woman "warmed up" by the primordial Mother will have to search for this mother again, but she will not miss her as eternally lost, as she meets her again in the *foreigner.* Freud deceptively called this doubling of the erotic object female "bisexuality," a premature diagnosis of the obscurity and mystery of object choice and its symptoms: "Some portion of what we men call the 'enigma of woman' may perhaps be derived from this expression of bisexuality in women's lives."[82] The extrinsic position of the simultaneously inside-outside original Mama is intelligently coded in the exogamy rule. In the model of *schizogamy,* it is made *explicit.*

The intimus comes from a group of nonhumans, those designated as *others,* as foreigners. Intimacy as a quality is found in being-inside, in interiority, in internalization. It emerges through the reactivation of the spatial figure of the primordial Mother (inner-being, becoming-inner). The eros of the girl combines this spatial figure with the as yet faceless foreigner and waits for them to rise from the unknown and nondifferentiable, from the nameless and without categories, and get into bed with her.

"And if, on this occasion, virgins had to spend their first night with total strangers, this too served to remove responsibility in a way familiar to us, once again, from sacrificial ritual. Sometimes it was the groom, in disguise, who assumed the stranger's role."[83] Burkert got the gist of it.

Xenological Anamnesis

Beyond the exogamy rule's political and social dimensions, it obviously outlines a form of forgetting rather than the form of memory found in Platonic love. The totemistic bride can neither *remember* the form of the first Mother, who originally contained her and carried her inside and out, nor recognize the figure of the approaching groom. Her question will be the gnostic one: "Who are you?"[84] Here, function dominates over form. If the prehuman Mother and the extrahuman groom are superimposed, there is a *change of form,* but the function remains constant (there is no change of object). There is rather a tension between the change of form and a *Xenon* that signifies lost or forgotten intimacy. In contrast to gnosis and to Platonism, the successful existence is conceived as a *breakthrough to the strange,* not an escape from it. The totemistic queens give us the possibility of a foreign man; he cannot be related nor can he become related, because his symbolic place is nonrelatedness as a paradoxically *intimate otherness.* Depending on whether you make someone your intimus, socius, or partner, different conclusions can be drawn. The formation of couples is subject to complicated interpretations. The world falls *grosso modo* into an exogamous and an endogamous camp. The endogamous approach, whose model is sibling marriage (or in any case an incestuous relationship), favors child marriage. The bride is brought into the household of her future husband and grows up with him like a sister. The exogamous approach, however, moves individuals into a state of continuous erotic alarm, because behind every *blind date* could be hiding the ultimate rendezvous. This noticeably raised level of excitement becomes a significant economic factor in modern societies. Without exogamous excitement, one cannot imagine lacking an object of desire as a permanent condition—a central theme of postmodern theory. Deleuze and Guattari were not entirely right when they strapped the Oedipus complex (the incestuous structure) onto the capitalist desiring machine, because Clytemnestra's complex also keeps the machine going. In modern societies, a mixture of exogamous and endogamous orientations give direction to the system. We seem to search for endogamous completion with the help of exogamous erotic bursts, ensuring the disquiet between the sexes and the incessancy of desire. One could say that searching for a partner today comes under the special protection of the *schadenfreude* of matrifugal Platonism. As a result, drive theory became the central theme of psychoanalysis, simultaneously capturing the *"animalistic"* parts of the erotic machinery but formulating them as an insult to those they drive, who are denied an insight into the causal depths of their emotional state. The totemistic condition pre-empts this dispossession of the "animal" drives by personifying the layer on which it rests. The coming together of the schizogamous couple stands under the patronage of the animal.

Thus, the sought man will be a foreigner in our story and—this is his social characteristic—will remain a foreigner. He will pay a courtesy visit and be prepared, as its essential condition, to dignify the constitutive principle of the queen. In literature we see what happens when this willingness for a courtesy visit and for reverence wanes, graphically played out in the dream hermeneutics of Orestes. From now on, humans who declare themselves the children of animals are suspect. If animals come too close to humans, or if an animal nurtures itself on the human breast like the snake on Clytemnestra, it seems obscene to the new technologists of hominization, the masterminds of the Greek *polis.* Humans are no longer certain they are human *extrinsically,* from the outside, by a *xenocratic* definition and demarcation of borders (*de-finition*), but by an internal formation of a group that allows the human to be derived from the human (*homo ab homine*). So far unnoticed, but nevertheless far-reaching prerequisites for modes of hominization are hidden in the rules for marriage. The exogamy rule that applied to Clytemnes-tra necessarily follows from an intuition that, as Bergson also confirms, appears as the coming near of the obvious. This is an intuition that connects us with the prehuman or nonhuman, from which we believe we came. This intuition is a state of indirect self-consciousness and coalesces with social consciousness.[85] Translated into its systemic mean-ing, this intuition implies that "all parasitical relations strive for a stabilization of symbiosis."[86]

That this attitude stands at the beginning of social activ-ity is also confirmed by a comment made by Gabriel Tarde, who makes the connection with the other, or rather the *imi-tation of the other,* the principle of his philosophical sociology. In his view, "self-imitation" is the assertion and mainte-nance of identity, but this process necessarily splits into self-imitation and *external*-imitation because memory can integrate otherness as sameness and vice versa, sublating modes or states of becoming in itself that are coded as past or as other and so are effectively a foreign self-ness [*Selbigkeit*].[87] The concept of the "other" is, however, too weak for our investigation. The problem encapsulated in totemism is less a matter of the dialectical difference between identity and otherness (i.e., differences occur-ring within a whole) than of a first great difference that produces inward compression (as *intimacy*) through its *repul-sion,* thereby making discrete unities consistent.[88] That the foreign was also an attractive idea in the metaphysical age can be seen in the concept of the foreign God, in the *deus absconditus,* but also *ex negativo* in the commandments that make foreign gods terrifying. Totemism employs foreign-ness, in the spirit of Gabriel Tarde, as having at once social and mnemotechnical (genealogical) meaning. The foreign operates less in the vertical, where the totally strange is bought to the Archimedean point of its greatest tension with the world, than in the horizontal, where on the level of interaction puzzling evidence appears and asks to be explained. That is why people give the most peculiar explanations about their descent, even though it seems obvious that they derive from humans. Only a philosophy that does not consider growing and becoming will remain indifferent to these enigmas. Only a philosophy that is only made by and for adults cannot begin to answer these questions.

Unconditional conditionality, or conditional unconditionality, is the signature of collective memory. It forms the logical and affective stage upon which totemism makes its grand entrance. Insofar as memory includes an other that represents the intersection of the other and the self-same, a principle is required that organizes what fades away, that organizes forgetting, a first amnesia that will initiate anamnesis. What is the principle of forgetting? The principle of forgetting is like the caterpillar the butterfly left behind, like the childhood the adult has outgrown. All arts of memory, philosophies of memory, and technologies of memory are based on a radical Platonism inasmuch as they involve remembering what can be known, whereas in totemism the preconscious, the unknowable, and the unknown are remembered. But then, how do we *recall* the foreign? Memory itself can be understood as the point where the a priori past meets the future like a *promise,* or in other words a first consciousness in its specific formation (primitive) meets a first Being (mighty, undifferentiated, containing the universe). A mother first embraces the child *like a living glass-house,* only after which does she actually hold them in her arms.[89] This image must always be taken from the *foreign,* because consciousness has always, both structurally and linguistically, left that level of experience behind. This congruence is therefore invoked as a *memory of the foreigner,* in expectation of a figure adequate to our first intimacy. This memory first functions erotically and then politically.

Totemistic "Objectification"

Curiously enough, the condition of possibility for the Athenian experiment, that is for political organization in its middle format, is a successful totemism that has standardized the "*imitation d'autrui*" to the point that sameness is projected beyond the parental borders of ascendance so as to identify the free (male) citizens of the *polis* as a homogenous group, as an *animalia politica* who tacitly agree to denounce the marriage rules of "prehistory." For this reason, it seems to me, the older versions of the drama emphasize the dream of Clytemnestra, while their numerous repetitions solidify a new hermeneutic that predicts her ruin rather than her glory. In this the great Athenian dramatists proved worthy of the task bestowed upon them. They allow subtle echoes of the causes of the rivalry between ascendance models to be heard, but they direct the limited attention span appropriate to propaganda to the political and legal incompatibility of matrilinear, uterine, and totemistic systems with the patrilinear concepts that absorb them. The possibility that this could provide a parable about the political ability or inability to associate with the foreign has, because of the *historicization of cultural phases,* remained foreclosed. The totemism complex and its symbol-forming function have been knocked down to a (nevertheless amazingly successful) subgenus of ethnological and intercultural folklore, and this has obstructed psychological, social, economic, and media-theoretical readings that would have made totemism into an efficient model of the contemporary situation. Even though the foreign, like few other concepts, has become central to cultural studies' preoccupation with the production of identities, and to contemporary politics and art, an inexplicable superficiality clings to it, for which an increasing sophism attempts to compensate. Kristeva's idea of self-alienation, or rather of a foreignness one feels in or against oneself, Derrida's attempts to smuggle into the philosophical canon the "guest" and "friendship" as figures of a process that reduces foreignness, has done little to change the current state of affairs. What is most evident, however, is the idiocy of a society that does not appreciate what has the highest value on its symbolic stock market, despite the fact that exoticism keeps it afloat. On the surface it seems as though the pre-oedipal, or rather the totemistic constellation, has lost its rights. But if it really contains a fundamental experience of the soul (nonmemory), whose persistence under different signs is precisely the object of our investigation, how could it ever not be within its rights? Instead, we must locate and present its symbolizations and the essential moments in which it appears *as an object.* Our analysis presumes that totemism is not a primitivism of specific groups but a symbolic politics rooted in the *pre-oedipality of the girl,* a girl who realizes the desire for the lost as a desire for the "foreigner." Now, what kind of foreigner can this be, and what kind of desire does she have for it? We will see what objects fulfill this need, this primary exoticism, today. If animals have served their totemistic function, then other mediums have to be found to satisfy this addiction or this simple desire. What can a social formation do in order to satisfy it? Which objects have sufficient exoticism to allow a form of immersion that resembles making contact with the foreigner and first-love? What kind of new totemism can easily win over modern societies because it arrives on a well-prepared terrain?

2

Radical Totemism
and Automatism

Theogenesis and the Twilight of Machines

Our task now is to relate certain elements of our contemporary use of media to the panorama on totemism,
so that the congruence of an archaic pre-oedipalism and
our "love" of devices [*Apparaten*] becomes apparent. We
will explore what kind of relationship with the nonhuman can actually be conceived in this case and in what
way it appears or plays a role. Today, the range of possible "relationship-catchers" has expanded immeasurably,
pushing aside the more general fetishism in favor of an
objecthood pertaining to the *schizogamic syndrome*. Our main
thesis is that totemism offers a model for the social and
cultural engagement with the foreign that illuminates the
overlooked connection between the imperative for collective animal ancestors and those exogamous practices found
in modern projects placing "desubjectivized" and thus
medial (i.e., reacting and responding) objects at the center of an expanding homogenization of "humanity." The
main obstacle to the analysis of this structure has been the
insistence on the connection between totemism and religion. While totemism's resemblance to religion has been

discussed by theology, anthropology, sociology, and structuralist thought, no media theory has ever been based upon it.[1] Only Bataille, in *Theory of Religion,* describes the gradual alignment of bodies, animals, and instruments in the mists of the birth of the main religions and their effect on the *status of objects*: "Only starting from the mythical representation of autonomous spirits does the body find itself on the side of things, insofar as it is not present in sovereign spirits. The real world remains as a residuum of the birth of the divine world: real animals and plants separated from their spiritual truth slowly rejoin the empty objectivity of tools."[2]

Our analysis will sharply diverge from those of Wilhelm Wundt, Arnold Gehlen, and Claude Lévi-Strauss, who were all ready to accept an *a priori* historicization of totemism as the condition for its scientific existence. Just the opposite, totemism outlines an utterly contemporary task, as Bruno Latour succinctly states: "If we are going to attempt to redraw the new institutions of democracy . . . , from here on we need to have access to the multiplicity of associations of humans and non-humans that the collective is precisely charged with *collecting.*"[3] It is likely that totemism in its specific form, a form favoring the animal and tailored around the prestige of a small group, is the "always already past" state of a political culture. But it is a matter of isolating, and working through, the motifs and elements of this historical "childhood" that continue to exist after the totemistic state had faded away, after the small totemistic group had been surpassed by larger social and political associations, which have put new solutions and configurations of these elements on their agenda.[4]

In my opinion, the pre-oedipal motor is still at work in our relationships with specific objects. Electra stands for a pre-oedipal erotic continuum in which the *form* of the primordial favorite may *change* while its function remains identical. Insofar as this relationship is intrinsically inextinguishable, it is constantly translated into new objectivizations/reifications. Besides the feminist "humanism" already described, totemism achieves a systemic stabilization when it compensates for the first amnesia, for the oblivion of descent. This systemic stabilization occurs by passing the imagination of a group through a point that remains external to it. This presupposes an exocratic or xenological operation that is more easily achieved when the primary totemistic condition ("childhood") is highly active. Stabilization succeeds when an exteriority, an *alien*, surrounds the curled-in intimacy of the group. This *alien*, or systemic partner of the group, watches over those inside, much like the caring and protecting presence of an ancestor. Frazer insisted on structural criteria for totemism that, first, explained origins, and second, did so in such a way that genealogical descent did not pass through any individual of the group. As soon as everyone has the same distance from an ancestor, the group is homogenized. The foreigner is not a monster from the beyond but rather the all-loving ancestor, a pure eye, a caregiver acting as a patron saint. If we are to track down contemporary totemism, we must look out for situations that manifest this form of cozy heteronomy in a deeper, medial sense. Where does phantasy lead when it rushes out of the open interface of a psyche eager to ground itself?

Between Leroi-Gourhan, who gave a shape to the technical organs emerging from the capital of the body, and Arthur Kroker, who was fond of an electrical flesh, a theoretical field has emerged in the last decades that is dedicated to the relationship between humans and their instruments, devices, and machines. Bourdieu and Leroi-Gourhan argue that even interhuman relationships are highly mechanized, machined, automated, and organized in habitual formulas and operational chains. Leibniz had already remarked on this in the *Monadology,* where he wrote: "Men act like beasts insofar as the sequence of their perceptions results from the principle of memory alone."[5] This comment annihilates a priori the sharp division made by humanists between a human–human relationship and that between humans and their devices. Consequently, media theory overlaps substantially with contemporary sociology, although this does not mean that it is able to confront the given problems. In the deep, subliminal layers of our relationship to devices a specific kind of regression becomes noticeable: a primary condition, an addiction, a hypnosis.[6] The investigation of this (expanded) condition demands an elongated perspective, one that media theory and sociology may not necessarily have at their disposal. The primitivism assumed in this relationship can only be interpreted when one has stopped concocting a theory of childlike states as the precursor to, and provisional state of, being grown-up. The relationship to the device does not *replace* those one wishes to have to desired objects but varies, completes, and deepens them. If humans have a fundamental tendency to mistake their wives for hats, then this follows the assumption that wife and hat are not different categories of object, and we thus drop the opposition of organic and inorganic, of subject and object, and of consciousness and unconsciousness.[7] Sacks's hero perceives his wife and hat as being *animated*; they blur together while signifying each other. On one side, it is necessary to investigate what objects and devices do with humans but also, and on the other, what humans do with them. Humans fall head over heels in love with them and have what Mario Perniola calls, following a notion of Walter Benjamin, "inorganic sex" with them.[8] Perniola demonstrates how people who get mixed up with "objects" fix their Eros on them as if falling in love. With this, even the Leibnizian thesis that humans behave like unreasonable animals is surpassed, when they now carry on like objects, like animated inorganic objects.

This transference allows these objects and devices to be so near to those humans "serving" them that they receive souls, becoming humanity's peculiar partners. Here, objects ascend to the status of qualified comrades, while reasonable subjects descend into childhood. "Inorganic sex" denotes a togetherness where subjectivity and personality exist in a regressive mode, allowing them to find the frequency of pre-oedipal relationships.[9] In inorganic sex, both subject and object are ecstatic and become *medial*. What we are dealing with here is a state of neither self-reflection nor self-awareness but an ecstatic being that a psychology of media must recognize as the principle mode of existence. This mode of being characterized by a fixation on objects can be designated as a *radical totemism*. Electra became the first director of the Office of Radical Totemism, she specialized in the dissimilar things that the human psyche showers upon itself and thereby animates itself. She specialized in inorganic sex.

If, as we have seen, such a dissimilar and "prehuman" thing can be anything at all, it nevertheless appears in a specific system and has its own times and places. There are, as is clearly the case with totemism, particular concentrations of interest in the dissimilar, which takes people (and often the most influential) out of themselves and makes them fall prey to entities or objects. These objects then begin to play a prominent role in the life of a group or a society.

Totem and Xenocracy

Structuralism considered totemism a linguistic system or grammar, and therefore neglected the *state* that affectively builds the totemistic mindset. As well as other specific characteristics, totemism is linked to a particular emotional level that appears in an abundance of shades and colors. This level welcomes a continuously changing cast of figures and objects in a cultural laboratory that *interprets and theatricalizes* the primordial or animal relationship. As long as the relationship with the animal is established in a culture, the members of a clan claim to be related to a certain animal whose spirit protects them.[10] In certain performances they transform into individuals of its kind, prefer hairstyles that resemble the animal's hair, decorate their objects with signs related to it, and sing and dance in its manner. Claude Lévi-Strauss presented and commented on the sociological functions of totemism, and in particular the connection of marriage rules to totemism, but he also documented how this relationship to the animal expresses *the ability to take something dissimilar as the cause of a specific and excessive mode of being.* It has the quality of a hypnosis or trance that at certain times is enacted performatively. The significance of this relationship is quite different to that established between humans and in fact supplies the latter with the energy to bond that it requires. The animal is the immortal founder of its clan, and in a world entirely organized through the kinship system and genealogy, was set in the highest rank. It is not simply the case, however, that a society's preoccupation with a certain animal is an entirely positive symptom. Odd notes can also be heard, like the jarring ambivalence of the prohibition, the taboo, against killing the animal concerned, and the simultaneous demand to *nevertheless* eat it at certain times and on certain occasions. Naturally, such things invite theoretical hypotheses, and Freud, for one, immediately saw the loved and hated primordial father of the horde resurrected in the totem animal. But things are not, however, so simple.

Lévi-Strauss took the enthusiasm for totemism, first of all, as expressing the state of the theoreticians who had fallen for it and in doing so believed he could declare a fairly longstanding theoretical delirium at an end.[11] In *Totemism* he dissects the errors that led to the "totemism syndrome" in ethnology, cultural theory, and in the history of religions, while simultaneously reducing the animal totem to a structural or, in other words, a differentiating and theological function. Essential within this theological function, Lévi-Strauss argues, is first of all the embodiment of a god by the animal and, second, the primordial relationship established between the ancestor and this animal being.[12] Insofar as our investigation has an issue with totemism, and even makes it the basis of a new media theory, it has to pick from totemism's many meanings those that coincide with pre-oedipal characteristics. Of these, certain constitutive points of view should be focused on: the explanation of descent, marriage rules, and the motif of foreignness.[13] Radical totemism is a nonspecific and simplified totemism, one that is essentially defined by its views on the foreign, on hypnosis, and on certain pre-oedipal objects. Lévi-Strauss's thesis that the totemism boom in ethnology and psychoanalysis (hysterically) paralleled the hysteria debate is, from the point of view of research into the pre-oedipal, an argument in favor of our understanding of totemism.[14] It has to be noted that between 1890 and 1920 the motif of heteronomy, of *xenocracy*, influenced a series of theories and diagnoses, to the point that exoticism and xenophilia were pushed to the extreme with great pleasure. Evidently the same impulse was at work in the endless discussions of hypnosis, in research into hysteria, in psychoanalysis, in theories of hallucination, and in experimental research into spiritualism. This period also (and perhaps not by coincidence) marks the beginning of the technical age in a strict sense, which reproduced the xenocratic hypnosis by new means.

Freud grasped totemism in order to design a masculine

memory, a primordial scene. This scene is the disfigure-
ment of the father after his sons had murdered him, which
Freud thought was prior to the political and propaedeutic
function of totemism emphasized by Wundt. He was probably drawn to the "primitive" in totemism as an expression
of the archaic soul. But his comparisons of "primitives" to
the "mentally ill" greatly restrict the value and use of his
work in this area. Nevertheless, to summarize the result
of Freud and Wundt's dispute over totemism, on a general level the cultic structure of totemism includes an Eros
directed toward the other as the better part, which forms
the condition of possibility for the political organization
of a group as *corporate identity*. This relates to Kantorowicz's
study of the two bodies of the king. Kantorowicz focuses
on the trickeries of medieval jurisprudence in its attempts
to cope with the problem of the dual king:

> The King has two Capacities, for he has two Bodies
> the one whereof is a Body natural, consisting of nat-
> ural Members as every other Man has, and in this he
> is subject to Passions and Death as other Men are; the
> other is a Body politic, and the Members thereof are his
> Subjects, and he and his Subjects together compose the
> Corporation, as Southcote said, and he is incorporated
> with them, and they with him, and he is the Head and
> they are the Members, and he has sole Government of
> them; and this Body is not subject to Passions as the
> other is, nor to Death, for as to this Body the King
> never dies, and his natural Death is not called in our
> Law (as Harper said), the Death of the King, but the
> Demise of the King, not signifying by the Word (*Demise*)
> that the Body politic of the King is dead, but that there
> is a Separation of the two Bodies.[15]

To some extent then, Kantorowicz understood the cen-

tral aspect of the logic of totemism (which he nevertheless does not mention) as the social constitution of the
totem in the form of the king and so launches it on the
path of anthropomorphization. But the king's body is
still distinguished from the bodies of all the other members of the community, as his body is the body of all, in
which the community unites. This body is the holy body,
the anointed body, the main object of state reasoning.
What for Kantorowicz is the king, is the totem for Wilhelm Wundt[16] and Arnold Gehlen,[17] who identify the far-
reaching religious and political functions of the totem in
human culture. This extrapolation of the body produces
symbolic containers that embrace groups socialized through
new forces of cohesion.

Animal Mummy and the Apparatus-Function

We will now consider the tasks and achievements of the
totem animal more closely. If Clytemnestra affirms her
descent from a dragon or a snake, which I suggest was the
oneirocritical interpretation of the central oracle of the
Oresteia, then this animal is neither common game nor an
especially gifted farm animal or pet. In fact, this animal
does not even have to actually exist where it is revered, as
the universal use of the lion in the attenuated heraldic
form demonstrates. Similarly, the totemistic relationship
does not necessarily require an individual friendship, like
the one between a little boy and a dog named Lassie. What
sets us on the right track is a reading of Iamblichus's tract
on the mysteries of the Egyptians. Iamblichus describes
how a theurgist—establishing contact with a god, trying to
align the god with his or her intentions—prepares a suitable arrangement of substances (a "favorite dish") into
which the god descends. This handling of the divine body
reveals it to be an apparatus constructed and functioning

according to certain rules and in which spiritual knowledge of the being concerned, along with physiological and
pharmacological knowledge, are condensed and represented. This arrangement operates as a god-trap and is
a tricky thing, an animal body, a sacrificial animal, a cult
animal. The extreme dissimilarity of the animal invites us
on a trip to the Plus Ultra, which in this case is the open
horizon of divine powers and their manifestations opening
above us.[18] The theurgist's primary apparatus is the animal, which in the hot phase of totemism saves his or her
insights through the *technology* of the *conserved animal* or, in
other words, as a mummy. Conserved animals represent
the ancestors, properly prepared for eternity, the grand-
mothers and fathers of the humanity that celebrates them.

Iamblichus writes, "'For why on earth is it necessary,'
according to your account, 'for the initiate who views the
rites to touch the dead, when most invocations are accomplished by means of dead animals?'"[19] And he continues:

> But if we consider, on its own terms, how divination is
> accomplished through sacred animals such as hawks, we
> must never say that the gods come to bodies in service,
> as attendants; for they do not preside over any particu-
> lar animal individually, or separately, or materially, or
> according to a certain condition. Rather, this kind of
> contact with the organs of divination should be ascribed
> to daemons and those such as are divided, to which an
> animal is individually allotted, and who govern partially
> in this manner, and have not been allotted an admin-
> istration that is entirely self-sufficient and immaterial.
> Or, if one wishes to maintain that a base must be allot-
> ted to (the daemons), of the kind through which they
> can associate with and be of help to human beings, in
> that case we must concede that this (base) should be
> pure from bodies, for no communion occurs between

the pure and its opposite. It makes greater sense that
this is brought into communion with human beings
through the soul of the animals; for this has a certain
affinity with human beings through the homogeneity
of life, but with daemons because it has been released
from bodies and exists in some way separate.[20]

One may marvel at an embalmed and bandaged Apis
bull, a crocodile, and a small mummified falcon from a
temple of Horus in the Egyptian collection of the Museum
of Art History in Vienna. For the cult, the animal mummy
represents what Iamblichus characterizes as "sympathetic
material."[21] The museum's publication concerning their
mummy collection does not even mention animal mummies, as their existence seems barely compatible with our
idea of a highly cultured Egypt.[22]

Far-reaching conclusions can be drawn from the
burial rites carried out on humans and animals: The animal functions as a specific and amplified proxy for the
human and includes a *communicative* dimension. Today, the
oft-cited permeable border between humans and animals
drawn under the auspices of genetic engineering and organ
transplants recalls the atmosphere of an Egyptian embalm-
ing factory and is more of an archaic postulate than a new
"danger." Its medium, or vehicle, is the artfully prepared
body that enables a primary curiosity to become "technoia."[23] At the time of totemistic alliances with the animal,
contact was made with a resonant body, which explained
what being-human was about and became the dispenser
and transmitter of the latest gospels, an oracular medium
prepared for the god to descend. The mummy worked like
a screen broadcasting a transmission. Thus, transgressing the boundary between species is totemism's declared
intention, achieved through a hermeneutic operation that
seeks to solve the urgent problem of identity. The animal

protects its descendants and embraces them within its *pure outside*. The inner consolidation can only take place if this *outside* appears benevolent, as the *good face,* as caring being. Who does not want a *guard* that is trained to deal with dangers one does not see? But access to this benevolent being does not come from the side of the human, who subordinates the animal to his or her purposes, but from the side of the animal that watches over the emergence of the human. Totemism *by definition* ignores the boundary separating species, meaning the animal is the First Human before it degenerates into being the first machine. But ignoring the boundaries between species does not mean allowing the difference between human and animal to become blurred, but as Socrates puts it, it means admitting that we *do not know what a human is.*

The convertibility of You and It therefore emerges in this passage through the animal–human relationship.[24] The mediality expressed in this relationship equals openness toward the dissimilar, because the animal enigmatically interferes with its human, and it actually communicates with him, it whispers to him, guides, protects, and informs him. The animal takes the place of sympathetic matter. It is the preindividual from which the human springs up, similar to Gilbert Simondon's theory of individuation, a theory increasingly important to contemporary political theory of the left.[25] Nevertheless, the animal drives individuation more obviously than a "preindividual substrate," a milieu, or the spheric, and it prevents destabilization through its enduring assistance.

The reason why totemism has not attracted much attention within media theory was perhaps the rather pompous thesis of the ancestral dignity of the totem animal. Contemporary intellectuals became bored when the discussion turned to ancestors, ghosts, and transcendence. But while such things were successfully kept away from the

surface of academic "business," in the underground, in
the parasitical sciences and an increasingly rampant therapy "business" it is about nothing else. So although one is
increasingly astonished by the consequences of the permeable boundary of the human species, and enjoys its pleas-
ing *side effects,* the university's philosophical business enjoys
its far-off exclusivity and allows the questions moving the
underground of the present to roll off it, professionally
untouched.

Those who think that the status of the animal is clearly
distinguished from that of devices, which can have anything foisted upon them except ancestor worship, are again
reminded that the recognition of the ancestral animal only
goes so far. Clan members placing themselves under their
protection ask for a classification of themselves only to
find that the zone of the imagination where ancestors have
their place is blurry and full of shadows. Identifying an
animal as an ancestor presupposes that the ancestor is a
scintillating, supraindividual image of a benevolent being
but *whose face is missing.* Thus, animals become *very old humans,*
establishing a ("anthropotheriological") relation that still
is drawn today to prehominid species, such as that between
human and ape (i.e., totemistic relations: humans stem
from apes or from a specific kind of ape). Totemism supposes an anti-Genesis, it is the *carnival of evolutionism.* The old
world, which invests its deepest knowledge in questions of
origins, directs the power of its imagination at the animal.
This discovery of the animal, which equals its *invention,* is,
on the one hand, a result of the blurry image of the ancestor produced by memory and, on the other, of the soul's
natural desire to overflow in excess.

The transformations that take place within totemism—
becoming-animal, becoming-mother, and becoming-
general—establish a complex system of *objectifications of empathic
knowledge* manifested in that special class of nonobjects we

call art. This is the moment when *ars/techne* emerges, along with those skills that will deposit knowledge into *objects*. In order to understand the ancestor as a limit that determines a series of similar things, one must recall its ability to produce the human species in the objectification of a cult. In accordance with primitive logic, this does not exclude eating the ancestor—a theme, incidentally, that the scholars of various disciplines (anthropology, paleontology, pre- and early history, paleopsychology) address with the greatest reluctance.

The question of origins is also a question about the mechanics of attention or, more precisely, about the search for positive echoes that forms the basis of *immunity*. The ancestor keeps permanent watch over his or her clan, but his or her power relates to the collective attention he or she receives from it. The complicated entanglement of openness, openness to the world, medial openness, and the echo belonging to totemism (and to every magical system) leads to a stable state of circulation and gives control over effluxes and influences. The perennial relationship to the totem subcutaneously reinforces the idea accompanying all acts at all times—namely, a collective superego (or *infraego*) that, for example manifest in the polite group or family howling pygmy songs, emphatically guarantees that one is neither alone nor forgotten. We begin to realize that what matters in the world of these relationships is maintaining the balance between radiation and being irradiated. The subtle economy of resonances encompassing exchange and sacrifice unfolds through a comprehensive system of rules. Rather than being a personalized guardian angel, who can secure only a limited number of social and political structures, the totem is a substrate upon which all group members equally thrive. Compared to a totem animal, a guardian angel looks like a nanny for a spoiled only child. The animal is there for the many, and this is its protopolitical mission. Its strong symbolic value allows totemic ancestral protection to bring the systemic stabilization of general memory to a mnemological point. Its protective capacity links up with the subject at that point where the subject's consciousness fades into historical groundlessness. At precisely this point the totem blazes with thetic power: "I am a flamingo."

As a result, the functions of the ancestor and the oracle coincide in the holy animal-apparatus. The corpse is deployed in the role of a high-frequency connection. The mummy—the first people's radio—drives the radiating soul waiting for its echo crazy. Mummies are like low-energy houses, like soul-economizing objects whose barely ensouled condition makes the high-level souls' blood boil. The sovereign immobility, the frozen eternity of the great secret that mummies represent, does not fail to make its impression on living souls. But mummies also induce excitement about "corporeality," to quote Gail Weiss's concept. Nothing is more fascinating than the transitory low-level soul object, a soul relic, which as a soul trap and echo surface eavesdrops on infinite space. The negative balance of a mummy's low-level soul, its stoic and self-consuming objecthood, makes high-level souls tremble. They become aware of their "soul-wealth," which low-level souls would gladly snatch for themselves. The mummy introduces the apparatus-function. The moment the totem becomes political, it becomes technical. The great animal-mother becomes an animal-machine, the animal-apparatus acting as the processor organizing large groups. Whereas the wild animal—one thinks of the Brazilian jaguar stories[26]—rarely steps out of the forest to communicate with humans, the animal mummy lies in its shrine in perpetual presence: the present of the beyond. The relationship between totemism and funerary cults has only been superficially analyzed. The cultic veneration of the mummy marks a late state of totemism where objectification (the transfer of the animal into the object world) is well advanced. The mummified animal becomes *pure projection trap,* a collector and reflector of surplus soul, an abduction and induction apparatus. What kind of body secret is revealed in this mummy, in the highest degree of technical and magical refinement? It is the machinery that is produced and sanctified in order to trap the soul. Phantasies of resurrection and immortality are expressed in the operational efficiency of the bioma-chine, as an apparatus of incarnation and vitalization. The body is the great magnet attracting souls and rendering them controllable; it is the document, the archive, and the truth of the soul. The mummy is not only the tightly wrapped spare body that excites and attracts excessive soul quanta but a research facility investigating intercorporeal sympathy or *experimental becoming.*

The clan organized around its totem animal, or within the sphere of the sacred body-preserves [*Leib-Konserve*], establishes a base model for the democratic rules of radi-ation by seeking to tune the irradiation of the protective "satellite body" into the frequency of its collective radi-ation. The conserved body reflects the collective phan-tasies that impact on it and its relative soullessness, and this is the pure structure of memory. Collective amnesia is precipitated in it, the nonmemory of the first object, as well as the projection that synchronizes the members of a community as the common beneficiaries of the redirected message.

The enigmatic and profound it-ness of the totem, its ownership of patents and privileges in relation to organic and genealogical structures, leads to its own collapse at this point, because it allows it to *also* be forgotten that col-lective memory does not derive from a system but from a problem that first demands systematic work. Having lost its privileged status, the animal directly exchanged its enig-

matic sublimity for the system of things, forming an equivalence with them, with the egalitarian mass of things. Its
foreignness, which had filled the space of the *id,* was now
absorbed by specific functional things. As Frazer testifies,
totems might also be artificial things such as a ball, a string,
or a net, or things like lightning or rain.[27] Frazer writes:
"It is more difficult to realise the relation between a man
and his totem when that totem is an inanimate object. But
such totems are rare."[28]

This late, postapotropaic phase of totemism is the
paranoid-technoid phase and is characterized by an imbalance between radiation and irradiation. The object concerned is showered with soul, but its echo and affirmation
do not follow. Its allocated demons no longer murmur
from the folds of the substitute body; the thing in itself
remains tacit.[29] The soul heats up while its objects are stub-
bornly silent, and it cannot help implanting resonance
devices within them. The postmagical age mobilizes technical phantasy in order to reconstruct the totemic aspect
of the receding objects and oracles. Engineers go to work
to systematically produce, and make available, the echo as
a technical effect, creating new objects that more clearly
and effectively deliver the desired reactions. Lynn Thorndike points out the contemporaneity of a technical boom
in both magic and natural science in the Renaissance.[30] As
a result, the career of the cultic animal body passes seam-
lessly into the machine as an oracle-giving and operable
animal. It is not, as Lévi-Strauss thought, that finally the
purely semiotic or structural purpose of the totem emerges,
cooled in the calm waters of a system of signs. There was,
and is, another dimension in the totem whose representation has continued to pose a problem, and that is its
capacity to envelop the group, its "marginal formation" in
favor of a positive and internal immunization (protection
by the ancestor). How might this positive immunization by

the animal-ancestor be accomplished after its collapse and defeat by Hellenistic antibarbarian propaganda? How will the fragile ecosocial equilibrium get over this debasement of its principal term? What kind of crisis will, first, the human and, second, the deity suffer if the animal loses its protective and pedagogical function?

Anthropomorphization of the Deity

Despite the tenacious survival of the prejudice that totemism is an *eccentricity* of savage and uncivilized societies, it is nevertheless agreed that the gods first took *animal forms,* as well as appearing with an animal as their recognizable symbol. Marija Gimbutas and others point out that between 20,000 and 5,000 BCE goddesses appeared with a variety of animals, goddesses she sought to systematize.[31] If this time period seems too obscure, then knowledge of Egyptian religion is widely available, and everybody knows about the animal forms of its gods. In Egyptian religion and culture, most of the deities are human–animal hybrids, represented as human figures with the heads of cats, dogs, crocodiles, cows, etc. The common explanation that these figures represent priests wearing masks and performing ritualized roles does not grasp the significance of these animals. This thesis of priestly deceit obscures the fact that the relationship to the animal could once have had greater importance than the interhuman relationship. For the gods, it was mandatory to appear as an animal or to legitimize themselves through it.

The Hindu gods mastered the practice of transforming themselves into an animal, like Vishnu who transformed into a boar. The Puranas report that Vishnu so enjoyed being a boar that he forgot who he really was and started a family with a lovely wild sow, until Shiva finally persuaded him to return to his original divine shape.[32] Shiva only

needs the spark of a vision in his blazing third eye to immediately take on its form. Finally, the Greek gods, the inhabitants of Olympus, distinguish themselves in the same way.
Thus, Zeus reveals his sublimity by transforming into the
dissimilar; he becomes a bull, a swan, or lightning, and
it is no accident that Zeus makes use of this ability when
stepping out as a suitor. Zeus also transforms himself into
other gods or heroes, whose privileges he enjoys in their
name and form, a transformation that is particularly odi-
ous to monotheistic religions and their demand for eternal
identity. Something similar occurs in Hinduism, where
there are beautiful examples of this. When the Olympians
appear theriomorphic, however, they only make use of the
animal without really *being* it.

The aurora of the new generation of gods rises in front
of the old animal's eyes, and the new nobles cannot help
but recall that the human relationship to animals had
once been the most significant concept of human society. Consequently, they present themselves as good friends
of these animals or even as almost animal. Through this
camouflage, parallel bodies emerge, dividing the "ancestor" into, on one side, a king and, on the other, a god.
In the course of this singular split the animal increasingly
loses its animal face and begins to look like its protégé,
like a human. It is therefore not only the Egyptian priests
who dress up like animals but even more the reverse, as
the animal begins to assimilate itself with its darlings: the
humans. The new divine identity was pleased to assimilate itself with the human race, increasingly flattening
the constitutive difference that, on the pre-oedipal level,
had defined the amount of the human in the prehuman.
The new gods chose the most highly *elevated human beauty* for
theophany. With this, a new chapter of hominization was
opened. Being-human is no longer deduced and legitimized through the dissimilar, in relation to the lords

encountered in their territories, the animals dwelling in
their niches, but through the most beautiful human, who
one imitates with all one's power. An "Apollonian" technics
of beautification now opposes the older Dionysian techniques of collective and medial hypnosis deriving from the
sacred animal. Frazer writes: "In short, the tribal totem
tends to pass into an anthropomorphic god. And as he
rises more and more to human form, so the subordinate
totems sink from the dignity of incarnations into the hum-
ble character of favourites and clients."[33]

The beautiful gods have barely arrived—garments shining like gold, covered in gems, with bronze feet and thun-
dering voices—and the totem animal falls into decline, left
to come back as a *stuffed animal*. What kind of switch is this?
What kind of comprehensive revolution aims to replace the
animal with these cosmetically perfect humans? This displacement manifests the repression of the symbolic order
of the mother. When an identification with those who
are great, beautiful, and humanlike supports becoming-
human, the age of the father has dawned. It is he, the
one who appears exclusively *human* and does not encompass the double of animal and human, container-You and
singular person. Furthermore, the increasing domestication of animals implies the annihilation of the hypnogenic valences sheltered by the wild and autonomous animal. Wundt and Freud both stress that the domesticated
pet could not have triggered the original reflex at work in
totemism.[34] In Jim Jarmusch's film *Ghost Dog*, an entirely
ordinary dog appears to be an over-friendly totem, but
it does not escape the viewer that this specimen, derived
in a simply ridiculous way from the degenerate species of
man's living-room companion, turns feral with ferocity
and freedom, with the enigmatic and internal autonomy
that was once possessed by the great totem animal. In the
human–animal partnership, these savage features disap-

pear, and the superiority of the animal fades away. Despite
this, the new gods cannot manage without the prerequisites
of totemism—sacrifice and salvation—and so they attempt
to establish them as a reaction, as if a new sacrifice, and
so a new salvation, could repair the deficiencies of the old
cult. The theotechnics that installs the new great-humans
as deities is, therefore, not substantially different from that
of totemism, but the balance of radiation and irradiation
defining the relation of those with a human shape to others
differs significantly from that of the human–animal equivalence. Under human-shaped deities, the female imaginary is put into a state of emergency, because women's
relationship with the prehuman "mother" can no longer be
symbolically grounded. In the name of a god who does not
maintain animal friendships, and does away with the difference between species, the question of origins no longer
appears endlessly open and waiting to be symbolized, but
is hyper- or dia-bolized. The human-shaped deity is too
big, too immense, too high, too beautiful, but one thing it
is surely not: It is *not foreign enough.* Its human form is sub-
tly affirmed in monotheistic theology, but the prestige of
this form is also limited. Moses Maimonides, for example, comments that the anthropomorphic images of God
are simple metaphors that are indispensable for compre-
hending the deity but do not by themselves give it form.[35]

In any case, the new garments of the deity, its new disguise, are insufficient to meet the demand for exoticism.
This deity may be attractive, elevating, inspiring, glorified, and nurture phantasies of union, but it is not foreign
enough to support a universal hypnosis. In fact, the divine
excess is to a certain extent a backlash, like an implosion
of human-being sparked by the better humans. Reserves
therefore build up, pebbles or follicles encapsulating the
unredeemed expectations directed at the great, sublime
foreignness. While the anthropomorphic deity hovers over

humanity, the suspicion grows that it is hiding something, something it is not inclined to communicate. There is something unarticulated, odd, curious, and unfathomable in it, an aspect that is defined by the obsessive idea of the *deus malignus.* Thus, if the deity is not foreign enough, being foreign turns into a paranoid allegation, because in a deity that is not sufficiently foreign its hidden aspect appears terrible and menacing. The god–human relationship is disturbed by this polarization of the divine image and saturated with suspicion. The human form of the deity reveals a history of projection, as Feuerbach so lucidly revealed. The anthropomorphic god finally degenerates into a weak god, uncanny like a Duane Hanson sculpture, a horrifying clone of a real person. Mike Kelley grasps this form of tautological representation very precisely in his project *The Uncanny.*[36] The synthesis of a human copy and the plastic medium, or sculpture, pushes the projection into a zone of closed off "reality" that removes the ground from (mytho)poiesis.

The uncanny anthropomorphic god is a posttotemistic antianimal. It is the primary object of the symbolic order of the father, revaluing the parts that have been shifted over from the symbolic order of the mother. These parts then *force* the anthropomorphic god to appear as a sufficiently "foreign" god, the one Dionysius Areopagite speaks of in *Nomina Deorum.*[37] This is the *Deus absconditus* of Renaissance theologians, who possesses or, better, hides any unintegrated parts of foreignness and otherness, which now pass into a *dissociated project.* This *dissociated project* of high theology creates an anthropomorphizing technology whose task is to collect the hypnotic features of the old animal and keep them away from the good, beautiful god. This technology of interactive devices and machines is nevertheless associated with the deity *ex post,* compensating for its lack of foreignness. The pre-oedipal frustration caused by the anthropomorphic god is cured by confronting a new technical challenge. The apparatus function of the mummy sets the structural standard for objects that will be technically produced but also ensouled. In order to catch souls such objects should have, like the mummy, as little soul as possible and relatively a lot of body. For the radiation economy— that is the proportion of radiation (vibrating and overflowing human souls) and irradiation (the echo from higher others and foreigners)—this means that part of the radiation that was originally released and directed toward the foreign god will be redirected onto suitable objects. This is the most important test of the postmagical engineers' phantasy: to catch radiation energy with the appropriate screens, nets, and reflectors. So, in monotheistic religions being influenced by the gods takes place either under conditions that otherwise apply for gambling—the echo is produced whenever the deity wills it, a phenomenon discussed with horror in the so-called grace controversy at the end of the Middle Ages—or God's radiation is successfully channeled and directed onto the desired course. Here machines and apparatuses, a whole technology facilitating irradiation emerges as a shadow theology securing the highest autonomy, inviolability, and frugality for the floating deity rotating within itself, while at the same time preserving the echo of the soul-radiating public.

The new apparatuses emerge as the animal fades away. The animal had emerged from that ambiguous point where the question of origins is enshrouded in amnesia, and insofar as it embodied or performed this constitutive amnesia, its position had always been quite precarious. But once the deity underwent anthropomorphization and beautification in the image of the father, it suffered its increasing *objectification*.

But a deity that represents an anthropomorphic superlative gets the irradiated subject into difficulties. The difference that *still* opened between the animal and the human is now that between superman and *man,* between greatness and the merely average. Theology of this type means that humans are in need of extreme improvement and redemption. Only the cheerful and heroic post-Franciscan hippies were ready to confront being compared with the beauty of Jesus.

The anthropomorphization of the deity revealed that a too emphatically human-shaped (man-shaped) divinity compels, on psychoeconomical grounds, an attenuated totemism. But as the Electra and Oedipus complexes reveal, the *"pre-oedipal" remnants* of the deity do not let themselves be simply extinguished. The inferiority and passivity of the group as opposed to their beautiful human-god, and their dependency on it bestowing its grace to them, motivate them to increase radiation activity by resonating with interactive objects. These objects must satisfy two demands: first, they have to be foreign enough to trigger ambivalent feelings, and second, they must enable a permanent relationship that, as is the case in the cult, is stabilized and deepened by the ritualistic repetition of directed acts. The totemistic disposition, therefore, sheds light on the technical structures that parallel cultic ones.

Apparatus or Weak Totem

An "apparatus" is an arrangement with the specific function of being a projection screen. It has to attract and invite the overflowing souls and know how to permanently bond with them. Tilmann Habermas's study of "loved objects" presents in detail the various ways humans are attracted to the most arbitrary things and define themselves *by them*.[38] How much more effectively will a thing deploy its power of bonding when it already functions by approaching and nestling next to humans? Frazer classifies the totems known to him, but their very significant differences present him with considerable problems. He does not find an explana-

tion for why, first of all, an animal, but then anything at
all, could be a totem. His intensified efforts in collecting
examples anticipated his cluelessness in interpreting them.

The minimal definition of the totem is that it is an *active
eccentric thing* with various prohibitions and orders starting
from the thing itself. Through this structure as an imperative, which implies the cultic act of *being attended to,* passivity
(of the object) and activity (of the subject) are balanced to
the point where human control includes its correlate of
being controlled. This ability to turn the tables is the classical characteristic of a medium, meaning not only that it is
the human that has the medium but the *medium has the human.*
Notably, media theory (in this respect, a product of the last
humanists) deplores how apparatuses, machines, appli-
ances, and programs take hold of humans and announce
the victory of the inhuman. In this respect, media theory obviously forgets, or considers inconsequential, that
the answers formulated by humanists concerning God
and the world have always had a hypnotic aspect tending
to pacify the self as a medium. Similarly, the researchers
who dealt with totemism did not think they had encountered the pinnacle of humanism.[39] They marveled at the
power granted to the animal, or to the object set up as the
totem, by those belonging to or affiliated with it. These
people seemed crazy,[40] connecting themselves to the totem
through porous membranes. They seemed, in retrospect,
to believe too easily and too much. It appeared as though
they showered their souls onto this appropriate object
oscillating between foreignness and familiarity and established it as a pole organizing their perception. Artifacts
were not excluded from such honorable treatment but were
in fact predestined to be showered with overflowing soul.
One might reasonably think that things made by humans
are not as stupefying as the strange and overbearing pecu-
liarity of an animal, but this is not in fact true. The question is not so much of the sensational appearance and

dramatic entanglement of things but of a deep, and at the same time flat, form of hypnotizing presence emanating from the impermeability of what is "beautifully made" and fabricated. The thing, insofar as it displays such eccentricity, "turns animal." That is, like the animal, it deviates from human nature.

Hypnosis, induced through contact with suitable objects, is not an outstanding state; it is not an agitation or stimulant of a consciousness in a state of high alert. Instead, it is calming down, falling asleep, a half-awake state of dozing and drowsiness. Here, we leave behind the level of thought favored by philosophy, the level of self-presence that is accountable to itself. We fall down a shaft whose upper end is called consciousness but whose lower depths are dark and open. Leibniz hits the mark when he designates this zone as "confused perception." But confused perception is not philosophically denounced, as one would expect, rather it is declared the way the monad has access to everything. Leibniz writes: "As a result, every body is affected by everything that happens in the universe, to such an extent that he who sees all can read in each thing what happens everywhere, and even what has happened or what will happen, by observing in the present what is remote in time as well as in space."⁴¹

This message from the paradise of universal sensation is followed by a restriction: "But a soul can read in itself only what is distinctly represented there; it cannot unfold all its folds at once, because they go to infinity."⁴²

Interpreting Leibniz's thought more freely, we could say that in this zone of confusion the soul extends into the infinite and toward the whole, knocking up against *objects* that themselves represent this form of perception. The weak totem functions as a condenser of such confused perceptions of the universe and so oscillates between diffuse hypnotic and authoritarian characteristics. It traps the activity of a soul that has descended into the shaft and exchanges clarity and distinctness for the flood of universal perception.

With this totem the world appears, the world one has and to which one belongs, although it is unclear, blurry, crumpled, and folded. It enables a simultaneous tuning-down (or regression) and hypnotic focusing of consciousness and the opening or, better, suffering of the "world" in its widest and universal sense, as tuning-in to the most general level of vibration. In this way the totem carries out the work of an "external operator" of consciousness and accomplishes an outflow or draining off of consciousness into the realm of the objective. The most general function of such objects is to unify the individuals turning toward them into a community that is constituted in the confused and blurry. This does not establish world citizenship in a rational sense but rather an electronically obsessed public that cultivates unclear ideas about the universal medium in which it is connected, well taken care of, and dissolved. It is remarkable that this highly depotentialized consciousness values its medial depotentialization positively or, in other words, understands and welcomes it as the condition of a literal immersion into a nebulous We. At this point, the disposition that appeared in a similar form with the mummy returns. Formally, it can be described as follows: An ensouled body feels drawn to and stimulated by what, in terms of its function, is another *dissimilar resembling* body. The overflowing soul, which pours itself (with *curiosity* rather than intention) into this soulless or more or less ensouled object, enters into a kind of *metabolism* with it that represents one of the most important stimulations, excitements, and agitations of the soul (in an aesthetic sense). "Metabolism" is here meant in precisely the way the architect Gottfried Semper used it, as the universal principle of artistic production.[43] Metabolism, therefore, does not mean *metamorphosis* or a change of form but *to take a place in another material* or *metasomatosis.* Metabolism means an interchangeable corporeality that makes use of at least two bodies: The overflowing soul takes its place in its second body.[44] As a result, metabolism presupposes an elementary schizosoma.

If we approach funerary practices from the point of view of a media theory of schizosoma, the services performed for the soulless body can be interpreted beyond the philosophical primitivism of the presence/absence or body/soul dualisms. In contrast to the soul, the corporeal is characterized by discretion (the distant concrete) and particularization. While the soul experiences continuous connection, conspiracy *ad infinitum,* for the body the law is separation, limitation, and segmentation. Thus, if schizophrenia demarcates the pathological level of the soul, a level of discord that resists the nature of psychic continuum, its universal conspiracy and empathy, then twofoldness, the *schize,* is the universal and given in the realm of the body. To be incarnated means to live a-part, as separated being. From this we can attribute to corporeal existence its *own* logic, that of a specific corporeal quality.

It is not only because of its rather worn out phonetic resemblance to *mommy* that we devote ourselves to the mummy. The mummy is a marvelous object of research from which the meaning of metabolism can be ascertained. In it flesh changes into its equivalents, into, for example, a composite of wax, sodium bicarbonate, turpentine, and bitumen. Mummification transforms the body into a statue, into a body-object. This process reflects the pre-oedipal state, whose central competence is its *empathy for another body.* In an illuminating article on mummification, Niwinski explores the possibility that bodies were macerated in a bath of special substances, a "lake of fire," and that clients were shown *painted wooden statues* revealing the state mummification would leave the body.[45] A kind of hot impregnation of the body with wax seemed to play an important role, hence the "lake of fire" in which bodies were treated according to the Egyptian Book of the Dead.[46] Similar to the cauldron of rebirth, the bath is interpreted as cleansing, a way of making contact with a universal fluid that removes our mortifying separation, a perfect immortality operation.[47] Whereas the soul had to successfully complete the journeys and tests stipulated by the Book of the Dead, the body was to be transformed through a process whose stages were not those of natural decomposition. The transformation into a statue represents an artificially controlled metabolism, which is why what comes first is the *showing of the statue* as a model. But why is decomposition, the decay into lower aggregates, resisted?

Morphosis, or *becoming-form,* preoccupies this type of imagination, and we will see how the double-body is placed at the beginning and end of this morphosis. Body splitting or split bodies organize an identity that places not only a great soul but at least two bodies as the ground of the social condition.

In order to understand this, we must dive deeper into the veiled history of the cultural and theoretical annihilation of the *plastic dimension of figuration.* One cannot comprehend what a totem as an artifact is, what schizosoma is, what the "two bodies of the King," or even an apparatus are meant to be as long as the nature of the sculptural, of the molded solid body, has not been grasped. We will now set off again through the territory of the pre-oedipal in order to analyze the loftiest of its objects, the *oracle-giving statue.*

3

Totemism and Sculpture

Preliminaries to a Theory of Schizosoma

> The sculptor who puts life into his object of art . . .
> is unconsciously restoring and re-creating the early
> loved people, whom he has in phantasy destroyed.
>
> —MELANIE KLEIN AND JOAN RIVIERE,
> *Love, Hate and Reparation: Two Lectures*

HANS BELTING ARGUES in both his book *Likeness and Presence*
and essay "Out of the Shadow of Death: The Beginnings
of Image and Body" that an *image* is irrevocably connected
to death, which is an important reason for the ongoing
relevance of the mummy as the core totemist artifact.[1]
Insofar as the image is constituted through absence, Belting claims, there is a notable antipode in every image, its
shadow being, something dead. "The enigma already surrounding the corpse has also logically become the enigma
of the image: this paradoxical absence speaks of both the
absence of the corpse and the present image."[2] Belting
concludes that portraiture has its origin in the cultic representation of the dead in the funerary cult and refers to
a series of clearly defined types in the history of images.

Yet, the thesis "that the icon formally and functionally

95

succeeds the antique funerary portrait"[3] suggests a logic of consecutive genres rather than every image having an inherent "relation to death." Apart from his universal claim of death as the reason for all images, Belting's failure to differentiate "flat" from "three-dimensional" images (i.e., an *image* from a *sculpture*) is also noteworthy. The vagueness or universality of Belting's ontology of images derives from the Greco-Roman concept of the imago, which refers to all forms of representations and artifacts, even to some that are less like portraits than those Belting considers. In fact, the Latin imago is such a broad concept that even the human itself could be conceived of as an imago, as when Jesus is considered the imago of his father in the trinity. A considerable amount of magical significance is attached to this idea of the image being a "child" of its object, and this will provide us with another opportunity to roll out the case for sculpture. Despite there being no distinction of three-dimensional from two-dimensional images in the imago—a differentiation that is anyway too geometrically abstract to be truly helpful—that every act of representation ends up with an image does not mean that every "image" can be taken as a representation in a modern sense. The Christological structures that are embedded in the Latin concept of imago recall the Platonic relation of the (primordial) image to the Idea, forming the ontological difference of the image within. But the prestige and, more importantly, the usefulness of this schema for our investigation is doubtful.

What interests us instead is *the girl,* so at least initially we will deal with life rather than death, although, of course, many discoveries about the living machine lie hidden in death or the dead body. The girl's phantasy concerns "children" that she believes are tucked up inside her and so repeats the relation she has to her own motherness, which defines her genealogically, generatively, and genitally. The potency of the girl lies in her potential for procreating and producing humans, making the plastic [*Plastisch*]—as the *prima materia of embodiment*—both the phantasmatic and real principle of her self-perception. The girl knows that she has *a body capable of creating bodies,* and this knowledge determines the construction of her world. As a result, the difference between sculpture [*Plastik*] and image must once again be forensically examined and made clear. A deconstruction of the far too general notion of the image is inevitable as the plastic obsessions of the girl do not emerge from it but, on the contrary, dissolve in it.

An examination of the votive image shall therefore be added to our discussion of the sepulchral art privileged by Belting in order to elaborate the intentions of the girl while retaining a sharp distinction between panel painting and sculpture.

In his essay "Out of the Shadow of Death," Belting comments on some skulls found in Jericho. These come from an ancestor cult of the so-called preceramic phase B Neolithic and have received special treatment: On the carefully cleaned skulls facial features are represented, or rather restored, through the application of plaster paste, and the empty eye sockets are filled with new eyeballs. This sculptural or plastic technique is a very specific kind of manipulation of the body, a reconstruction and imitation of it that presupposes *knowledge of the body.* It is no coincidence that this sculpture developed in the context of a funerary cult motivated by the enigmas of the body: What is a body, what goes on in it, what constitutes its life, and how does it present this in spatial figures, what does it express? Through this progression of questions Belting touches upon the concept of the mask and notes: "Images first expressed acts carried out on the body, they were masks, paintings and costumes before they disengaged from the body and duplicated it in the shape of the doll or the fetish."[4] To describe masks and costumes as "images" seems premature, as if applying the concept *retrospectively* on these primitive interventions on the body was in fact a *deduction* of it. In this way, Belting is able to interpret the image ontologically as part of a genealogy of cults or, rather, of culture and media: "The mask," he writes, "was an epochal invention in which the famous ambivalence of every image is established once and for all: it takes the place of those who must be absent, so they can be present in the image."[5] Quite justifiably then, older material is drawn upon to shed light on the essence of the image, but in doing so it is subordinated to the image it in fact produces. The particularity of this older material, namely its *plastic dimension,* is in this way *theoretically* ignored.

While Belting does not make the plasticity of the body a separate category, Jean-Pierre Vernant clearly distinguished this corporeality from the image in a strict sense, as Belting well knows.[6] According to Vernant, an image-body (an image that *has* a body) must be clearly distinguished from an image that only *refers* to a body. After the Platonic turn, as Belting verifies, the relation between body and soul reverses and the body becomes something futile and fugitive, while the soul is attributed eternal life: "Although images are now measured according to their beauty and mimetic power, they became incapable of the active use that first gave them significance as bodies of exchange. Passive imitation only allows for the memory of bodies, and excludes images taking on a new presence."[7]

Belting's premise is clearly under the spell of a concept of the image stressed in both modern and postmodern media theories of painting, photography, and film. From our perspective this is a severe deficiency. What this concept lacks, despite its theoretical focus on the body, is a *strong concept* of plastic forms [*Plastischen*]. The conclusion that the image addresses an absent corpse may also mean that this supposedly *dead body* actually represents the *theoret-*

ically lost body. So even if all creation in the fine arts has its origin in the enigma of the body, media theory's simplified understanding of this in the 1990s—that the relation between a body and a (flat) image was the emergence of something phantasmatic, barbaric, and uncanny—has to be withdrawn.[8] In fact, the body is not simulated by "flat" images but by sculpture and plastic form. The history of the plastic art of shaping bodies runs from the interventions made on the Jericho skull to the miracle-working and oracle-giving sculptures of the great antique sanctuaries.

The image has a privileged relation to thought—this was the point in Platonism—while sculpture has a privileged relation to the body. This somewhat heavy-handed distinction shall become more refined through our critique of the relation between the body (as a dead one) and the image dominant in current theory. The proxy bodies or metabolic bodies found in sculpture will be made part of a theory of functional objects or of the apparatus. The proxy body, the *double* of the body, is the missing link in a series of spatial modes that contain the living body in space by pushing in between it and the objects appearing as its "world." We will investigate the contemporary effectiveness and significance of this archaic equivalence—namely, that of the living "birth" body to its proxy or metabolic bodies. Even if the "image" is unthinkable without sepulchral art, the "absent body–mimetic image" relation that currently constitutes the image must be replaced by the "intercorporeal" relation between *present* bodies found in votive sculpture. These present but dissociated bodies communicate through a schizosomatic operation, through the mutual self-enfolding of their "split off" and individualized bodies. These bodies can be, for example, the viewer, a sculpture, or even a present corpse (I say a "present corpse" because corpses are too quickly categorized as "absent"). The question then is whether and how certain elements of *theopathy* (the attempt to sense as god), which inspired the fabrication of divine statues (mummies, pharmacological machines), have passed over to *polipathy* (being absorbed in a political project), to associating and touching, inventing and restructuring a *social* body. In this sense there is a connection between the extreme practices of the funerary cult, the passionate interest in the nature of sacral sculpture, and the construction of social and political homogeneity. To conclude from these complex relations that images equal the absence of bodies and thus spooks and "mediatic corpses," ignores the significance of the problem. Instead, the point is to understand how sacral sculpture formed the center of the Babylonian, Egyptian, Assyrian, Greek, and Roman cults because it was their principal medium, inextricable from their ritual practices and religious propaganda. Sculpture was the *"pagan" hominization machine,* the technology of the "Great Secret."[9]

Exploring the theoretical horizon of sculpture as experimental metabolism, one is supported by the fact that three-dimensional representation of humans is the main instrument or vehicle of pagan cults, which has been under fierce attack from religious nomothetes ever since the Judeo-Christian primal scene (Aaron casting a golden calf in Moses's absence from the gold of the Jews, who then dance around the artifact). The diatribes of early Christianity and Gregory the Great's bulls of excommunication (such things pour out of religious propagandists from the first century on) carry this political *ressentiment* against sculpture even further. The idea that the body of the deity is the central object of cults and the arts, of their operational and liturgical experiments, has never really been overthrown (as can be seen in the ongoing controversy over whether God's divine nature is present in flesh and blood). But insofar as a specific place or a specific material (*this* tree, *this* stone, *this* metal) adheres to cultic sculpture, it is a medium of chthonic finitization, and deities use it as the vehicle transporting them to earth. This idea is opposed to monotheistic theology emphasizing the divinity of a mobile, omnipresent *numen* independent of earth. It is therefore no coincidence that the zealous theologian tries to make the faithful abhor the cheapness of the divine bodies before which they pray:

> But if any one were to present to his mind with what instruments and with what machinery every image is formed, he would blush that he had feared matter, treated after his fancy by the artificer to make a god. For a god of wood, a portion perhaps of a pile, or of an unlucky log, is hung up, is cut, is hewn, is planed; and a god of brass or of silver, often from an impure vessel, as was done by the Egyptian king, is fused, is beaten with hammers and forged on anvils; and the god of stone is cut, is sculptured, and is polished by some abandoned man, nor feels the injury done to him in his nativity, any more than afterwards it feels the worship flowing from your veneration.[10]

This vilification of the materials offered to the divine so that it could enter a proxy body meant that living flesh also became discredited as cheap. Those who lament this lost value rightly accuse Christianity of helping the anti-Egyptian sentiments of Judaism gain a second life: Thou shalt not make a carved or cast (*tzelem*) work of me.[11] This means: You shalt not trust sculptural propaganda, you shalt not believe in the body and least of all in the "reserve-body," you shalt not order anything from a sculptor, and you shalt wipe out the sculpture schools.

The philosophy of art influenced by Christianity always held a veto against sculpture and stirred up reservations about it. Consequently, every strongish theory of the plastic arts goes directly into that danger zone, into that taboo realm where it is accused of magic and idolatry and its author excommunicated. According to this media logic, rather than for religio-political reasons, it was better to overlook sculpture and fixate instead on the image, to see sculpture as a transitory moment (at most a *starting point*), an archaism in the genealogical development of the image. That sculpture is something to be overcome or something outdated could also be said of its pagan impulses, but unfortunately after the absorption of paganism those who still liked sculpture were not inclined to renounce the sensations produced by its "pagan" use. Instead, they produced *defiant sculptures* that effectively violated religion's artistic canon.

Wherever this religious hostility toward sculpture weakened, or where a certain subversive, antireligious moment was given a chance (in an obstinate popular piety and in political cults), these defiant sculptures once more proliferated. They were surrounded with an aura of popularity and an *improper* theory that gave more credit to empirical effects and the continuation of tradition than to the opinion of experts. Their fascination was appreciated, conserved by a languid layer of cultural memory to which one gave oneself willingly and without guilt. Insofar as sculpture remained artistically relevant into the twentieth century, it had to put up with being theoretically denigrated as the most harmless of arts and humbly make ever smaller and more inconspicuous things found in stalls selling pilgrims' mementos and in tourist souvenir shops, in craft markets and outdated workshops in remote alpine villages [*Oberammergau*]. Sculpture's theoretical status is defined by anachronism, and the definition of sculpture approved by the fine art academies codifies this trivialization of what is in fact a wild and hot medium. The mantra of belittlement: Sculpture is "Form in Space." This dogma neutralizes the meaning of sculpture's cultic use in its tautological formula. Sculpture is reduced to a pure formalism and as such finds it difficult to enflame contemporary theory. The slogan "Form in Space" is the crowning of four thousand years of Judeo-Christian propaganda. This lazy concept of the sculptural arts [*Bildhauerei*] is expanded, diversified, and transmitted in all directions by contemporary art historians and the authors of art school curriculums. In doing so, they take the side of the great propagandists and agitators of the Judeo-Christian continuum, which, if they realized, would deeply embarrass them.

Metabolism and Therapeutic Schizosoma

According to Belting the image was installed at graves, those magnificent places of absence, to bring back the dead. At the abyss of that deprivation, that bereavement through death, an image-carrier was set up in a perceivable protest. As well as the saints and the mother of God, these *votive images* also depict benefactors who were certainly *not dead* at the time of their donation. In this way, the votive images discussed by Belting perform the cultic act of the *promise,* they are gifts that present a request pictorially, they are a medium that coincides with its *message.* The depicted benefactor, just like the beseeched patron, appears according to the logic of reflection, giving the donor portrait, and in particular the votive sculpture (a *double* in the proper sense of the word), an important place among votive offerings.[12]

What then is the function of the votive sculpture as a double of the donor? In Ernst Buschor's opinion the origin of Greek sculpture is the *Kouros,* a grave sculpture depicting a young man that doubles the deceased who is divinized in the sculpture.[13] The sculpture of the dead person, who now becomes *immortal,* is the real certificate of a *transformation.* Thus, before discussing the relation of sculpture to the image, we must consider this *category of transformation* (i.e., its *metabolism*).

For the votive donor who is not actually dead such a claim is not without consequences, because the image of the benefactor is also subject to the principle of transformation. In this way votive sculpture prefigures the transformation that is later found in painterly representations. The doubling of the dead *and the living* has the same transformative intention. If we focus on the lower half of a donor image where the pious are found standing in line and gazing up to heaven, we see that the image (contrary to Belting) is a strategy for magically giving a *living person* a second body and assigning certain tasks (such as praying) to this doppelgänger. This desire for transformation is the main reason for this kind of representation, which depicts *reconstruction and a new life*. Healing is its central function, which in a similar and derivative manner also inspires the medical "doubling" of anatomical and genetic models of humans. The votive offers an artificial and explicitly *better* body, giving a simple kind of physical and *nonlinguistic* suggestion as to which direction its reconstruction by the "sculptural" force should go. The votive offering, designed either as a complete image of the donor or as a body part (an arm, a leg, an organ), is an *effective schizosoma* that must be placed in the vicinity of a beneficent deity. That this votive offering was really a *sculptural* project rather than simply an image is evident in those offerings that did not portray someone living but invited someone to *come to life*: "The bishop Benno II (1068–1088) was given to his parents as a gift after they had made a pilgrimage to the apostolic princes in Rome and asked to be blessed with a child. They had commissioned a talented artist to make an image of a little boy from purest silver and took it along with them, in order to better submit their heart's desire to Christ and the apostles in this way, rather than in words."[14] Thus, one first gave birth to a child in a *plastic form* in order to inspire human "sculptural" activity to produce the desired child.

Or similarly: "Duke Wladislaus I (1079–1102) of Poland
sent the golden image of a little boy (*ymaginem auream infan-
tuli*), as well as other gifts, to the church of St. Aegidius,
otherwise known as St. Gilles in Provence, because he was
not blessed with children."[15]

No corpse is called up and no dead person is commemorated in these gifts, rather they anticipate the awakening of life. From the perspective of this transformational
schizosoma sculpture appears in a new light. Sculpture
as an effective operator of schizosoma is *also* extremely,
but not *exclusively,* suitable for use in the vicinity of death.
Conversely, sculptures of the dead (grave monuments and
mummies) appear in a new light in relation to this schizosomatic potency of sculptural action, as they too contain
something of *the force that wants to make things live* that animated
the gifts "for successful births."[16]

Belting, however, traces this votive function of sculpture through the example of *effigies,* examining the use of a
doll of the king in the funeral ceremony. Even though he
clearly stresses *the effigies' antithetical* relation to death, he nevertheless maintains that *death* is the most important aspect
of the shaping function. Belting argues (as Reinle does)
that *effigies,* like votive sculpture, were suppressed by art
history because they belonged to the "low" arts.[17]

The function and techniques of ersatz- or doubling-
procedures are not generally discussed by mainstream academic art history. Because of the recent turn to new dis-
positives of the apparatus and media, however, Julius von
Schlosser's highly relevant studies have regained respect
and been the object of renewed interest. I remain convinced that sculpture as a surrogate image can *be just as easily
derived from a cult of life as from a funerary cult* and that sculpture's
function in funerary cults is only one of its possible functions. Further, it is *biopathy,* or the passion and sympathy
the pre-oedipal child has for her mother's body in the first

schizosoma that in fact provides the model for necropathy or empathy for the dead.

Pre-oedipality as a "Plastic Phase"

A quick glance into the children's room will confirm our thesis. On the *lower* level of the waxy leg of the votive we find stuffed animals and rubber duckies, which today industrial sculpture produces *en masse* for the little ones. We still lack an intelligent theory of toys (although this would be one because it avoids the banality of both a functionalist theory of learning and the sophism *praecox* of a psychoanalytical coding of toys), but one could nevertheless attempt a loose classification of its elements. Like other theoreticians who left the care of children to women, Lacan paid too little attention to what was going on in the children's rooms where, as all mothers know, things pile up, and he underestimated the identificatory value these small or large toys have for infants and toddlers. These toys are put into children's hands as soon as they can grasp them, and these bizarre, more or less grotesque theriomorphic or anthropomorphic things stare back at them, provoking ecstatic elation. This experience with three-dimensional [*plastisch*] toys (the dodo, the teddy bear, the corner of the blanket without which the baby cannot fall asleep and whose loss is consequently far worse than all your credit cards being stolen) has been ignored by theoreticians of corporeal identification.[18] Precisely here a wonderful niche market opens up for an entrepreneur operating *beyond* pedagogical guidelines: the industrial production of *miniature sculptures* of the *inhabitants of alternative worlds* and *stuffed animals*. The child touches the plastic form of the toy and feels that corporeal or, rather, consistent plastic beings exist with whom she feels a strategic intimacy and complicity. These objects are able to give a security that enables a comprehension of living wholeness, a certainty the child could never draw from interacting with her mother or another *caretaker,* whose bodies appear as enormous continents with unexplored and unknowable zones, which the child cannot hold and turn with the same competence she does her stuffed animals. In this toy we have the prototype of a votive offering, a *plastic form for becoming-being* [*Seinwerden*], for *being as a project.* The child forms a binomial with this figure, this sculpture, becoming its sibling or schizosomatic twin. The meaning embedded in the stuffed toy can be understood (although as with the doll only secondarily) in terms of the transitional object. Its first significance is its primitive function as a sculptural double equipped with faciality, which will then have, beyond its imaginary or symbolic meaning, a great effect on the mature sculpture of cultic and high art. Just as votive sculpture, according to Reinle, is missing from art history, so too the plastic form of the child's toy lacks a serious theoretical category, despite the fact that outstanding artists have used it. In recent contemporary art the stuffed animal has appeared as a revenant of the lost genre of plastic form: as pickles in work by Gelatin or as a trophy in Gregor Zivic's photographs. As soon as we note the successful synthesis of the tactile and the visual in this toy, sculpture as exclusively dedicated to the thanatosophic recollection or even resurrection of a dead person *willfully annuls itself.* The essence of these objects instead draws upon the boundless prestige of life, which demands that nothing dead shall exist. Ignored by the linear discourse of art and media theory, the islands of plastic schizosomatic identification—those gorgeous scenes of the pre-oedipal world—flourish beyond the threshold of children's rooms.

If one carefully reconstructs the art historical and anthropological conditions of Lacan's theory of the mirror stage, it becomes easier to evade the disciplinary boundaries of contemporary theory. The latent assumptions of this theory and their contingency—its conditioning conditionality—must be questioned. As we know, Lacan's theory of the mirror stage is of fundamental significance to the concept of corporeality and has been the object of intense intellectual debate for the last twenty-five years.[19] One could even say that the configuration of body and mirror in Lacan's identity-forming primal scene has organized the theoretical approach to the body in an *exemplary fashion*. In fact, media theory and anthropology used it in horrifying ways and, quite frankly, profited from this monstrous doubling of the body in the (mirror) image. From McLuhan, Flusser, von Braun, Kittler, and Kamper, to Därmann and Belting, a broad spectrum of commentators saw the production of an integrated corporeal self-awareness through the mirror or image to be terrifying or even impossible. Similarly, in contemporary art a new wave of body performance has attempted an ideological liberation from the terror of the image and in its subtler formulations reclaimed a deeper, reality-enriched, and reality-endowing mode of perception. In our view it is therefore suspicious. Unlike Viennese Actionism and other performance art of the 1960s, which at least opposed the forgetful and reactionary postwar state and its Christian morality, *performativity* in art is only a *medial* reaction. The body is asked to physically and personally react to the imposition of the mirror and the image, to withdraw physically and personally from the image by expanding its means of expression and refusing all privileges. Rather than providing clarity, this short-winded dialectic itself requires explanation, as the deeper reasons for its sentimental body-lament remain unclear. This problematic body traverses the difficult changes in media and ideology that have emerged in various social and political spheres. It is a story full of anticyclic phases, retardations, and anomalies, and so in order to be clear we will exaggerate and sharply spotlight our position, without considering more carefully many aspects of these processes. To begin, it seems necessary to ask a few key questions about Lacan's construction of the mirror stage: First, is the mirror really a useful medium for the production of a schema of (corporeal) integrity, or are there other, perhaps more useful ones? Second, to which media theories or canon of media is Lacan referring when he claims a medium is a *constituens* in the sense of an anthropological constant? Third, what is the significance of the mother's presentation of the child within the mirror scene, and what is the difference between a Lacanian mirror-child and a *Freudian Narcissus*? And fourth, when does a mirror actually come into play historically, and what (contingent) roles does it fulfill at this historical moment of its invention?

In his version of the mirror stage Lacan highlights two things: First, that the (self-)perception of the child's physical self is critical, chaotic, and dissociated; and second, that the integration of this dissociated body is achieved through being-seen, by the child becoming-an-image, for which she needs the support, or the medium, of the external gaze (the commenting gaze of the mother). The constellation described by Lacan is therefore a special kind of interpreting intersection of gazes that has its locus in the mirror. The mirror creates a pure "from-outside" for the ego, its symbolic meaning thereby going far beyond that of actual mirrors, as did the reflecting surface used by Narcissus as described by the Greek mythic poets. The story of Narcissus and that of the child in the Lacanian mirror stage are essentially different, however, because Narcissus gazes alone into his mirror while the child needs a helper to carry out the act. Jacqueline Lichtenstein uses a copper engraving by Hendrik Goltzius that resembles the primal scene as the frontispiece of her book *The Blind Spot*; a man caresses a lady's breast and their gazes apparently meet in the mirror he holds, although its reflective side is averted from the viewer.[20] The etching is one of five representing the senses, but rather than showing "the sense of sight," as one might expect, reveals instead "*le toucher*" (touch). Lichtenstein begins her extensive discussion of *sculpture's* relation to painting with an analysis of this engraving. Lichtenstein calls her book *The Blind Spot* because it shows how sculpture, as the older and more authentic medium for the imaginary integration of the body, is *now missing as such*. For various reasons, sculpture and its objects have been surpassed, because they were too heavy or too close to the order of representation or were replaced by more mobile, freer, and lighter means of expression. But is that the whole story?

The background animosity toward Egyptian cult ideology in the paragone controversy of the fifteenth and sixteenth centuries is more or less forgotten today.[21] Within the pathos of the awakening aesthetic there was agreement about the excellence of painting, which could simulate bodies so well that birds flying past wanted to eat Zeuxis's grapes. An important phase in the internalization of media was completed, as images were seen as better at *simulating the body*. A religio-political conflict became media theoretical and yielded to historical prejudice: Sculpture is without spirit, is hostile to the spirit and materially heavy, while painting is superior because it is closer to the imagination. Lichtenstein shows how this debate has been fervently continued and how modernity was premised on the superiority of the media of images, which it tried to claim through a variety of *multimedia* figures. In the 1960s the classical notion of sculpture is finally overcome as sculpture expands into multimedia.

It is no accident that Lacan's theory of the mirror stage is formulated at about the same time, and in the history of science the introduction of a suitable metaphor often blazes the trail for a "discovery." For example, Schrödinger's initial description of genes as a biological "clock" obscured the significance of his discovery, which only emerged after he started describing them as a kind of "writing."[22] Similarly, Lacan's mirror explicitly utilizes the overdetermined medium of vision to frame his scene. As can be gathered from the text "What Is a Picture [*tableau*]?" Lacan was particularly interested in the flat screenlike image, or image-producing media, which a small diagram shows lying between the gaze and the "subject of representation."[23] This interest is not without reason and owes itself, as the text progressively reveals, to painting. "For me, it is at the radical principle of the function of this fine art that I am trying to place myself."[24] Lacan refers to Merleau-Ponty, who had already inverted the canonical relations between eye and spirit in painting. "Nothing new is introduced in this respect by the epoch which André Malraux distinguishes as the modern, that which comes to be dominated by what he calls '*the incomparable monster,*' namely, the gaze of the painter, which claims to impose itself as being the only gaze."[25] This construction of a mediating screen—of a *tableau*—is perhaps indispensable to understanding an imagining desire, making the mirror worthy of discussion because through it the production *of an integrated image of the bodily self* is accomplished.

It is informative to draw an analogy or parallel between the transformation of the arts and Lacan's theory of bodily integration. Lacan developed his model of the mirror stage based on the art or, rather, the artistic practice of his time that he found in the *structure* and *nomenclature* of *painting*. The "statuesque" art of the body-double was replaced in the fifties and sixties by *installation* in the widest sense. There was, in other words, a kind of dissociated and discontinuous distribution of hot zones and cold things, of slanting porch swings and felt and fat, of preserved chocolate,

stones, and newspapers, etc. *Installation* took up the inheritance of sculpture, and this introduced a significant change
in the way the body was treated.

The body is no longer seen as an oracle-antenna, as a
sensitive mass, but as a set of arranged objects from the
worlds of the commodity and the media through which
a fluid, shapeless body of sensation flows. "On the one
hand, one cannot deny the voluminous body as we see and
know it from outside, with its great zones: trunk, legs,
hands, etc. On the other, we add the operative level: if
I close my eyes I could localize myself and find my way,
even if I was completely ignorant of the first body. But
because we live with or on two bodies, with the objective
one and with the one that we feel, if these two bodies no
longer correspond they can produce a pathology that is
based on dissociation."[26] This dissociation Dagognet talks
about is not between the two bodies that we are concerned
with but rather that between body and soul but *in new clothes.*
The preference is clearly for what was formerly called the
"soul," for a substance that tends to go beyond the body.
From this disguised or inverted body–soul construction
the devaluation of the "*corps volumique*" inevitably follows.
The ecstasies of Greek sculpture have been completely
forgotten, and the schizosomatic construction placing a
double volumique next to the *corps volumique* now seems obso-
lete. This is because—and here the theorist gives himself
away—the voluminous body is only seen from outside and
so falls under the hegemony of the gaze. Its voluminousness appears (as the paragone controversy anticipated) as
something random, as an ontological coincidence without
any claim to its own aesthetic category, and so as a *sign of inferiority.* What has *volume* is already suspicious because it pro-
claims its steadfastness, its ontological stability, through
this aspect of itself alone. The child in the mirror is also

seen from outside and is therefore immediately subject to the merciless dictatorship of the logic of volume. In *becoming seen* she reveals her voluminousness. But she also sees, she *gazes back*. Now what is the relationship between these gazing *"corps volumiques"*?

We have already mentioned sculpture's original relationship to theurgical or religious techniques (those bracketed out by the paragone controversy), but examining the prehistory of the mirror will provide even greater clarity. Besides its property as an optical, visual fetish, noted by theologians, metaphysicians, and philosophers alike, the mirror is, and probably from soon after its "invention," primarily a powerful *magical* thing. Lacan uses the mirror to describe a historic moment (the moment of the *gaze*) and opens, at least potentially, a perspective on the history of reflection. Unlike with other significant metaphorical objects (e.g., Plato's "sun"), Lacan does not carry out a historical-critical investigation of the metaphor of the mirror (qua principle of reflection). Consequently, the fate of the mirror parallels that of sculpture, remaining imperceivable within the genealogy of concepts for the body. In the history of sculpture, as in the history of the mirror, there is a great affinity with problems of corporeal identification. It is usually claimed that in early cultures the mirror first appeared as a bowl allowing a portable version of the reflection given by the water's surface. The Chinese sign for mirror is the same as that for seeing a reflection, or mirroring, and shows a figure bending over a container that is obviously filled with water. This sign appears significantly earlier than any object corresponding to the term mirror. Significantly, the Chinese gained knowledge of the mirror from their nomadic neighbors, who used copper mirrors for the ritual reflection of the sun and for making fire. As well, the bronze material with

which the Chinese produced mirrors had already been
in use making various other objects for about a thousand years. People's constant desire for an "outer" image
of themselves was therefore only loosely associated with
the technical possibilities of its achievement, and in every
case the dating of the drive that supposedly powered the
desiring-machine of "reflection in the mirror image" is
earlier than thought. While it is clearly not necessary to
own a mirror to fulfill this almost innate desire for an
image of oneself, those who had a mirror do not seem to
have used it for the mirror stage, otherwise the nomadic
invention would have immediately led to a cultural revolution in ancient China. The mirror becomes an important instrument only after the end of the dynasties of the
second Bronze Age, when a new cosmology, and with it a
new political model, gains importance. Bronze Age society
was totemistic, with the body of the ancestor at the center
of the concepts of the public and of the legitimacy of the
sovereign. This was a divine body in which the descending
gods and the ascending worldly powers met, and society of
the time understood itself through an identification with
this body and its uninterrupted line of legitimate children.
The decline of totemistic society is marked by the introduction of the mirror for ritualistic purposes, where a new
reintegration of the body was achieved by catching the soul
and the body within it. What the mirror had *seen* was conserved within it, and this finally explains its widespread use
in funerary cults and as a burial object.[27] The mirror was
thus the instrument of a distinguished gaze, the *preserved
remains* [*Konserve*] of a gaze, which protected and secured
the identity of the group members coming afterward. In
funerary cults the uninterrupted line between the ancestors and their descendants seems to have been secured by
a ritual mirror that transmitted the ancestral gaze to new

generations, ensuring the connection of those present with those absent. The crossing of gazes introduced by Lacan therefore calls upon a dimension of the mirror-drama that was already highly significant. The mirror lying on the heart of the deceased secures his or her integrity, as the mirror-image does for the child in the mirror-stage. But only the a posteriori, posttotemist connection to the ancestor emphasizes the significance of the one who shows (*this is you*), and this faculty of genealogical reason, the universal "Mama–Papa," consequently returns in psychoanalysis. Lacan connected the mute symbolic transactions of a prior history to his model by having a *female ancestor* (in the shape of the mother) direct the mirror-gaze onto the child, thereby going beyond the protoreflexive scene of Narcissus. Lacan, a bit in love with painting, understood the surface of the image as the level of the symptom and, in his preference for the mirror, repressed the older plastic regimes of bodily identification and integration. But in doing so he connected, at least *implicitly*, to that historical-critical moment of physical identification when the sign of the father (the outside gaze) becomes law. In place of the magical receptacles produced by the plastic arts, the mirror reflects the integrity of the body as its *pseudo-container* and is a pure magic surface. Lacan indirectly picks up on the archaic relation securing the genealogical continuity *between two bodies,* which was found in a mirror declared to be a magic receptacle (a *container,* therefore *also a body-double*) and where the larger and older body sends benevolent signals to the smaller securing its existence and identity. Sculpture's objectifying function produces humans within which (bodies that can produce) bodies display themselves, but this function is suspended in front of the mirror, even if Lacan still claims that the mother's role of *female witness is that of a female producer* [*Zeugin als Erzeugerin*].

Excursus: Plasma, Forming, Sculpture [plasma, plassein, Plastik]

> The analyst is allowed in this way into the child's
> inner world, where there is a tremendous contention
> between forces, where magic controls, and where the
> good is constantly in danger from the bad. It feels
> mad to be in the child's inner world.
>
> —D. W. WINNICOTT, *Human Nature*

> Man resembles the universe like an artist's statuette of
> a holy animal resembles it.
>
> —RICHARD REITZENSTEIN,
> *Das iranische Erlösungsmysterium*

> The process by which we displace love from the first
> people we cherish to other people is extended from
> earliest childhood onwards to things.
>
> —MELANIE KLEIN AND JOAN RIVIERE,
> *Love, Hate and Reparation*

In order to respond to a certain weakness in the theory of
sculpture, a clarification of the concepts just introduced is
necessary. In the Prometheus myth the *fashioning of man* takes
place in a *plasma*; plasma is the source material, although
it is not precisely explained what this universal material
is.[28] It is a moldable matter, a first becoming of form and
shape, while the making as such is described as an activity of *ekplasen*. The commentary specifies that Prometheus,
just like the Babylonian Mami and the Jewish God of creation, made man out of clay (*limus terrae*), something soft, a
putty. Clay is the plasma of the first sculptors. Reading these
creation stories it becomes clear that sculptural creation,
insofar as it is the art of "the beginning," is an archaic,
primordial activity, the work of a craftsman-god or female

potters, who appear as self-assured masters of their art. Taking on and giving form overlap within this moldable material, which as the amorphous, as abyss or chaos (that is, as the swamp where the terrible creatures of primeval phantasy dwell: the crocodile-like Behemoth hiding in the reeds or Leviathan rising from the mud), represents the womb of all forms. The *plastes* who handles this soft material is the fine artist, the sculptor, the image-maker. *Plasso,* Greek for "I form/shape" also means "to build/shape something from a soft matter," to create something, fabricate something, but significantly it also means "*to compose* (a poem), cause, make up,*" which then means "to define a form by finding/inventing it." *Plasis* thus refers to all types of form-giving that change the shape of a substrate, it refers to the forming of soft matter, to imitation, to the forms and images themselves, to the figure and to the power of imagination that for the Greeks, trained in the cultic logic of the Orient, proceeds according to the *model of plastic forms*. The adjective *plastos* refers not only to the sculptural designs of fine art, as well as everything else shaped and formed, but also to creatures of the imagination and phantasy, to fictional creation, to invention in the sense of the beautifully conceived, as well as to the lie, the false and the fake, and so to everything that is rooted in phantasy rather than being. It is therefore clear that plasma is the material of creators and engineers, of artists, technicians, and poets, whose appearance in stories and theories of creation indicates that the creation of the world formulates *a first theory of art.*[29] The relation established in the concept of *plasma,* as in the plastic medium, between a soft and entirely moldable material and the phantastical or imaginary design of the world (i.e., poetic power), confirms the overriding significance of the sculptural for creative activity, for the intention to conquer, rebuild, and secure one's world as a habitable horizon. If one understands how tightly this knot was tied one gets an idea of the effort necessary to loosen, weaken, and finally dissolve it.

Next to the *plastic* is the *sculptural* and the *caelamen,* which describe similar categories of images. Unlike plastic form, sculpture is made by removing matter, by the *sculpere* of wood, ivory, marble, and other precious or nonprecious stones. The tools that sculptors use are made of polished iron: a graver, carving knife, bit, or chisel. So while plastic form, even when only imagined, is seen as an ectype of a rather fluid matter, or as the transitory shape of an endlessly mutable plasma, the sculpture, by its choice of materials, is a hard and durable thing that results from form being given to a solid, resistant material or its form being the result of a long period of geological or botanical time. Sculpture always resonates with these long periods of earth's history, and sculptors are as likeable as Stone Age fossils. Wooden sculpture belongs to the realm of chloroplastic time, which runs a bit faster than, but still exceeds, the human life span. Insofar as sculpture is *earth art* or *geo-techne,* its radical primitivism has been rejected or adored, depending on whether Uranians or Earthlings encountered it. In any case, those dedicated to their granite monoliths, such as Franz Xaver Ölzant, seem curious, like people of another or older kind. Sculpture, as a metaphor for the abilities of the soul, implies *permanence.* Often the verb *insculpo* is used to describe the imprinting of something into the soul or into *memory.* One then speaks of someone *in mentibus insculpsit,* memorizing or impressing something into their mind (carving it like letters into the bark of a tree). This mode of memorizing has its origin in early forms of *script* such as cuneiform that used tools similar to sculpture and that was in fact *a kind of sculpture.*

McLuhan carefully studied the work of the *caleators* and explored its significance for media theory, but despite this few today seem to know what a *caelamen* is.[30] According to its dictionary definition, *caleators* are producers of relief, engravers, those who decorate things with carvings. The *caelamen* is a half-raised image, a bas-relief. It has a position between sculpture and the image because it takes from both; it possesses the special spatiality or corporeality of sculpture, but it contracts this corporeality, compresses it, radically shortens its perspective and thereby anticipates the spatial logic of the image and its fabulous two-dimensional effects. An interesting example of this kind of hybrid image is a Madonna panel from the thirteenth century that Belting discusses in *Likeness and Presence*. It shows an enthroned mother with child in relief, surrounded by painted angels, saints, and scenes from Mary's life.[31] Belting calls this work a "hybrid of sculpture and painting."[32] Here the task of the relief is to remind the viewer that the main figure "was once a sculpture."[33] Thus the painting *invokes* a sculpture, which in this context appears like a *token*. In the *caelamen* the sculptural is worked into the surface of the image, so to speak, and for this reason McLuhan found it especially useful for explaining how the surface of medieval script still "glowed" with the elevation (in a technical sense, from being raised) of reliefs. If it is the case, as McLuhan thought, that even script—a not insignificant medium of communication—retains a connection to the plastic medium in the depths of its own prehistory, how much more important will this reference to the sculptural be in the case of *intercorporeal* communication?

The Statue Delivering Oracles

"This image full of my form
this imitation of Daidalos lacks only a voice. I bring these
(as) a well-won ornament to the god
a well-made votive.

It would challenge my own mother!
For seeing it she would clearly
turn and (wail)
thinking it to be me, whom she raised.
So similar is it (to me)."[34]
"I am Hermes with a voice from Daidalos
made of wood (but) I came here by walking on my own."[35]
"Don't be afraid, old man, it's nothing.
All the statues of Daidalos appear to move
and see, so clever is the man."[36]

The totemist age is the *age of the plastic*. Totemism expresses
the pre-oedipal constellation in its preference for the plastic medium. One could even say that the pre-oedipal constellation is obsessed with the plastic medium, to which its
fevered imagination *ascribes vitality*. Both the treatise "The
Book of the Seven Statues" by Apollonius of Tyana, which
is available despite its complicated reception history, and
"The Torch of the Thirty Statues" by Giordano Bruno, a
title that plays with the title of Apollonius's text, support
this thesis.

Apollonius's text describes *seven statues* built from seven
Uranian materials. Each of the statues—the Sun, Jupiter,
Venus, Mars, Mercury, the Moon, and Saturn—occupy
their own temples. The text reproduces *speeches* given by the
statues, which Henry Corbin argues means that the statues
were priests in their own temples.[37] On his account, the
"priest" ecstatically recites emphatic salutations to a divine
father, and his description as a "statue" simply reflects the
intimate connection between the temple and its priest,
who is part of the temple's inventory. But greater honor is
given to the text if it is understood *literally*. Neoplatonism is
a tradition of extremely bizarre ideas, and while it is quite
conceivable that the text talks of priests reciting the names
of their Heavenly Father, as well as of other pneumatic,
angelological, and demonological topics, the fact that the

priests are called "statues" and not priests would nevertheless be very unusual. But if one understands these statues
as, in fact, statues, we approach a *hierophantic practice* that is
central to ancient cultures. Lucian's or pseudo-Lucian's
magnificent text on the Syrian goddess and her cult in
Hierapolis explicitly mentions "speaking" statues answer-
ing priests' questions, the distinction between statue and
priest being entirely obvious even if unclearly articulated.
The literal interpretation of Apollonius's text along these
lines reveals the significance of cult sculpture and, more
precisely, its social, political, and communicative significance. These statues, if they speak, are oracles. Statues
make *statements* [*Statuen* statuieren]. "The proof of this,"
Corbin writes, "is that the statue first becomes a statue
after one has taken it out of the vein of stone from which
it grew. It first becomes a statue blessed with a body after
a series of labors, treatments, and operations. Only then
does one erect a shrine for it, and it proceeds through its
various degrees up to the highest. Only when it has become
spiritual, human, angelic, solar, enlightened and radiant
can it express its condition with the highest eloquence."[38]

These peculiar bodies have the specific characteristic of
delivering messages from themselves in order to help the intuition
of groups take off.

The statue functions—just as Lucian described it—like
an electromagnetic field or terrestrial antenna that allows
the message to "come down" or "come across." It is a *theur-
gic apparatus.*[39] It is remarkable that a *statue* plays the leading role in this collective, mantic practice. This specific,
formed and solid object therefore activates a virulent schizosoma, maneuvering the group toward an "expanded mental state" that liberates its superfluous "soul substance."
This excess is then "captured" or collected and then echoed
by the higher and effective medium of the statue. This
interpretation reveals a characteristic of living bodies and

their type of knowledge, an *oracular knowledge* that emerges
in stark contrast to noetic knowledge. Thus *bodies pronounce
oracles,* but in order to make them do so systematically the
schizosomatic machinery of the Mycenaean, Cretan, and
pre-oedipal worlds must be started up. Then, the unbro-
ken resonance of the pre-oedipal human with its mother's body makes it a "prophet of the mother." Children
remain in resonance with that large protective body, and
this establishes the political credo of the *territorial motherland.*
The *prophets and prophetesses of the mother* take up the frequency
of the large body of the earth in order to refine their oracular reason, their intuition, and their visionary talent that
erupts (it is vulvic, volcanic) from below. Their profes-
sional exemplar is the sibyl.

Corbin's reservations about the possibility of speaking
statues are possibly because of their description by Grégorie
Loukianoff, from which he draws.[40] These statues are artifacts, automata whose sophisticated mechanisms allow
them to speak or move. Derek J. de Solla Price lists among
these automata the Colossus of Rhodes, a jackal god now
in the Louvre, figures allegedly invented by Daedalus that
walked back and forth in front of the labyrinth, a flying
dove made by Archytas from Tarentum, Roman oracular
statues, Pygmalion's statue, Don Juan's father-in-law, and,
finally, the golem. One of the most spectacular automata
was commissioned by Mark Antony after the murder of
Caesar. It is said that it slowly raised itself from the bed
to show its thirty-three bleeding wounds to the people,
shocking them to the bone.[41]

As Solla Price emphasizes, this sculptural art ("plastic
urge") is driven by a desire "to simulate the world."[42] So
is the statue who is a speaking god an instance of the pre-
oedipal world, a world people wanted to simulate? Without
knowing the *prehistory* of *natural oraculating* bodies, however,
the origin of these automata is hard to pin down. The his-

tory of technology must be preceded by a *pre-oedipal history of enthusiasm* in order to explain the overpowering that occurs through coming-into-the-body. It is this that first ignites technical curiosity.

A primal scene of the technical career of the oraculating body is the ritualistic opening of the mouth of a mummy.

> The opening of the mouth enabled the spirit to visit. Slowly this ritual spread to other domains that could receive the heavenly spirit: to other statues that were allowed to participate in the eating of sacrificial offerings; to the figureheads of sacred boats; to carved figures on temple doors (in order to bring their reliefs to life); to scarab amulets. Already very early, from the Thinite Period onward, corpses were brought to life in the same way. The ceremony was carried out on the mummy itself, and subsequently on its sarcophagus and on the grave statuettes representing it. The purpose was to give life-energy back to the body, the life spark that had escaped from it, and to return to the deceased the use of the mouth so he or she could eat and drink, speak and breath again.[43]

The ceremony was modeled on gestures used in the "gold house," the sculptor's workshop: "The priest touched all the openings of the head with a small adze-like instrument to simulate the carving of a sculpture."[44] As well as the statue of the distinguished deceased, an "army" of ushabti figures were brought to the animation ceremony in order to attend to their lord. The Egyptians, like other peoples, believed that a representation of a person or an animal could be animated. The focus on the mouth already indicates that such representations were expected to be able to speak and express themselves. The provision of food is an "amplifier" of the utterance, because arousing the appetite produces a vital inner movement. Statues of gods were treated like noble people, they were awakened by priests in the morning, washed, dressed, censed, and fed. On feast days they were carried around their domain in sedan chairs and asked questions. Plutarch tells of a cult image that stood in the temple of Heliopolis and was covered with signs, the semeion, and at prescribed times was carried to the sea in a solemn procession and bathed.[45]

Plastic objects speak because they have caught *pneuma*. In this way, statues *really* speak with priests in the Heliopolis, as the dolls and toy figures in children's rooms *really* speak to them. The engineer tries to solve the enigma of this speech by giving the statue or doll a mechanism *that makes this break through to its soul obvious.* This vivification of the statue repeats and objectifies generation and birth as the *primary concerns of the pre-oedipal world,* while symbolically warding off any offense the child may feel from not being present at her own conception, and so being dispossessed of her own origin. Why else would moving and speaking statues have been produced? Admittedly, this technical accomplishment establishes Daedalian heroism, but it does so only after pre-oedipal phantasy has built a second, oracular body for statues. The statue, formed from a material that enables the doppelgängery of flesh, objectifies the essence of making humans (generativity, genitality) and introduces a body that will survive and outlast them. This is the body of the *longue durée* and represents a superior body. It anticipates the immortal body, the *deified* body, and if it is built from the "stuff of large bodies" (e.g., wood and stone from the earth, gold from the sun), then this metabolism also carries information of a higher order.

The "inner statue" described by Giordano Bruno shares with the statues of Apollonius of Tyana a relationship to what Corbin calls an "active imagination." In his text *Lampas triginta statuarum,* Bruno describes various forms of searching and re-peating in terms of *re-colligere* or remembering. First, what is to be remembered should be given a strong outline, so it can be easily retrieved, and second, this retrieval should be based on an emotional or organic automatism. What is to be remembered has to be attractive to imagination and phantasy, so that they simultaneously arrange themselves around it. Bruno thought there were different ways to *search for* (*investigandi*) something, and what follows in his text (and no wonder Bruno scholars are sometimes at a loss) is a description of various ways of *producing a statue.*[46] First, by pressing wax into a model; second, by applying parts to or, as the case may be, a physical substance around an "*atomon spiritualis*"; and third, the combination of parts as in building a house. This obscure text also explains how to extract material from something shapeless until the desired form appears, along with a few other methods. The first, Bruno continues, is suitable for everything to do with the composition of speeches, the second is a process of nature that is useful for searching and finding, the third imitates the workings of the soul, and the fourth appears in the combinatory system of Raimund Lull. Bruno's theory of statues clearly illustrates how archaic sculptural practices were maintained in later mnemonic operating systems and, in particular, that of Renaissance mnemotechnics.

Mnemotechnics sets out to build an artificial memory on top of a natural one and seeks to use the reflex-like contributions of the older, sedimented layers of memoria in a "technical" manner. The "first events" or primary facts structuring memory are sought in these sediments. Mnemotechnics explains how remembering and memorizing function and suggests how their functioning can be improved through the internal organization of memory. This is why Bruno, in the midst of the emergence of the image as the artistic principle of the Renaissance, insists

on the importance of *statues* and gives them unlimited credit
within his theory. He wants to use the gifts of "*statua quippe
sensibilis, visibilis, imaginabilis*" in order to activate memory and
retrieve the things it contains.[47] The statues' *corporeality* sta-
bilizes the deeper layers of memory, and with the help of
these distinguished objects the imagination is able to nav-
igate the deepest layers of *memoria*.[48] As well as its role in
memorizing, the statue also has a function in relation to
the "collective soul." The statue acts as a specially prepared
"bait" guiding the "soul-substance," a role that made it
politically explosive. Bruno's mnemotechnics shows how
a statue can combine a personal memory with a public and
general memory. The durability of its materials makes it
able to be shown not only to the multitude, as every body
can, but also to the multitudes of successive generations.
The statue has a *durée* (duration) and even the *longue durée*
that, as Bergson argues in *Matter and Memory,* is the foremost
quality at memory's disposal. Bruno's text clearly elabo-
rates this function of the statue in terms of its effective
archaism. Its role in collective memory makes it a mnemological principal, and as such Bruno sets it apart from
the image, which also has extensive mnemotechnical tasks
to perform. The *oldest memories* adhere in the statue because
it belongs to "antiquity," which means the statue-principle
is a function that can unlock the "deepest past." The statue
is the *effective mnemotechnical operator* of the pre-oedipal world.

The Two-Body Doctrine

The mummy or the artfully prepared corpse, along with
durable statues, make it necessary to revise the concept
of death. If these things really were perceived as simply
"dead," then they would never have attracted such intense,
open curiosity in the first place and had such an abundance of projections attached to them. The deadness of

the exquisite conserved body is its privilege, and if sacrifice
is also in play then it is a matter of an *artwork of deification*.
Obviously a dualism has been introduced here, but unlike
those *en courant* in philosophy such as the body–soul dualism, this is a *body–body dualism* that inspires the phantasy of
a world that does not know death but only a *body exchange* (as
metabolism), the transfer from one body to another. The
body–body dualism is materialized by plastic technologies,
while its sublime form unfurls in doctrines of the immortal body built on a phantasy of a paradise that reflects the
happy mood of prenatal symbiosis. In a footnote to the
two introductory chapters of *Spiritual Body and Celestial Earth*[49]
that explains the role of the earth angel, of the *Ange de la
Terre* or Spenta Armaiti,[50] Henry Corbin assumes that this
strong presence is a divine female; tellurian, garden-like,
and paradisiacal, and connected to matriarchal ideas of
the pre-Aryan period.[51] While this historical projection is
perhaps doubtful,[52] Corbin nevertheless provides us with
Iranian mystical texts that help us tunnel into the mountain of interpretations concerning the powers of the body.
The images arising from this historical and psychic depth
make the pre-oedipal world accessible to us as the world of
the *blessed body*. The poetic treatment of the earth's body in
the texts presented by Corbin leads us to a stratum emanating corporeal bliss. The Iranian mystics assume that
the body's true characteristics can be explained as a great
blessed earth, whose bliss rises to meet them. This earthly
place from which our physical happiness derives has beautiful waters, mysteriously formed trees, meandering paths,
and wandering lines of hills; there are magnificent rare
birds in the branches who chirp and hum, delicious fruits
growing on the strong trees, and the air is filled with the
perfume of gorgeous blossoms of all shapes and colors.
This place is called *Xvarnah,* paradise.[53] Here, everything is
nourishing, a "milieu" from which bodies "separate" like

curdling milk: "The paradise of the faithful believer is his own body."[54]

From these texts we can deduce the main elements of a *pharmacology* or *physiology* of the resurrected body, of the body that transforms into a divine body. If the statue suspends death, and if this surviving second body is created through the explication of the natal, then we can assume that the body has *in principle doubled*. Indeed, in the texts translated by Henry Corbin such a concept emerges in sharp relief. The two-body doctrine, which is eventually developed into a theory of *four* bodies, distinguishes a mortal earthly body from the resurrected body of heavenly earth: "I shall answer him as follows: know that the 'material body' (*jasad*) which is in the human being is in reality made up of two bodies."[55] One of the two bodies that belong to a human is transient, the other is not.[56] This is the quintessence of Neoplatonic theories of paradise.

The second body is not to be understood simply as a metaphor, as an idea of an afterlife modeled on the body, instead it is (as is always pointed out) an actually formed body. The body is the organ of blessedness and damnation, and everyone constructs this second body with the power of the imagination through everything they do. The first body is a kind of ground control directing but also forming the second body; they are interlocked and interrelated, and what happens in one also effects the other. Disembodiment is *not at all* part of the plan. The early scholars reflected on this task of worldly existence—to build a body from heavenly earth—and stressed the paramount importance of imagination. Any contempt for the imagination must be abandoned, and the suggestion of Shaik Ahmad Ahsa'i concerning the connection between *active imagination* and the *resurrection body* should be followed.[57] In a conversation with Mullah Sadra Shirazi he says: "The imaginative power in man . . . is a substance existing independently, as regards its essence and its operation. . . . As we already said, at the moment when the bodily mold is annihilated, it survives—obliteration and dissolution have no effect on it; . . . *post mortem* it continues to see itself as a human being with dimensions and shape corresponding to those that were its own in this world."[58]

That the body "survives" or is preserved in its grave, while shaking off the earthly dust that made it opaque, presupposes that it enters a place with "dimensions" and "form."[59] If the earthly body contains a paradisiacal body to which it can finally "return," then this must be true in an exemplary fashion for the body that "produces" the individual bodies, the *body of the earth*. The earth carries paradise *within itself* as an immortal "second body" called Gaia Sophia, as earth wisdom or as the *earth angel*.

> By assuming this nature, the human being is then, in the true sense, the son of the Angel of the Earth, and so able to have a mental vision of her. . . . Around Daena, who is the daughter of Spenta Armaiti . . . are clustered the figures of Angel-Goddesses whose hierophanies are described in the Avesta in marvellous terms. . . . Here experience is schematized in conformity with the fundamental angelology of the Mazdean vision of the world. The presence of a feminine Archangel of the Earth in the celestial pleroma was recognized and experienced. This relationship establishes the Mazdean *sacramentum Terrae*, the Sophianic mystery of the Earth.[60]

The enormous, transformed, and paradisiacal body of the earth establishes or grounds the dignity of all smaller individuated bodies,[61] which shine like cut diamonds as a result.[62] The undertones of an *earth logic* can still be heard in the depths of this agrarian and territorial history, despite its consistent and brilliant sublimation in the pneumatological superimposition. Everything that happens to the body is geo-graphy, communicating an earth-text, the life of the earth. Humans arise as earthlings, from the earth, their life is not a *life-toward-death* but a *life-toward-the-earth.* Corbin comments: "Here we already glimpse that what the soul perceives through its *Imago Terrae* is actually both its own archetypal Image and the enactment of its own mental dramaturgy."[63] The transformation of the body expresses the true power of the earth to *produce diverse bodies.* This *femininity* of the earth is an echo of an initial motherhood that both fabricates and reduplicates bodies. The logos of the earth as such is the body, which finds itself in a drama that traverses the stages of its transformation. The geosophy of the paradise-earth requires no anti-earth, no hell or any other Ahrimanian stopover, but instead outlines the unfolding of a single place, of one body whose form is an *artwork* created by the one imagining it, passing through different states.[64] The immortality of bodies came before the invention of the immortality of the soul (which philosophers found so difficult to defend) and was achieved through a sequence of diversifications and transformations of their materials grounded on an ultimate and divine superbody (for the Iranian mystics this was the earth). The resurrection the body awaits in its tomb is not a transformation into impersonal elements and particles, something *being* cannot anticipate with joy, but a bodily refinement of unprecedented quality.[65] The sequence of transformations the body must undergo to achieve a paradisiacal body are (al)chemically defined. One could imagine the beautification of the resurrected body as similar to that of silicon and potash, which initially look like opaque sand but after melting turn into glass. If a white elixir is added to this glass one gains its more precious form, the radiant crystal. This in turn, through a further dose of the same elixir, becomes a diamond. Additionally, a stonelike body can also be obtained by adding white elixir to copper, turning it into silver, which a dose of red elixir then turns into gold. With a second dose of red elixir the gold undergoes the highest transformation and becomes *Lapis philosophorum,* the "philosopher's stone."[66]

Among doctrines of resurrection the more biological preach a dissolution into base elements, a decomposition into tiny particles whose life is eternal. In contrast, the heavenly earth described in the writings made available by Henry Corbin is the mother of form and shape and remains the same whatever dangers are faced.[67] With form, *individuality* is secured, and everyone can prepare their own personal paradise and hell. Once this principle is understood, the cult to which these doctrines of resurrection belong emerges more clearly. If the grave is a kind of scheduled stop on one's journey that allows you to change into a better and more attractive suit, then this place should be prepared with the highest care and in the most beautiful way. In it the soul sings this song: "I walk towards my image, and my image walks towards me. It caresses and embraces me, as though I have just returned from captivity."[68]

The One and the Many

We have seen how *plasma* is relevant to the question of origins, to the creation of both the world and its human artifacts, and how the transfiguration of the body was its happy ending. The task of the "plasma" surrogate is to make these aesthetic preparations, the "cosmetics" of the second body, palpable and visible. This will bring together the moral and spiritual dimensions developed in the texts that Corbin has given us with the political and social aspects of *plasma.* As we have seen, imagination is crucial for the "cosmetics" applied to the resurrected body, and so an art form emerges within the culture of immortality that practices this imaginary operation on an "immortality mannequin."

The existence of cult sculptures as secondary bodies, or as schizosoma, is the *immediate expression* of the theory of the *glorified* and *deified* body. The laboratory of art practices these *imaginary* designs, where the ideals of transubstantiation are plasmatically anticipated. But unlike funeral cults, an artificial second body is not produced for every body. Insofar as it stands at the center of a cult, the imaginary body, the body of active imagination or the resurrected body, stands as *one for many*. The cultic artwork is therefore a prototype or veritable model for the many. The *ars deformationum* are practiced on the artwork, testing which plasma best inspires the general imagination and in what form. Sculpture, as the art of schizosoma, is thus always moral, it has something of a norm about it, of a being-supposed-to, and for this reason was often the preferred artistic instrument of authoritarian politics.

There are two distinct artistic laboratories of the immortal body. One of them is dedicated to a schizosoma that can be collectivized because it has veered off from *humanité*. Here, *animal shapes* are produced, beginning the long history of nonhuman sculpture: of fetishes, masks, hybrid beings, and heraldic signs. The forms of theriomorphic sculpture return in a weakened state in the biomorphic lines of abstract sculpture. The second laboratory is dedicated to the truly great cosmetic project, the *production of supermen* [*Übermenschen*].

Plastic mass and its duplication are, as nature impressively demonstrates, quite different from the image. As Giordano Bruno realized, sculpture is often produced through a technology of molding (the impression) or casting, by which many examples can be made from one form or, to put it another way, an original prototype is reproduced through a kind of *techno–democratization*. Even if sculptures were produced from stone or wood, and were by nature unique items, by developing production line workflows and the repetition of similar components, a kind of serialization became possible. This preindustrial standardization of production was well advanced in sculpture, a fact unfortunately unnoticed in Benjamin's famous essay on mechanical reproduction. In particular, small souvenir figurines resembling venerated statues were produced in large numbers, without the faithful lamenting any loss of aura in these takeaway figures. On the contrary, the potency of cult sculpture was thought to be increased by its proliferation in copies. People carried this small figure, this talisman, because of the way it operated like an antenna, allowing an essence to attach to it, despite the doubts of those who love the original.

The suppression of important aspects of the theory of creative activity means that the reproduction of cult sculptures, which begins in the metallurgic culture of the Bronze Age, has been largely ignored. In fact, the discovery that certain substances could be liquidized and changed into another form through the use of molds is a *technical fact of the utmost importance.* The relationship to the magical gesture of touch is essential rather than merely extrinsic. In melting and pouring, in the synthesis of the two forms (one after the other) into a single substance, the technical simulation of "imprintability" [*Abdrücklichkeit*] as a mode of expressibility [*Ausdrücklichkeit*] is achieved: The form is poured out of the cast, and the body of the cast is restored. This technology of the imprint translates the moment of magical touch into a concept or "frame." As such, it inspired the great cosmological narratives of the Upanishads, which interpret the universe as a gigantic smelting cauldron where forms are melted down in a blast furnace or as a cooking pot where the *prima materia* simmers as the primal pulp of form. This metallurgical method of creating forms is found even more clearly in Ovid's *Metamorphoses.* The introduction describes the principle of transformation as melting something down and forming it anew, and the interactions between the protagonists of the stories reflect this power of cohesion that is founded on that of the particles of primal matter.

The further development of the Bronze Age technologies of smelting and casting led to the production of the rigid metal membrane, which defined public (i.e., political) sculpture into the twentieth century. The origin of the cast membrane of the Schiller monument in front of the Academy of Fine Arts in Vienna in the magic of touch, for example, can only be deduced in a roundabout way. Nevertheless, the objectification and stiffening of the sculpture's membrane was produced by two bodies pressing themselves together: first, the modeled clay body leaves its mark in plaster, producing a form, and then a second body emerges by casting this form in bronze.

The imprint is the bridge to the *second body* that reveals *intercorporeal communication* as the beginning of all things, it is the pre-form of the *schizosoma* with which it shares a primitive body sense. The extremities, the five points of the human pentagram, are especially suitable for or even desire the imprint, because they are the "feelers" along which we move through the world and so concentrate our *sensitivity*. In a culture whose perceptual organization is not exclusively optical, a culture where the "male gaze" (as a pure *outside*) dominates, sensation is the zone of contact between "feeler" and object. This is where the symbolic order of the mother finds her "beloved essential things." This explains why rocks with an unusual surface or silhouette became cult sites in prehistoric times. A sensitivity for fault lines in the surface, for recesses, incisions, and scratches in the earth (geo-metry) characterizes not only the Australian Indigenous peoples, who are wonderful trackers of the landscape, but all the early hunter and gatherers.[69] Later, pigments and colored pastes were applied to imprints, adding a third and contrasting element to the initial juxtaposition of hard bodies and a soft medium. In this context, while the confrontation of the body with the materials of painting in *Viennese Actionism* was an attempt to explode the standards of academic art through contact with older, more primitive forms of expression, it in fact acted as their restriction, because behind these "typological attempts" to attain an imprint of the body is an effort to limit the archaic dyad of an archetype (of performing bodies) and a *soft material* (such as clay) to mere pigment. In religious use the *imprint* was a magical means of visualizing the saint and the benefactor, it served as a substrate of what we call the *magic of touch,* a kind of *hotline* between the beyond and the here and now of the worshiper.

It is important to note that the *imprint* initially appeared as a "prelogical assurance of self" and was subject to the desire of primary narcissism. In the miracle of the dissimilar left behind by a body rolling in pigment, and so honoring "something of itself," a specific significance is attributed to the tactile sense, to the pressure of the first intrauterine dwelling, the pressure of the first sustained embrace (holding and being held), and to the subsequent joyful unrolling of the self in a trusting acceptance of the world. Didi-Huberman gives, quite correctly, a genealogical interpretation of this type of similarity that involves physical immersion and the imprinting of oneself into another substance: "For the imprint physically—and not just optically—transfers the similarity of the thing or person of whom a cast is made. The analogy to sexual reproduction is clear: first, there belongs to the process of imprinting an intimate contact, the pressure of the object being pushed onto the substrate or intruding into it; then, the result does not disappear as a mirror image, but it is literally 'born' as a body, born through the act of imprinting."[70] Here, the organic ego, the skin ego described by

Didier Anzieu comes to the fore, an ego that regulates its communication and operation through pressure and counterpressure.[71] The first touch is not so tender after all.

The imprint is narcissistic insofar as the skin ego only has knowledge about itself through what is shown on its sensitive surfaces, even if they emerge in various folds, faults, evaginations, and invaginations. Through painting, that is by transferring itself to another surface, the skin ego obtains a blind mirror image that is saturated with the bed-warmth of the self. This self-imprinted self is thus—to employ a concept specifically used by Artaud and Deleuze—intense and without organs because it is not "instrumentalized," it has not yet entered into the neurotic classifications of organ fixation and is not yet dominated by that overly privileged valve *through which every expression modifies itself*. It is therefore magical, primitive, physical, and plastic in the proper sense.

The history of the imprint gives an idea of the true geo- and physiopsychological age of the sculptural. Groping *for the other body* belongs to binomial schizosoma, and since its advent humans have reproduced themselves through "inner statues."

Social Sculpture

The open crossovers between the ego and the universe established by the pre-oedipal world are prerequisites for the symbolizations that finally make the sculptural project both *pedagogical* and *political*. Three things demand attention here. First, the focus of the group's imagination on a shared object that produces a strong *center of projection,* a "construct" to which everyone has the same relationship. Second, the *synchronization* of the group members in a ritual, or in liturgy and its effect. Third, the *relationship of the projection centers* or "poles of synchronization" among themselves, which are a result of *attraction and repulsion* between the groups and, even if it sounds odd, of attractions and repulsions among the deities themselves.

This phase of religion appears with radical totemism and sets up a fragile relationship to the foreign. The totem animal establishes kinship among the members of its group through its excellence and exceptional status, making the characteristic of this group its *kinship to a nonhuman*. Subjects achieve a *stage of political organization* in totemism when their biological parents start to compete with a powerful surrogate. The eventual replacement of biological parents by the totem prepares the way for a homogenous formatting of subjects that marks the approach of the *political age*. The totem is initially represented by a *paidagogos,* who also takes on the role of a parent. As the appearance of the *paidagogos* in Sophocles's *Electra* indicates, it is a question of making the child love the pedagogue as an ersatz father, even if the child naturally wants their parents despite them being useless and incompetent. Thus it is a story of *weaning*.[72] It is no coincidence that in the biography of the child oedipalization and the admission to preschool coincide. The *paidagogos* shows his foster child Orestes "the old land" and, more precisely, the "market place, that bears the wolf god's name,"[73] both behaving in a fatherly manner and referring to a totemic past. The children of the *paidagogoi,* like those of totemic ancestors, are adopted by *secondary* but nevertheless politically real "parents." Through weaning the first bond undergoes declension, it undergoes a purposeful and *collectivizing inflection*. When the first bond is thus understood as a copula elaborated according to semantic rules, a new genre of design emerges, the *design of the bond,* which establishes a *Surrogat-parenté* or artificial parent modeled on the child's relationship with the spirit- or animal-mother.

All higher beings profit from this breach opened by the totem animal, because further bonds can be made according to its model, connecting those previously unrelated in a kind of *a priori primal kinship,* one that repeats the hierarchical tendencies of the first "primal kinship." The totem animal therefore marks the invention of *corporate identity,* of a symbolic body where, as is also the case with the head and limbs of the church, ordinary anatomy ends and a *second, extended body* is phantasized by the entire group. This higher being, although polarizing the group, ensures that it maintains a metastable balance as one *multiple body.* As a pole of this system the higher being builds an "over-body" above the entire group, a "satellite body" that always and everywhere guarantees their primordial relationship. This body builds a bridge over the individuals gathered beneath it, like Nut the Egyptian goddess of heaven arching over her charges as the firmament. One could object that this satellite body is merely a *projection,* like the totem animal had been for early humanity, but the oscillations of group members under the assembling arch happens in *spite of this.* In fact, a *group soul* emerges between these individuals synchronized and socialized around the same pole and becomes stronger through their interaction. Although there are other aspects of the cult, it has surely patented this creation of a group soul, even if it also loans it out for less holy purposes.

The condition and first step of synchronization is aligning a community around something, whether an animal, a deity, or an abstract ideal. Then a broad range of instruments encourages group members to carry out the same gestures, rituals, and prayers, deepening and stabilizing the synchronization through repetition. In a choir, individuals become stronger and the less talented sing better. A "choir" or "choral song" expresses the *frequency of the group soul,* of a social cohesion produced by cultic practice and that emerges like an overtone from ritual and the forms of activity associated with it. Unfortunately, neither contemporary sociology nor the theory of communicative action concern themselves with these *musical forms of interac-*

tion. Unsurprisingly, psychoanalysis only sees a superego in the satellite body and its complex, exaggerated movements around the father.

There has been a great deal of speculation about *synchronization,* although one wonders why because if two or three people do something with determination it is natural that others will follow. The group's mutual and *continuous infection (inward)* immunizes them endogenously and acts as an *active repulsion (outward),* allowing their higher soul to cohere. This causes the various forms of fanaticism, fundamentalism, patriotism, dogmatism, and chauvinism and means that the creators of these states—the gods themselves—have, and indeed desire, only very restricted contact between themselves. In this way theological systems are able to prevent the arbitrary circulation of information and exchange.

The gods place great importance on preventing the *wrong people* from becoming enthusiastic about them. The economy of synchronization and enthusiasm only operates—and this is a universal principle expressed by every religion—through the gods, through *absolutely the best,* and the best are jealous. Everywhere formal arrangements are made and bastions are fortified. Cults and religions are entities constituted by enthusiasm and strive to protect themselves by building invisible fences of effective taboos. It is not so much the belligerent believers who sound the attack but the deities themselves, who infect their followers with their own aversions via their *monopoly on synchronization.* The deities are under inconceivable pressure to perform, a pressure all the greater the more similarities they share with other contemporary or extinct deities. Confusions between the best must be entirely avoided, and so when such similarities emerge they fall victim to the *condamnatio memoriae,* the suppression within the public memory. As a result, any similarities between Mary the mother of God and the Egyptian Isis, between Christmas, the Germanic festival of

immortality, and the mysteries of Mithras, appear scandalous. To suggest such similarities means being immediately
considered a believer in nothing and even being disqual-
ified as a *cultural studies scholar.*

In this light, banishing the animal from the center
of the cult was an act of jealousy by the younger, rising
gods, who wanted to give their disciples pre-eminence.
But this annulment of the older, foreign gods simply does
not work, because devalued gods are "nondisposable" and
remain as *problematic or hazardous waste.* This uncomfortable
situation is certainly, although perhaps only faintly, clear
to the groups who convert to the (new) best, because it
remains inscribed in the construction of their religion,
annoying and enflaming them, and so communicating
this irritation to their "satellite body," the god. Thus it
is less an appeal to humanity, to the new Kantian mood,
that prevents the followers of the world's religions from
attacking each other than an awareness of their lavish consumption of symbolic bodies, satellite bodies, and poles of
synchronization, which produces an endless succession of
the highly revered, the devalued, and, finally, the spat out.
If theology, for once, was adequate to its task of being a
science of universal waste and repression, the guiding star of a new
solution might rise.

As the older gods cannot be easily got rid of, their
devaluation or depreciation is in fact a *transvaluation,* which
is why divine "objects" appear in a circle and supersede
one another according to a principle of rotation. The
motor function of cultures and of cultural memory (the
sequence and periodicity of cultural levels and cultural
forms), could also be seen as a displacement of *media* within
a theogony resulting from its immanent pressure of differentiation, its symbols inadequately papering over the *gap
in memory* that opens where the old beliefs had been. This
relationship to *constitutive amnesia* produces a series of sym-

bolic patches that establish spaces of *creative nonunderstanding* explored through the following questions: How could the first being appear when I saw it, without knowing that it was the first being, and even now that I see it? What was I before I was a human? What was the staffage of the pre-oedipal world, a world with a *totally different normality*? These lines of flight are a kind of fleet-footed delirium creating a transit space of aesthetically exciting objects that bridge the abyss of primordial memory.

It is not only cultural or religious projects that follow the rules of totemism. A dimension of excessively overdetermined *hyperfunctional objects* also appears that offers connections to an older but veiled truth. These objects give human beings a first intuition of their solidity (as individual bodies that have fallen out of their "medium") and enable them to identify with surrogate and immortal bodies, in an instantaneous corporeal understanding or cultural automatism.

The cognitive faculty that occupies this space of creative nonunderstanding is an archaic and shapeless *sympathy* or *pan-pathy* ("the one that feels with the universe"), and its corresponding state resembles somnambulism or hypnosis, states that are prevalent today in our everyday consumption of information media.

These *hypnotizing media* are perpetually changing. At one point an animal gazed steadfastly back at us, then a mummy, a statue, a doll, a monument, and finally, and no less enchanting, we are faced with an interactive device. But even if we distinguish these things, the suspicion arises that in their diffusion and confusion one can be taken for the other.

This is unsurprising given that on the level of symbolic construction living beings and their apparatuses run parallel to each other. On one point however, humanist criticism (or perhaps one should say humanist discomfort) is correct, that older apparatuses did not maximize the potential *output of influence* (i.e., an object's absorption of intense and excessive psychic "showering"). The animal, as we have seen, defines a benevolent level where *maternal calories* are always freely available, but while the attentive (*caretaking*) side of this apparatus is perfect, from the perspective of its cult it is neutral and without love. So while the animal brought warmth to the relationship, it had to accept that people returned to it because it was one of the great and certainly older ones but tended to amuse themselves with it before turning away satisfied. This is quite different to the newer apparatuses, where one has the frustrating feeling of having to leave shortly before they fulfil their promise. The interactive device, however, catches the aspect of the older gods that their new anthropomorphic generation are not willing to manifest and translates it into a general function. As a result, the device is the happy object on whom meditative energy is focused. The humanist camp is therefore rightly suspicious of the device, because it embodies a "knowledge from below," a knowledge sunk into a pure corporeality that is only lucid under its own disreputable conditions, as an advanced form of *absentmindedness, of being-outside-of-oneself, of being-mechanical.*

These modes of materialization—where "materialization" means an alienating, *xenological objectification*—become recognizable as a symbolic sequence: the animal first appears as a mummified animal and fetish; these are followed by *statues*, initially animal-shaped but increasingly anthropomorphic. The statue appears as a human-shaped *deity* and then degenerates into its weaker manifestation as a *doll* and finally into *oracular automata*. With these, the *apparatus* is divided into the little containers where its functions are hidden.

The sequence of the three essential functions of ANIMAL/GOD/APPARATUS are combined and variegated within a human (within a *girl-human: g-human*,[74] thus within a *being who is not subordinated to the symbolic order of the father*) in the following way:

G-HUMAN<=>Animal

(Human recognizes its origin in the animal)

G-HUMAN<=>ANIMAL+God

(Human regards the animal as a deity)

G-HUMAN<=>GOD+Animal

(Human ascribes an animal form to the deity)

G-HUMAN<=>GOD

(Human acknowledges the deity's change into human form => doll)

G-HUMAN<=>GOD+Apparatus

(Human simulates the god through a machine, which compensates for the god being insufficiently foreign)

G-HUMAN<=>APPARATUS+God

(Human is opposed to the apparatus as an extrinsic and purely enigmatic function)

G-HUMAN<=>APPARATUS

(Human forms a binomial with the disenchanted function)

G-HUMAN<=>APPARATUS+Animal

(Human once again ascribes "animalistic" abilities to the apparatus, animalistic powers are projected into it)

The human–animal couple is the beginning. As soon as

the animal is "weak," a new terminus must be introduced
in order to support the inner logic of the dispositive. Symbolic values that were initially stored in the animal are
rescued and put into interim storage. As the expiring animal form of the deity required preservation in the apparatus (i.e., had to be revalued), the weakening of the god
ends in a strengthening of the apparatus. The apparatus—
magnificent, universal, and strong—finally replaces the god
but carries *the animal behind it* (as it did in the older substitu-
tions or compensations agreed to by animal and apparatus),
introducing it once more like an atavistic reflex. At first a
weak animal appears, a kitschy, subordinated, or demented
animal, an animal of poisonous green plush with huge eyes
and pink ears. This animal now haunts civilization, broadcast from the depths of its devices and their hypnotizing
surfaces. Cute animals do the rounds: mice, fawns, pup-
pies and ponies, Grzimek's Daktari. Then birds and flies
freak out, hairy animal countenances emerge from bel-
lies, mountains of cattle corpses flicker across the screen,
a goat fetus suffers through an intrauterine pregnancy.[75]
Digital transformations turn humans into animals, give
life to things with skin, horns, and hooves, computer mice
consisting of organic material make animal sounds. Animation degenerates and enters a stage of *animalization. Anor-
ganic sex* with devices heats up as the organic returns within
them, as organisms are resurrected through them, because
the showering of an object with soul potentially makes it a
low organism, a primitive species of soul owner. If the animal
returns, it returns objectified, as the animal downgraded
to an object, and it struggles to recapture its old glory as
the mother of all humanity. Animals initially lend their
face to the empty, reflecting surfaces that steer the inner
immunity of groups. Appearing according to the *bottom-up*
principle, they first become visible to those who are still
small, to the *pre-oedipal population.* Children's rooms have

never seen their stables as crammed full of stuffed animals as they are today.[76] The weak animal gains ground. In
the children's room the Great Animal reigns, the totemic
Mama, and next to her an animal patron, who for psy-
choeconomic reasons (the stabilization of a memory gone
haywire) presents *herself on a small scale* in the stuffed animal,
in these multicolored and mass-produced animals about
which no one comments but that are there to warm up the
connections of our apparatus addiction.

4

The Labyrinth

General Theory of Schizosoma

ANALYZING THE MOST DISTINGUISHED objects of the Cretan-Minoan (and hence the pre-oedipal) world, the figure of the labyrinth must be considered along with the invention of *schizosomatic sculpture* and its examples of *totems, mummies,* and cultic sculptures, given that the prototype of the prophesying statue was also supposedly invented by Daedalus. While the labyrinth has already been extensively researched and discussed, in my opinion it has not yet been recognized as a major part of the pre-oedipal world.

The labyrinth displays the peculiar spatiality underlying female identification. The interfering spheres of inside and outside that constitute the labyrinth are interpreted as the human-animal in the *primordial Mama,* making it the principal cultic space of pre-oedipal societies. That it must be a space or a spatial structure follows from the principle of the body-producing body, the *generative* body that defines the pre-oedipal constellation. Experiences of a "prehuman" caring being are transferred to the labyrinth, where they are "machinized" or "standardized." If we follow Mary Jacobus's lead and interpret myths as *structures of memory* as such, rather than as memories of childhood, the labyrinth is more than an image, it is a generator of memory. According to Jacobus, the memory of the pre-oedipal mother is simultaneously contained and containing, the content and structure of memory, which this *mother* produces as *its sense*.[1] Jacobus emphasizes that in relation to the pre-oedipal mother the identification of content with the form of the *container* is imperative. A concept of this *container* simultaneously posits the inside and outside, enabling what is on the inside to realize itself as content beyond the semantic or figurative connotations of spatiality (and those of literary studies). The labyrinth is thus a first space, one with the complex organization of a heterotopia.

The labyrinth simultaneously folds in and out (it implies and explicates), it both pairs and synchronizes the inside and outside and in this way gives natality, as the premise of memory, its first *topos*. From the perspective of natality memory thus seeks itself via the container, being both its substance [*Gehalt*] and content [*Inhalt*]. In the labyrinth memory *and* the weakness of memory (the impossibility of separating the spheres of containing and contained) become concrete. Pre-oedipality does not mean only attending to the mother at the expense of the potent and polarizing affects of the separation to come; it means being within the interminable and searching movement that translates memory into *space*. The labyrinth is where this movement takes place; it is interminable because it is identical with the *container*. Yet, the stories woven around the Cretan labyrinth recount everything but the bliss of birth. The labyrinth invented by Daedalus erects a *monument* to the perishing pre-oedipal society, where the human-animal creature the Minotaur is *locked up*. Daedalus's monument configures pre-oedipal memory into an architectonic apparatus but in doing so revalues it: The human-animal Minotaur now appears as the *sacrificer* who kills the virgins assigned to him by lot. The sacrifice of the girl in the

Daedalian labyrinth therefore takes place in a natal space where semantic and affective omens are exchanged. This labyrinth is a *space of horror* where girls are eaten by a human-animal, an act that nevertheless also refers to an *original equivalence* (girl = unit of value = human-animal). So instead of performing an initiation rite to Motherhood this pairing of girl and human-animal represents the *annihilation of the girl*. The Electra complex is basically caused by this fact. If the primeval Mother symbolized by the labyrinth devours the girl, her rescue by the symbolic order of the Father offers a way out. The critical position of the girl *who is tricked out of her pre-oedipality* becomes significant with Electra, the younger sister of Iphigenia. Insofar as she must, as a girl, be in the labyrinth, which now no longer represents the birth-mother but rather the devouring-mother, she exemplifies this revaluation. The hopelessness of this situation where she is offered her own extinction will, quite logically, make her want to kill her own mother. The labyrinth created by Daedalus is therefore an instrument that simultaneously reveals and conceals a memory that does not reach its end.

Only one girl escapes this labyrinthine machinery: *Ariadne*. As the Minotaur's sister it seems likely that she *knows her way around the place*. Perhaps she is *his feminine aspect*? Is the Minotaur a "man" only because his/her totem of the bull (*taurus*) gave him a *male family name*? *Together* the Minotaur and Ariadne form the totemistic binomial that engenders female identification. They are both separate and one and the same. But Ariadne comes, as does Electra, at the *end* of the maternal lineage, leaving the hypogeum behind and saying goodbye forever. She decides to follow the hero Theseus who allegedly murders the "sacrificer." His killing of the killer accomplishes the concealment and revaluation of the human-animal, putting an end to its realm of immanence and leading the girl into the pure *outside of the Father.* Ariadne *gets out,* following her thread, but her luck does not last. Ariadne's Electra complex has obviously not taken root deeply enough, and on Naxos, grief-stricken over the disappearance of Theseus, she is fair game for the biggest vagabond of them all. She promptly marries the wild Dionysus, the unborn god whom Zeus had sewn into his calf. Of course, the remains of the human-animal were still present in him, explaining perhaps why, in a moving scene, Ariadne immediately falls for him. As Friedrich Nietzsche has Dionysus tell Ariadne: *"I am thy labyrinth."*[2]

Pasiphae's Cow

Ariadne's mother is Pasiphae, who mated with the white bull who emerged from the sea. Through this coupling Pasiphae belongs to the circle of goddesses escorted by an animal. Horned animals are especially prominent as companions of the goddess—for instance, Ishtar's goat or the appearance of Hathor as a cow. Most of the goddesses who date from between 30,000 and 2000 BCE and were found either in southwest Asia or in the area of the supposed old Danube cultures are recognized by their animal (as if by a code) and are interchangeable with it. The goddess and the animal are related through totemic *replacement.* Horned animals are generally assigned the moon aspect of the deity, and the goddess may carry a calendar in the form of a notched horn, as can be seen in the famous cave carvings at Laussel. Before her defamation, Pasiphae and the bull represent the ideal divine couple: the moon goddess together with the white oceanic bull. Their devaluation occurs at the moment when their "wedding" is no longer a totemistic doubling, a figure of totemistic schizosoma, but is considered a real ritual founding state and family and involving a coitus that is also real. To "progressive" cultures the difference between the partners seems to have raised imaginary problems that had to be practically overcome by a *homo faber,* by an engineer. Daedalus takes on the task, without understanding its background or significance, as he was not Cretan by origin, but arrives having fled *Athens* after the murder of Talos, his extremely talented apprentice.[3] King Minos welcomes the ingenious blacksmith to his kingdom and grants him his favor, at least until he finds out that Daedalus invented a wooden cow that allowed the Queen to practice "adultery" with the animal. Suddenly the story takes a moral turn, one that is obviously a later addition, a commentary *post factum.* Certain cultural misunderstandings slip into Daedalus's product design, but these misunderstandings are *productive.* He literally *fabricates* the misunderstandings and makes from them a veritable framework. From a mythopoetic perspective, for example, his wooden copulation machine is an insult to the majesty of the goddess escorted by her animal. But Daedalus is uninterested in how this animal mediates between the "prehuman Mother" as a hieroglyph for our first intimacy and the groom, and concentrates instead on its supposed rivalry to the king. Pasiphae abdicates her position as a great moon goddess at the moment when Daedalus presents to the interested public the machine that will allow the divine bull to mount her.

At this point the connection between schizosomatic totemistic practice and machinic genius emerges once more, a connection we have already discussed in terms of totemism's relevance to contemporary media theory. The animal is *misunderstood* and disfigured by a forbidden coitus, by sodomy and perversion, as its companionship with the goddess is technically analyzed and the phantasized union banishes her to the wooden cow. The wooden cow clearly paved the way for a long history of the serious deferral of, and *disfigurements* to, the nature of the female goddess. What makes the technical object so monstrous is its ignorant attempt to reduce the liaison between the goddess and her animal to a horizontal affair. Both the goddess and the animal suffer from this negative projection; the goddess becomes a misguided, perverse queen and the animal a disfigured creature lured into a trap, deceived by skillful mimicry.

The deeper meaning of this peculiar alliance (which we find in countless examples of goddesses accompanied by animals) is the "literal intersection of the dissimilar," which symbolizes the experimental part of human nature promoting risky evolutionary or revolutionary movements. Here, the emergence of a specific surface activity in animality tends to transgress its own limits. The animal companion is the sovereign expression of the goddess's dependence on her substrate or plane of emergence. The animal companion is therefore not a nasty escort service but, as we have seen, the symbol of pre-oedipal femininity, matrilineal ascendance, and unconditional, earthbound loyalty to the mother. The companion therefore has the decorum of the being it *replaces* because of its deep totemistic affinity with the great and principal subject. The animal symbolically bridges the gap in the process producing identities.[4] Furthermore, this constellation reveals a kind of reciprocal observation or consideration that allows *for orientation,* because in a conjugated subjectivity the eyes of one watch and protect the other to give him or her security.[5] The *accompanied goddess* represents the structure of the *totemistic socius*, with the disparity of the partners conditioning both ascendancy and partner choice. From the limit to here, through *the other,* the mother/spouse, the ancestor, helper and equal among clan members, gives the human being its shape. Why is Daedalus ignorant of this "intercourse" between the goddess and the bull? Why did he consider this "intercourse" pathological, an interpretation that made his intervention as a foreign specialist necessary? And why did Daedalus, like a foolish child who is ignorant of coital gadgets, give this strange interpretation that while hardly pouring glory on the King or his kingdom nevertheless demanded his goodwill?

What does this story really tell us? Could it be that it retraces the history of "electrification"? Its purely salacious reading disguises the intersection that inscribes the parable of origin. It circles the dissimilar couple too tightly, preventing the unveiling of totemistic generativity. The couple of Pasiphae and her bull are not, as in the pre-oedipal state, allowed to be "three," so they will transfer their problems onto *a new third*, onto *the coming child*. In the totemistic couple the other who gives identity was an ancestor, the nonhuman or prehuman "foreign half" of the partner that allowed a "humane" countervalue or equivalent to emerge. The totemistic "marriage" itself was organized in a triangular form, like the roof of a house. This *pre-oedipal triangle* has an entirely different meaning to Freud's oedipal triangle and operates according to an entirely different physics of relationships. The organigram of totemistic marriage having mutated into *Daedalus's framework* the child-being that was previously *undisturbed* under totemism's threefold roof now had to perform new tasks co-organizing the marriage. It now had, for systemic reasons, to occupy the lower point of the *nontotemistic* marriage triangle, but as this marriage was constituted by a "pair" or twofoldness this proved *impossible* to achieve, and its position is pitiful. The child must operate as a buffer between the *eo ipso* irreconcilable parents (despite their phantasized merging), and so it plays the role of the *alien* from another time, another culture, another world in order to introduce *exonerating strangeness* into the construction of the binome of the pair. From now on the child bears the burden of the animal with which it is connected (what kind of *circle* is this?). There is *an old solidarity* that motivates the child to sacrifice itself for the benefit of the animal. This is called subverting a culture, inasmuch as one simply turns its structure upside down.

That Daedalus murdered his apprentice because the boy learned too well and threatened to surpass his master reveals his character in stark relief. By profession he was the *great jealous one* intolerant of competition. The *elimination of the third* secretly motivates all his machinations. Already in Athens he strived to be the best and the most loved of the skilled. Once in Crete, he finds a wondrous paradise of primordial trinity where a king "cohabits" with his wife and her bull, and takes it as a challenge to introduce Athenian modernity. The copulation apparatus is a miracle cure reducing the primordial trinity to a comedy of manners. Inspired by this great technical success, he tackles the problem that is its direct result, the status of the child it produces. Having invented the copulation apparatus for Minos's wife, he then sets about building the labyrinth where the human-animal Minotaur, Pasiphae's child from her connection to the white bull, shall be locked up. Here the abomination or, in other words, the atrocious totemistic affiliation (at least to the well-groomed Athenian) remains hidden from the eyes of the world. The labyrinth is a spatial representation of the *collision of heteronomous cultural spheres*: The Athenian crashes into the Cretan-Minoan and the *political* conception of society and government (derived from the Greek *polis*) collides with the totemistic clan society of old Crete. The architect, a foreigner who knows how to profit from the exogamous atmosphere of a realm that appreciates the foreign, creates a spatial work that certifies *his* condition, *his* understanding of the task. He resolves the reading difficulties resulting from semantics being a mnemotechnics as well as a foreigner can (where there is no sign there is no memory): by designing a space for infinite research. But the labyrinth is not just a simple machine, a *scrutinium*, a search-system. *The misunderstood child of the queen* is locked up in this compound, one can no longer "see" her because it carries the features of its totemistic parents: It is *animal and human.* Its parents must be ashamed of their child, according to Daedalus's *reading difficulties,* and banish it to a structure from which it is never supposed to escape. The labyrinth myth codifies the *end of the pre-oedipal* in a capriccio telling of a monster losing itself in a confusing construction. The Cretan-Minoan experiment is stopped, and *being-lost* becomes the child's destiny. The child is caught in the machine of being unborn and as a fact of memory, following an expression of Hinderk M. Emrich, is "actively deactivated." The "inside-outside" of matricentric totemistic existence, the complicated *container* of the human-animal, is no longer the maternal palace inherited by the girl but the technically refined dungeon in which the forgotten is trapped.[6]

But beneath Daedalus's labyrinth, in its gaping depths, lies the lowest stratum, which owes as little to a feat of *engineering* as Pasiphae's animal. This pre-Daedalian labyrinth was that of the girl, who possessed sovereignty over it as *mistress of the statue, mistress of the sculptural, mistress of the Great Stuffed Animal and of plastic figurines.* Daedalus, who had already stage-managed the disgusting reputation of the girl's mother, also casts the child's sovereignty in an unfavorable light, giving enough credible evidence to put the child-monster behind the bars he had ingeniously invented. Just as he could not bear Talos *being better* than him, so he did not want to give up his mastery over the twisted space and the plastic realm to the child. Only he *himself* should be celebrated as the master of the living statue, *as sculptor, as inventor of automata and movable dolls.*[7]

Besides this technical makeover of cultural structures, the labyrinth poses the interlacing of cultures *as a problem of memory,* or as the process replacing an older regime with a younger one. Within the architecture of personal memory this process correlates to Freud's description of the transition from the pre-oedipal to the oedipal. To descend beneath the agoras of Athens means descending into what remains hidden; into the labyrinth, into the underworld, into the pre-world of corporeal and spatial sensitivities (*souterrain*).

The horizontalization of the primal *potency of becoming-human* that was originally split between the goddess and her animal can only be achieved by an engineer and inventor, by a figure unimpressed by that separation of powers implying the dissemination and "hypersocialization" of knowledge. This setting embeds knowledge into the arms of a caring nature allowing the human to only have a fraction of it, which means the knowledge *left over* by nature or the gods is *modernized* by Daedalus. The position of the animal that had appeared with its peculiar face softly veiling the knowledge of ancestry is annexed by a *bricolage* animal, a fabricated, *techno-animal.*

Clearly, the intention is to technically *compensate* for those parts escaping the totality of knowledge—namely, those parts that were previously accessible through a specific form of partnership. "Horizontalization" in this context means deleting the dimension that synthesizes the two related, nonidentical subjects in a third term that overrides them, granting them a symbolic and an ontological rank. The wooden cow consumes the energy of this third term, and the terrain is leveled out. Under the weight of the horizontal "terrace" where the "modern" posttotemistic parental couple sits enthroned, the child, almost crushed, will offer familiar symptoms as it cries for help.

The Satellite

The books by Hocke and Kern on the labyrinth include all its possible interpretations.[8] Their studies examine such a

wide range of mythological and literary motifs and explanations that one is tempted to leave this field of research
to them, uncontested. One of the most significant interpretations is of the labyrinth-dance.[9] This is a line dance,
a wound-up polonaise made up of a human band circling
in and out, in which the lead dancer must ensure the band
does not get tangled up.

But what the dance unleashes or signifies remains open,
and so does its cognitive potential. The dance puts great
emphasis on the big toe, bending the body forward and
creating an expectation of moving deeply into space. This
activates the spatial radar that enables our *independent bipedal
movement,* by which the human literally escaped the prehominid stage.[10] According to leading anthropologists,
these physical abilities make the human a runner rather
than a thrower, which for Leroi-Gourhan was the most
important ability of early humans.[11] The running human
achieves two things: first, an accentuated feeling of competence, or happiness, an *endorphinization* achieved by capturing space through moving on the ball of the foot. The
fleet-footed, two-legged bodies of dancing and running
recall this condition of the species' success: the ability that
led humans out of their natural environment. So-called
hominization continued these tested, physiologically effective
techniques of getting carried away with oneself and recognized the importance of the delight emanating from the
movement of dancing and running. Second, during running and dancing, as with all risky accelerated movements,
a kind of *satellite* regulates the runner's positioning. Leroi-
Gourhan's model of the "automation chain" would therefore have to be augmented by an overriding dimension,
a "surveillance station" from which movements are controlled, no matter how automatic, unconscious, or trance-
like. This entity may be imagined as something hovering
above the moving subject with which it maintains an echo,
a kind of *reflection of its movement.* Apparatuses are interesting

insofar as they operate in favor of *somebody* who designs, operates, or admires their (self) movement. Apparatuses (in relation to this [self] *movement* they could be understood as *automata*) only make sense if there are *allomats,* or systemic parts of the automat that perpetuate the first press of the button in ongoing impulses.

This world divided in two consists of a zone for *surveillance,* for the unblinking divine gaze, and another for what *lies beneath* it. Accordingly, votive images would be information gleaned from the labyrinthine, visual, and semantic inheritance of the intelligent running bipedal animal that moves into the world through its *automated self-perception* and under its inborn "satellite." By initially imagining itself as a disparate pair, the "labyrinthine" subject comes up with an explanation for itself, providing a riddle to explain the latent origins of a key competence. Shamans, along with priestesses and priests enforce the potential of the satellite's *surveillance-intelligence and* attempt to explore this *surveillance-intelligence.* The core of cults and religions has to do with this attempt to subsume not only one or two but as many as possible subjects under the satellite's higher being in order to achieve a collective subject under the auspices of a patron god. The group's identity is thereby regulated by the deity who protects them, remaining irreplaceable for the individuals belonging to this group, even under the conditions of enlightenment. This theoretical approach enriches the witty postenlightenment and panecumenical theses by thinkers such as Derrida and Vattimo that are currently popular by analyzing the enigma of religious group identity without canceling it.[12]

What is the advantage of dancing together rather than solo? In the homogenization of the *multitude,* to use a concept from Toni Negri and Michael Hardt, synchronization is achieved by rhythmicizing and multiplying a small movement in order to unleash energy. An individual who submits to a *surveillance*-authority is in this way both contained and aligned by the "cover of the group" [*Gruppenglocke*]. Perhaps this also explains why the famous argument against the conflict of religions (that, in the end, everyone has one and the same god) never really penetrated the mentality of the deeply pious. The pious trust in being subordinated to an authority defined by its relationship to a specific group therefore becomes exclusive and noninterchangeable. The cult commits a deity to looking after its worshippers, making it complicit with them. So, while the deity is the *double,* the perennial and *unsleeping support of those who pray,* the opposite is also true, and the one who prays is the *double* of god. Theologians who were not afraid to look at *theurgy* affirmed this often-unnoticed double aspect of religions.[13]

Therefore, for the totemic organization a *central shrine* containing enormous sculptures was mandatory, and we have seen that the Cretan totemistic artwork, the shrine of the animal-human, preceded Daedalus's technoid interpretation of it as a dungeon for the monstrous child. With brilliant foresight, Daedalus sensed that architecture would be the most appropriate instrument to disseminate his propaganda for the new politics.

The relationship between the totemistic body and the members of a group was and is the object and purpose of technological phantasy, seeking to reveal the energy flows that connect them. The totemistic project consequently first turned political and then energetic. It became electric and electronic.

What is the difference between the symbolic and technical versions of the labyrinth? In contemporary neototemistic media, devices take the place of the animal, and like the cult statues that have been produced since the Bronze Age, broadcast *the same in the many* and become a magnet for postcultic gatherings. This "horizontal" reprise of the traditional territorial gathering and exchanging of information is enhanced by the invisible omnipresence of networks able to grant *everyone* a connection. The group body of the assembled multitude is an electronic halo [*elektronische Glocke*] reflecting the echo of the individual: *the satellite.* As the doubled labyrinthine space is electrically repeated in this structure, the spatial coding of existence again becomes important. The central question is not "Who am I?" but "*Where* am I?" If the universal wireless connection to everything is realized, the determination of spatial coordinates is a message that the medium itself demands of its *users.* Satellite-controlled communication regularly sends a test signal to those in range to see if they still know where they are, and it is only a small step to the satellite body, which originates in the pre-oedipal world, providing an immediate answer to this check-up on existence. Indeed, satellite navigation systems have already taken this step. Blindly trusting this outside monitoring, the group follows its electronic instructions, technically mastering the labyrinth of the world. The satellite is the new totem, the *allomat of all automata.* Unlike technical mastery, which transforms the authority of surveillance into a *Daedalic apparatus,* the labyrinth-dance offered orientation coming *from below.* Earth's archaic announcements brought the pythonic oracle up from the *hypogeal* satellite. The information service of the *underworld* is now reprojected by the technical mirror of the satellite circling the earth (through the "outside"). This pushes the *earth back into an altered field of echoes and oracles* evoking older oracular regimes. The double-world, the world of *surveillance* embodied by the satellite, mimics the schizosomatic oracular condition. The dramaturgy of salvation through an *external authority* paints the stay in the labyrinth in gloomy colors.[14] Salvation, however, as the story of Ariadne informs us, depends on either the statistically unlikely event of finding the missing persons or their ability to locate themselves (by means of a pretechnical thing— *the thread*). What would you have told the rescuer anyway? How could he have discovered her coordinates if Ariadne herself would not have known where she was? How does one summon an emergency medic to an unknown place? This means *practicing* emergency. The turning passages of the labyrinth are simulated by the spins that start the *game of blindman's buff* and thoroughly disorientate the player. In this game the old orientation exercise lives on. Does blindman's buff not recall the Minotaur? Here, he would finally truly appear as *female.*

As Daedalus manipulated the meaning of the holy connection between Pasiphae and the bull through the technical addition of the wooden cow, so his search engine isolates the relationship between "the authority of the other" and the self-moving subject from the symbolic order of the mother and supplies it with a *double* mode of subjective *search*: search and search for the self, which means the *self-positioning of the searcher.*[15] But the difficulties in synthesizing these distant and differentiated poles of self-localization, while projecting them onto a *single* diagrammatic level, causes *turbulence on that spot*; its whorls and curvatures speak of a diagrammatic plane curled up in kinks and spirals, a result of what repels each other now becoming bedfellows. The collisions between these separated semantic spheres of the subject and its *surveillance*-authority lead the lines to rebel. The labyrinth becomes the epitome of extravagance, eccentricity, and the mannered. In it, pressure (loss) and counterpressure (search) produce a representation of the uneven balance of this systemic convulsion. Incidentally, the rest of the myth reports that Daedalus finally rescued himself and his son by flying out of the labyrinth.[16] If the labyrinth is a construction where delinquents can be "confined" without having to lock a door (i.e., the Minotaur), then its designer's escape should have been less risky. In this narrative twist Daedalus's engineering achievement returns to a state prior to the diagrammatic, and as the panicked architect grasps his last resort he simultaneously reveals the primary process behind his construction's "business secret." His final flight from the labyrinth echoes the motif concealed by its construction, as *he himself* becomes the motherly *surveillance*-authority hovering above the whole.[17]

The cryptic world illustrated by the labyrinth reaches its Daedalian apex in the plastic electronic medium of a world-encompassing, satellite-controlled network. The principle of xenological hypnosis is transformed into an absolute technological surveillance through impersonal ("transhuman") apparatuses. Within it the loving care and nourishment received from a primordial awareness of the mother becomes mere automatism, depotentialized into discrete forms of interactivity. In the plastic electronic medium that structures the world, the Electra complex has become a global syndrome. The interpretation of the earth as "Mother" is revalued by the symbolic order of the Father and effectively liquidated. She is deleted as the true site of competent bodies and autochthonous consciousness, and in her place the existential performance (self-positioning, self-search) of the earth-logos is automated as if he was defective. A humanity that does not want to "inherit" anything from the earth polarizes itself against it and resists the embodiment of the "Mother." *In this, all humanity therefore suffers from the symptom the Electra complex attributes to the girl*, inasmuch as the Electra complex makes it imperative to leave behind pre-oedipal symbiosis. This traps humanity in an awkward situation. From this point on, their stay on earth became *inauthentic* and the primary abilities of schizosomatic identification, oracular competence, and labyrinthine reason, which had been lost in the exodus from the Mother, were transferred *to technical objects*. But this transfer nevertheless gives rise to reconstruction, one that allows us to *once more discern* the pre-oedipal constellation that was only modified, not canceled.

5

The Four Pre-oedipal Objects

A GREAT DEAL HAS BEEN WRITTEN about phallic objects. The story of Daedalus, however, presents the prominent objects symbolizing the maternal genitalia pre-oedipality circles. Contrary to Deleuze and Guattari's *schizoanalytical square* (constructed from the machinic phylum, the flux of libido and capital, the immanent constellations, and the territory) the *schizosomatic square of pre-oedipality* contains *objects*: three-dimensional things of machinic vitality, things of vital natural machinism. There are four Daedalian objects: the labyrinth, the living statues,[1] Pasiphae's copulation apparatus, and the satellite.[2] Next to the labyrinth being an architectural interpretation of and substitute for the world, the engineer also has automata or living sculptures marching back and forth in front of it. These two objects, the labyrinth and the automata, together present *maternal genitality* in the mode of the toy: The mobile and oraculating sculptures belong to the prehuman Mother embodied in the labyrinth, they emanate from her and walk around "in front of the entrance." The third object, Pasiphae's copulation apparatus, *objectifies* the totemistic logic of the pre-oedipal imaginary, producing the parallel series of humans and animals and connecting them (copulation as "copula"). This apparatus, as with all objects that undergo

163

technical development, will be radically improved by and have a decisive role in *electrification*. The fourth pre-oedipal object explicates an essential systemic quality of the labyrinth. According to the myth, *Daedalus himself* rises from the labyrinth and flies off, embodying the "external observer" as a *deus ex machina* who provides orientation to the disoriented.[3] As the labyrinth's engineer he ensures its complexity, since he is simultaneously inside and outside of it. Recent Daedalian phantasy has transformed this fourth pre-oedipal object into an apparatus, into the satellite. Daedalus's interpretations of the pre-oedipal horizon fabricate objects from contingencies, objects that archive the essential scenes of "intercorporeal" communication, scenes the (child) body specializes in.

Electra's world, the world of territorialized totemistic daughters, is labyrinthine, because some parts of these daughters remain forever "inside of the mother" while others are "born" and move "outside." These daughters excel in stereo sensation (the schizosomatic competency of oracles), enabling them to "read" the states of other bodies. As far as they are "in the mother" they integrate into the prehuman continuum and are animals. This living schizosomatic sculpture that girls *are* equals the "animal in the labyrinth." This level of the girl's perception is, however, left behind the moment it is reflected and technically simulated by the Daedalian objects. Yet, the Daedalian objects assist us to recall and appropriate the history contained in them, it being precisely the decomposition of this history that led to their invention as its especially effective preservatives.[4]

The girl's place in the system has been colonized many times, as when the animal enclosed in the labyrinth is interpreted as a *sacrificer*. Pasiphae's copulation apparatus suppresses the animal's significant role in the totemistic order, making Pasiphae seem quite disoriented by the strange pairing it enables, similar to the story of a Russian princess who was allegedly in love with a horse. The *disfiguring* interpretation of the human-animal as a sacrificer assumes that the animal will *vanish* from posttotemistic logic, and as a result the girl loses an essential part of her identification with her mother (which is why the appearance of the sacrificer is entirely logical, the part of the girl that remains in the labyrinth is *sacrificed*). The Minotaur in the labyrinth is the *child of Pasiphae* who "devours" girls. As a Japanese fairy tale has it: "Every year a virgin of the village younger than twenty should be dressed in a white silk dress, sat in a large unvarnished chest, and sacrificed to the deity."[5] An itinerant preacher promises to rescue the girl who has been chosen by lot and together with his valiant dog gets into the chest in her place. After the villagers place him in front of the temple and then flee in panic, he hears strange sounds before the chest is finally smashed: "The monsters were entirely surprised and confused. He beat them. They were large baboons who must have been many decades old, and they fiercely attacked him."[6] The largest baboon is said to "have been so big that moss grew on his back."[7] This *mean* human-animal (an animal of a prehominid species) is *not* identical with the totemistic groom, onto whom the animal-form of the prehuman and primeval Mother is projected. He is not that groom who appears to the girl in the labyrinth, though the structural similarities of marriage by capture and "marriage by sacrifice" (prefigured in the rape-marriage of Persephone to Hades) are expressed by the same word for "nuptial chamber" and "grave" in Greek: *thalamos*.[8] The transformation of the human-animal into the girl's executioner clearly shows how the symbolic order of the mother is revalued, perverting the girl's obligation to be sacrificed. While the projection of the "animal" parts of the mother onto the "animal" groom may once have given rise to cave marriage or underworld celebrations, this *descent into the grave* as the girl's wedding is something entirely different. This grave (as place of extinction) contains the "dead" part of the girl, the part, in other words, that *always,* although certainly under better conditions, will remain *inside of the mother.* In her descent into the "Mother," the bride would have had to "visit" this "part" again, because this part enables her to procreate and thus be the *origin of both sexes.* In being executed by the human-animal a double privation therefore takes place, degrading both the girl and the primeval Mother at the same time (a privation of signifier in *genitivus objectivus* and *possesivus,* as is finally seen in Theseus's heroic act). The basis of the queen's power over her territory was the primeval Mother's ability to produce the different genders. Now she is reduced to a passive furrow in a field,[9] where the man sows homunculi.[10] What we call the *Electra complex* doubtlessly emerges on the level of immolation through/ by the human-animal. The relationship to the prehuman Mother is canceled, and the complicity with the animal that signifies her (introducing gender difference) is simultaneously suppressed—i.e., the animal's structuring and bonding effects now operate within *humanity itself.* Interhuman or familial sacrifice is then required for reasons of stabilization. When a member of the human community is institutionalized as a principle of the symbolic order and therefore becomes politically viable, a compulsion for equilibrium develops that demands sacrifice.

The sacrifice of/through the human-animal is the beginning of human sacrifice. This is why Agamben's analysis of the *homo sacer* as the human who is killed but must not be sacrificed puts him back on the trail of the *human-animal difference*. Abraham killing the ram in place of his son should in fact be read in the opposite direction: The sacrifice of the ram reveals that the disappearance of the animal from the symbolic order was "guilty" of establishing human sacrifice.[11] Anthropologists assume that hunters emerged before farmers and that it was their respectful complicity with their prey that created the animal deity.[12] The importance of the animal in this protopolitical form of social organization put its differentiating power under increasing pressure, so in totemism sacrifice tends to be inherent. The Dionysian hominization succeeds on condition of complicity with the animal and at its expense.

Failing Equalization and the Emergence of the Complex

In the Oedipus complex the relationship between mother and son is primarily dominant and secondarily aimed at. This is why the mother–son couple represents the incestuous model of an autonomous "genital" mother creating her own phallus—a thesis in line with both Otto Weininger and Freud. The symbolically "sacrificed" daughter will, if she ever obtains the place of the maternal signifier, invest the paranoid remnants of her adolescence in the project of sacrificing the king. This results in the cyclical coupling of the incestuous mother with her son and of a paranoid sacrificed female with an enslaved male. As long as the mother–son couple triumphs in founding culture, father and daughter will turn out to be victims. The holy sacrificial king and the sacrificial virgin "pay" for the smooth operation of the symbolic order of the mother, which they will overthrow for this very reason. Vice versa, in the symbolic order of the father dawning in Athenian modernity mother and son become sacrificial material, something that will become explicit in Christianity.

The Electra complex is therefore the *first symptom* of the sacrificial system. This is not the entirely inevitable fate of the girl but rather the role imposed on her when the mother identifies with her territory, and thus with the earth, seeking to ensure her power. The Electra complex is the political symptom of the mother–daughter symbiosis, consuming the daughter in order to preserve the mother's disproportionate power. Demeter and Persephone are an excellent example. *Electra's fixation on her father* is dramatic only when it is assumed that she is a victim and is even emphasized by knowing that the girl will never follow in her mother's footsteps, despite her sacrifice, because Athenian politics no longer allows it. Although the prohibition against human sacrifice announced in the story of Iphigenia at Tauris may have ended cultic sacrifice, the order given by it was nevertheless *internalized* as psychological drama.

On the level of the symbolic orders, as soon as they are constituted *politically* (i.e., without any function of the animal) one parent is always dominant and must be supported by the child of the opposite gender to balance the weakening of the partner of the opposite sex. The strong mother "pays" with her daughter, *whereas the strengthening of the father implies the strengthening of the daughter* (the Electra complex) and the simultaneous weakening of son and mother. This formation, this machinery that creates the bourgeois couple, is rightly called the *battle of the sexes,* and it is only fair to assume that suspending gender difference will end it, as contemporary debates definitively attempt.[13] If the pressure of the difference between mother and father is passed on to the children, the monstrous situations expressed in the Electra complex and the Oedipus complex occur. In both "complexes" the negative consequences for the daughter and the son code the malicious memories of the sacrificial order. Both "complexes" program the failure to form a couple, because the younger generation can only compensate for the systemic disagreement of the older one.

Electrification

> First of the gods I honour in my prayer is Mother Earth,
> the first of the gods to prophesy.
>
> —AESCHYLUS, *The Eumenides*

In order to understand the Mother-*power* as the condition of the girl's sacrifice, we must explore more deeply the forces of the earth. The writings of the Iranian mystics have shown us an earthly paradise in possession of the elements of blessed bodies. But how is the power of the Mother related to Earth as territorial power? Does the totem of the Mother's power consist in the earth's body that is addressed as "Mother Earth"? On which productive forces is the Mother's power based? Speaking of territoriality, what exactly is "terra"? Is there still reason to sing the holy song of the Earth, after the exodus that has taken place between 4000 and 1500 BCE, the migration of the great agricultural societies leaving the formerly fertile grounds of the northeast, which had begun to desiccate?[14] Is agriculture the *lost* culture? Certainly, its intention has fundamentally changed. Voluminous research in the early twentieth century by physiologists, geochemists, and geomathematicians scrutinized the interrelations constituting life on earth. Their writing is permeated by an elevated tone that seems suitable for the immensity of the topic. But the symbolism and *anthropomorphization* that pervaded the agricultural definition of the earth as *Mother* is no longer in evidence. Instead, their view is of a *system of the earth* whose population includes humanity in a rather neutral sense. Alfred Lotka (1880–1949), for example, in his widely read *Elements of Physical Biology* (1925), argues that the entire living population of the earth constitutes a single system, an environment whose activity is sustained through the daily influx of solar energy.[15] According to Lotka, individuals

within this system consist of the various chemical compounds making up a defined form, each having the capacity to grow or, in other words, acquire a milieu through
chemical reactions. In this way, individuals coagulate the
properties of their environment.[16] The Russian geochemist
Vladimir I. Vernadsky (1863–1945), the visionary author
of *The Biosphere,* claims that in a biological sense "nature" as
milieu is the *Green* stuff, the carrier of chlorophyll or *synthe-
sized solar energy.* Vernadsky focuses on this green part of life
to which the entire living world is closely and inextricably
connected, as even beings that do not contain chlorophyll
develop through the chemical compounds produced by the
Green. In this sense, all beings constitute a layer of development that profits from the transformation of *solar energy
into active planetary forces.*[17]

As much space as possible is taken up with chloroplasts—
living green matter also expands upward through the tree's
growth technologies—because the vital principle is the *principle of multiplication.* Life proliferates through multiplication. According to Vernadsky, living matter moves through
two different processes: through respiration (i.e., in gas
exchange, by which living beings are intimately connected
with "green matter") and through multiplication (transporting both "green matter" and energy).[18] Transport
as both expansion and growth therefore occurs through
effective proliferation. For Vernadsky the *concept of energy* is
crucial in understanding this system, as it exploits cosmic radiation to enable the emergence and proliferation
of individuals. The community of individuals is set up
through the *continuum of energy*, which corresponds to Gilbert Simondon's general theory of individuation: "In any
case we have arrived at the idea that a science of the human
must be based on a theory of human energy. A morphology
is very important, but a theory of energy is necessary."[19]

Collective participation in the flow of energy ensures its maximum use and transformation.

If theoreticians of the biosphere are right in claiming that the earth and all the organisms it contains constitutes a *single living system,* how can humans break out of this system? The distinction of nature from culture that has legitimized human dissidence is undermined by the postulate of *systemic unity,* forcing us to describe being-in-the-world in a new way. The fiction saying that humanity is "external" to earth as a system must be overcome, yet the systemic intertwining of humans and the world has to be outlined. Tracing humans from humans, or from "humanity," seems anachronistic or even scandalous in light of the systemic unity of nature and culture. Deriving the human from the human (and the genus "human" gets annoying) suppresses the fact that human bodies *only partly* come into existence through the activity of *human* bodies. In human descent, and particularly in relation to nourishment and the production of the body, anthropophagy has been made to symbolically play a core role. It is in fact anthropophagy that symbolically accounts for the contribution of the "prehuman" Mother to the production of the body (the echo of schizosomatic symbiosis can still be sensed in the child that "anthropophagically" devours the body that nurtures it). But right at the moment anthropophagy is projected into the symbolic order of the father, a monstrous experiment begins. By this form of anthropophagy the fact *that humans once born become unborn again* cannot be grasped. That is to say, when humans stop eating the body of the Mother, they eat the *body-producing* macro-body of the Earth, within a *system they dwell in as if unborn.* That is why humans are simultaneously *born and unborn,* and as being-in the system of the Earth they collectively approach the psychological position of the girl. The biblical imperative to not live on bread

alone but rather on the logos of heaven weakens the significance of geophagy. When anthropophagy becomes part
of the order of the father, the totemistic meal, the geo-
phagic meal, or "communion with the earth" is dispensed
with. Cannibalism thus turned out to be the truly sacred
form of eating under the guiding star of the Father and was
made the center of Christianity as the ultimate human sacrifice, overcoming the sacrificial regime. Anthropophagy
was transformed into *theophagy,* as this specific meal must be
called, and that has been extensively studied by Jan Kott.[20]
Comparing theophagy to anthropophagy, anthropophagy
represents a relatively sublime form of humanism. Theophagy, however, makes the old sacrificial order return like
a ghostly revenant. Trust in the consumption of Jesus (*Iesum
edere*) to unlock the gates to paradise. Through the obedi-
ence of Christ who, faithful to the father, delivers himself
to sacrifice, paradise is restored. A paradise that, according to John Milton, was lost through Adam's disobedience.
Doing away with the consumption of prohibited fruits,
theophagy aspires to be the summit and perfection of food,
offering a reconciliation with the father on his level.[21] Milton depicts the victory of good over evil, and of Christ over
the devil, as a medieval university disputation in the course
of which the poor orator talks himself to defeat:

> Perplexed and troubled at his bad success
> The temptor stood, nor had what to reply
> Discovered in his fraud, thrown from his hope
> So oft, and the persuasive rhetoric
> That sleeked his tongue, and so much on Eve,
> so little here, nay lost.[22]

Nevertheless, the purpose of this conversation is clear,
it is about the enticing dish that seduces, indulges, and
rewards. The motif of forbidden fruit repeatedly appears,

and a new kind of food source is hinted at: an *extraterrestrial food that comes from heaven.*

> "But, if thou be the Son of God, command
> That out of these hard stones be made thee bread;
> So shalt thou save thyself, and us relieve
> With food, whereof we wretched seldom taste."
> He ended, and the Son of God replied:
> "Think'st thou such force in bread? Is it not written
> (For I discern thee other than thou seem'st)
> Man lives not bread only, but each word
> Proceeding from the mouth of God, who fed
> Our fathers here with manna? In the mount
> Moses was forty days, nor eat nor drank."[23]

We can sense here that there is repressed content in dietary imperatives that either include or erase a politics of implicit solidarity. The prohibition/commandment presented in the scene of paradise, and truly lost in Milton's phantasy of it being regained, concerns *feeding on plants,* which remain colorless and undramatic even though they are the most powerful and *momentous* of all foods. This *feeding* brings *self*-awareness, meaning the holy couple's residence permit for the garden was revoked. The totemistic food prohibition is attractive because it implies the *prohibition of coitus* with one's closest relatives. Does the prohibition on eating the apple include similar rules? If there is a correlation between rules governing relationships and rules governing eating, as in the totemistic food prohibition, the rules of kinship and the rules governing the communion of food, what does a *prohibition of vegetables*—the *forbidden apple*—mean in terms of political organization? This food prohibition echoes the archaic identification of motherhood with the nurturing chloroplast milieu, thus extending primordial Motherhood to the burgeoning body of the

Earth. This symbolic extension is "invented" during the Neolithic revolution and equals the discovery of the *galaxy of Demeter.* These people are exemplary of those in the *schizo-somatic, or pre-oedipal state*; they reveal *the human with his or her macro-body—i.e., with the macro-body–producing body.* The metastable configuration of a group of farmers feeding on the primary energy of the Green, can be seen as the children of Earth, as those found *in Earth.* The earth itself provides the totem for these children of Earth, and because of its vast dimensions it is represented by animals in the same way as the prehuman Mama is represented by stuffed toys *for very small children.*[24] Perhaps there is a gentle inclination to allow the paradise of *Greenness* to emerge together with the *great geo-totem,* to celebrate the eternal Earth Mother and to relish her grass. But one should remember that the *geo-totem's* prestige was connected to a monumental representation of the Mother whose politics ("Mother Earth") required the girl's sacrifice. One should recall that in Elysium, Kore—*the girl*—defined the exchange value that ritually compensated for the return of vegetation. The life and death partnership established in Elysium between the Green and the human was founded on the sacrifice of the girl. In Persephone's story a girl has to descend underground (into the underworld) so that the corn Mother could accomplish her task.[25] The girl (body of a body-producing body—"Mother") and the fruit of the Earth (body of a body-producing body—"Earth") generate ontological *convertibilia*[26] that enter into a symbolic exchange: the human daughter goes into the Earth Mother (into the grave), the Earth's daughter (the corn, the apple) goes to the human mother who thereby (*machenschaftlich* [in a technical way], as Heidegger would say[27]) secures her position as the origin of all *nourishment* (anthropophagous and geophagous). The girl is the significant political figure, it was her sacrifice that has supported the *mythology of "Mother Earth" up until today.*[28] Only if she returns alive, if we celebrate *her* resurrection, does the *pathological* time of the symbolic order(s) expire.[29]

> Should one have to assume that the magnet can possibly have an effect upon a person, then it would not appear strange if this person in turn influences a second; just as a magnetized piece of soft iron acquires the property of attracting a second. To be sure, this analogy does not diminish the miraculousness of the fact that one nervous system can influence another nervous system by other means than the sensory perceptions known to us. One must rather concede that a confirmation of these experiments would add something new, hitherto unrecognized, to our Weltanshauung, and expand the borders of the personality as it were.[30]

If the earth is "Mother," then what relation do her "children" have to her today? What kind of relationship do the human inhabitants of the earth actually have with this "Mother"? In the continuum of the "forbidden apple" this Mother's capacity for nourishment, her nutritional value, is simultaneously totemistically fixed and abolished. This symbol of "Mother Earth" was too strongly invested in and provoked continual protest from the symbolic order of the father, a kind of stubborn disavowal of the Earth that compensated for the *hypertrophy of the position of the girl.* This ambivalent form of earthly existence is psychologically manifested in *being born* and *being unborn,* and philosophically in inclusive and exclusive modes of being (immanence and transcendence),[31] and it expresses the concealed *universal girl* (which is only secondarily effective, because it is under paternal law) rather than the Oedipus complex and the idea of an incestuous relationship to Mama. The girl necessarily followed the strengthening father, and became a symbolic figure of the same scale, but she "plays" according to her own rules. This "girl" appears indexically as a playground that the children have abandoned and is manifested in the four Daedalian objects that form the framework of the *universal girl*. It seems as though humans, insofar as the children of the Earth turned out to be subsumed by the symbolic order of the father, manifest against the Mother a permanent, culturally elevated *Electra syndrome* garnished with Daedalian objects.[32] The father holds the power, but the girl and her "toys" introduce a schizosomatic relationship with the Mother into the system and *precisely in this way support the Father's politics.*

The synchronicity of the hysteria debate and of the ethnological and psychoanalytical totemistic hype, as Lévi-Strauss has diagnosed it, is certainly no coincidence. The profound shifts in the representation and self-perception of the psyche occurring at the turn of the century were caused by recent technical (mainly electrical) inventions and have been extensively studied and discussed. Might it be that "Electra" and "electricity" have something to do with each other? The female hysterics who were the objects of the male diagnostic gaze, or the machines of techno-heroes such as *Future Eve*,[33] were symptoms that expressed the girl in the time of electrification. Short-circuiting the feeling of nature and the schizosomatic competence of the girl reintroduced an old identification. Josef Breuer writes about female hysterics: "I shall scarcely be suspected of identifying nervous excitation with electricity, if I return once more to the comparison with an electrical system. If the tension in such a system becomes excessively high, there is a danger of a break occurring at weak points in the insulation."[34] The girl sympathizing with the "mother" also suffered her electrical convulsions. The petrified situation started to move in a way that finally made even an electrical shock seem the ideal therapy. Electra is "high voltage." The "mother" she sympathizes with is, for the female hysteric, the *uterus* [*Gebärmutter*], whose autonomous movements give her cramps and make her faint.[35] This auto-mobile mother is the animal, *la bête noire*.[36] These women winding themselves into hysterical bows display what it means to be an electrical conductor stretched between powerful poles. The woman, with her supposedly intimate relationship with nature, once more became famous for her sensitivity, for her greater than average feeling, and for her ability to be magnetized. Electrical energy seemed to tune her into her natural affective frequency, illuminating her inferiority in relation to the active but insensitive male grasp. In any case, hysteria introduced a new tension into gender relations and has not ceased enthralling the imagination since its discovery.[37] Under the title "Behold the Madwoman" Georges Didi-Huberman describes a female hysteric who goes "dancing by," but in fact it is *Electra* passing: "The children chase her with stones, as if she were a blackbird. Men chase her with their gaze."[38]

In 1877 Thomas Alva Edison produced a useable electric light bulb, which was followed by a revolution in street lighting and the construction of large electricity grids. This "democratization" of electricity was the culmination of a long series of earlier inventions. Electricity turned it into a fundamental aspect of everyday life.

> *Ô feu subtil, âme du monde,*
> *Bienfaisante électricité*
> *Tu remplis l'air, la terre, l'onde*
> *Le ciel et son immensité.*[39]

Of course the story goes back much further. The Greeks knew of amber's electrostatic charge, which gave Electra her name. A Parthian clay vessel from the first century BCE, found by Wilhelm König in 1936 near Bagdad, contained an iron rod and a copper cylinder isolated with asphalt. Experiments carried out at the Roemer-Pelizaeus Museum in Hildesheim demonstrated that this device, that was apparently used for galvanizing gilding, generated charges of up to 0.5 volts with the help of grape juice acting as an electrolyte. Similarly, the pre-oedipal toy of Pasiphae's copulation machine generated "electricity" by coital friction.[40] Daedalus's achievement was to suspend the dominance of the symbolic Mother in this apparatus (in a technical way [*machenschaftlich*]) without losing its "function" (genital friction). As the collision between the symbolic order of the Mother and the symbolic order of the Father was rooted in the fight for genital power, for exclusive procreative power, it had to be safeguarded firstly in neutral terrain. Daedalus must therefore be fully acknowledged as having taken the first step in its machinization and the suspension of the fight. Electrical generators are advanced procreation machines, and with their help, as one can see in the phantasies of *Metropolis* or *Frankenstein, life can be injected into statues.* The properties of electrical charges in conductors is consequently analyzed by *solid state physics,* the key science of the plastic realm, forming part of the constellation of pre-oedipal phantasy. The affinity *bodies* have for each other is "electrically" expressed as the energy of schizosomatic affection.

The lesson of electrification can only be learned when the (hysterical) symptoms of the girl cool down. When she is no longer under high voltage tension the "electrical current" may flow freely again, and the privileges of energy production escape both the motherly or fatherly monopolies that had previously administered them. The conclusion to be drawn is the *revaluation of the earth* itself: It cannot be *Mother*. It (or should we now say, in plural, THEY?) must find its/their way back to being an enormous, double-poled electromagnet, to its/their hermaphrodite nature that first enabled it/them to become a transformer and generator of energy. A bipolar earth that builds magnetic fields and electrifies its ionosphere is already a double-body generat-

ing friction, an exquisite transformation machine, a pro-
liferating paradise, a double-poled miracle of energy, a
rounded couple or two-gendered Platonic primordial body
without arms and legs.

Earth itself has specialized in the production of these
sexual bodies, which are due to the same double-poled Earth
energy, bodies that emerge through the process of cell division, in meiosis and mitosis, even if these have been *variously equipped.* For this reason Earth itself, as the primordial
horizon of all creatures, must *also* be allowed its fatherly
and masculine aspect. It is not the "fault" of humans that
the Earth-female and the Earth-male express themselves
in their bodies, nor is it their task to fight for the pre-
cedence of one over the other. The orchestration of the
human sexes can and should be based on the Earth-logical
parenté and so again become a game, a *children's game.* It is
Earth "pervading" the human body that owns the patent
to and the privilege of inventing sexual difference, and
the responsibility for this idea and this work returns to
her/them. In the rearview mirror, the conflict between
the sexes looks doubly mistaken. The time has come for
the children's game. In any case, through the electrification that was named after her, Electra was very intensely
reminded of her toys.

Appendix

Solyanka State Gallery: Les Ballets Russes
Presents *Anti-Electra* by Elisabeth von Samsonow

1909 VIENNA DRESDEN: Hugo von Hofmannsthal stages his drama *Electra* in Dresden, music by Richard Strauss

1913 MOSCOW PARIS: Les Ballets Russes stage *Le Sacre du printemps,* music by Igor Stravinsky, choreography by Vaslav Nijinski

2017 VIENNA MOSCOW: Elisabeth von Samsonow performs *Anti-Electra*, a critical-revolutionary hybrid of *Electra* and *Le Sacre du printemps*

First Day 28th of June PART I: NO!!! (Thesis)
Second Day 29th of June PART II: ??ANTI (Antithesis)
Third Day 30th of June PART III: YES!! (Synthesis)

PART I: NO!!!

The girl is the victim
The girl is complicated
The girl is hysterical
The girl must serve
The girl is the gift that must be given
The girl is an exchange value
The girl does not belong to itself

181

The girl is the grease of economy

The girl is a production site

The girl has the body of excellency

The girl must obey

The girl must be beautiful

The girl must not resist

The girl from the Rites of Spring has to surrender

Its destiny is to be sacrificed

Electra is lost

Electra is a victim

Electra is psychopathic

Is there a difference between sacrifice and victim?

Electra is hysterical

The girl and Electra perform hysteria

Their bodies become hysterical

(I mourn for Electra

I mourn for the girl of the Rites of Spring)

The girl has no voice

The girl has no choice

The girl must work

She must be busy

The girl is subjected to the law of reproduction

She is an agricultural item

The sacrifice of the girl makes nature work

Without sacrifice of the girl no harvest

The girl is the standard of natural reproduction rates

The girl is seized and eaten by the Earth

The Earth is seized and eaten by humans

The sacred exchange standard is operated through
    death

The girl and death make a pair

The best must be given

Only the best are worthy of being sacrificed

(I mourn for Electra and the girl of the Rites of Spring)

PART II: ??ANTI

Why should the girl be victim or sacrified?

The girl from the Rites of Spring and Electra, do they
belong to the same agricultural continuum?

The hysterical girl is made the symptom of the fear of
starving

The hysterical girl is made the symptom of the fear of
reproduction/sex

Hysteria is a form of protest

The hysterical girl is an artist

Under the condition of industrial production the sacrifice of the girl becomes murder

The industrial interest in the girl is problematic

The girl is a projection surface

The girl serves as a trap and as a victim

I protest ANTI

I protest against the industrial (ab)use of the girl as a
projection surface of publicity

The girl is the signifier of production

Without girl no human

Can the girl decide on her own?

The girl guarantees the reproduction of labor man-
power, not the reproduction of nature (no need)

The sacrifice of the girl is murder

Long live Persephone

I protest against the sacrifice of the girl

Denis Diderot: you all die at the age of sixteen

The girl represents an anomaly

The girl has a body-producing body

The girl is a transhuman reproductive accomplice of
the Earth

The girl is the sine qua non condition of humanity

Girl grabbing equals land grabbing

Beware of land grabbing

Beware of girl grabbing

The girl has no knowledge?

The girl is directed/manipulated by amnesiac collectives
who do not remember

Things must be changed

Release the girl from Thanatos's service

The girl is not living money

Life is not money

Time is life

Free the girl

Comfort Electra

This is the end of anorexic protest politics

This is the end of diet psychosis

This is the end of the perverse food standard dictatorship

Psychoanalysis was wrong

Diet problems in girls do not manifest protest against the mother

Diet problems manifest protest against the role of the girl

Diet problems manifest protest against the economizing of the girl under capitalist industrial conditions

Girl=food standard becomes living money

DIETETIC PROTEST

GIRLS BECOME THIN

DO NOT EAT

EAT CONSCIOUSLY

EATING IS DANGEROUS

Short circuit of capitalism and Earth

=Digital Earth

Land grabbing=girl grabbing

The girl is busy

The girl is business

GIRLS BUSINESS

The girl serves as a ground for industry

Let me do this for you I will do this for you

O EARTH

O ELECTRA

O DEAR NONVICTIM

O FREEDOM OF THE GIRL

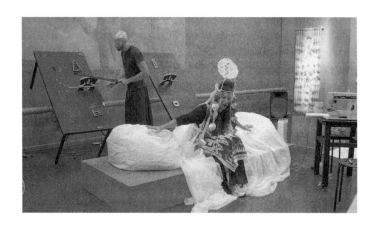

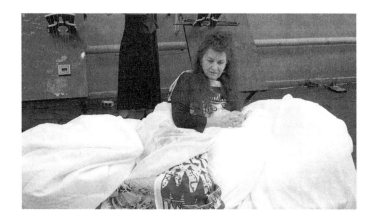

PART III: YES!!

The girl has a voice of its own
The girl is THE BEYOND
The girl is the revolutionary nongender
The girl is universal
The girl=ecology

Earth understanding=girlism

Girlism is universal

Girlism is knowledge and love

Anti-Electra is freedom

Anti-Electra is life

Anti-Electra is creative

She is the origin of nice things

She is specialized in body-body relations

A schizosomatic expert

She can feel you

She can feel everything

She feels the world

She recreated the World

Everybody can be Anti-Electra

The clouds the houses the chemicals the men the boys
the horses the insects everything can be Anti-Electra

Solyanka State Gallery can be Anti-Electra

Moscow can be Anti-Electra

Vienna can be Anti-Electra

Anti-Electra is beyond and below

Anti-Electra=social infrastructure

Anti-Electra is playfulness

Anti-Electra is allover life

Anti-Electra strips herself of use and abuse

Anti-Electra is revolutionary knowledge

Anti-Electra is ecology

Anti-Electra is pre-oedipal affirmation YES!

Anti-Electra is a transplant

Anti-Electra practices photosynthetic philosophy

Every gesture is a ceremony

Ceremony of Life

YES ceremony of Life!

A body with new organs

A body filled with precious organs

A body with funny organs

A funny genital body
O LIFE!
O LOVE!
O SEWING MACHINE!
O SOWING MACHINE!
Remember and free yourself
Open your mouth
Sacrifice becomes ARTIFICE
The end of sacrifice
The end of abuse
The ARTIFICE'S EON
Art is the transformer
Anti-Electra is the transformer
Anti-Electra is the artist
Anti-Electra is art
Enter the garden
Come to the world
HALLELUJAH
The girl of the Rites of Spring enjoys herself
She is playing
She sews her own fate
She is still dancing
She is not busy
She is no business
The value of the girl consists in herself
End of ritual evaluation and psychotic abuse
HALLELUJAH
The spring springs up
The well springs up
The fountain of life unbound
Anti-Electra is singing
The girl is an atmosphere
the girl is the sphere
the future
the presence

O RELEASE
O SOLUTION
O TAILOR OF LOVE
O UNIVERSAL MACHINE DU DÉSIR

Notes

Preface to the English Language Edition

1. Luce Irigaray, *Das Geschlecht, das nicht eins ist* (Berlin: Merve Verlag, 1979), originally published as *Ce sexe qui n'en n'est pas un* (Paris: Éditions de Minuit, 1977); Christina von Braun, *Nicht Ich: Logik, Lüge, Libido* (Frankfurt: Verlag Neue Kritik, 1985; repr., Berlin: Aufbau Verlag, 2009).

2. Levi Bryant, *The Democracy of Objects* (Ann Arbor, Mich.: Open Humanities Press, 2011); Graham Harman, *Object-Oriented Ontology: A New Theory of Everything* (London: Penguin Books, 2018).

3. Cary Wolfe, *What Is Posthumanism?* (Minneapolis: University of Minnesota Press, 2009).

4. Rosi Braidotti, *Nomadic Subjects: Embodiment and Sexual Difference in Contemporary Feminist Theory* (New York: Columbia University Press, 1994), 173.

5. Laboria Cuboniks, *Xenofeminist Manifesto: A Politics for Alienation*, quoted in Helen Hester and Armen Avanessian, *Dea ex Machina* (Berlin: Merve Verlag), 2005. Article 0x04: There should be a "right for all to speak as nobody defined" (Recht für Alle, als niemand Bestimmtes zu sprechen). See also "XF Xenofeminism: Politics for Alienation," Laboria Cuboniks, http://www.laboriacuboniks.net/; and Laboria Cuboniks, *The Xenofeminist Manifesto* (London: Verso, 2018).

6. Tiqqun, *Preliminary Materials for a Theory of the Young-Girl*, trans. Ariana Reines (Los Angeles: Semiotext(e), 2012).

7. Elisabeth von Samsonow, "Latency: Biography of an Omniscient Spy," in *Epidemic Subjects—Radical Ontology,* ed. Elisabeth von Samsonow (Zurich: Diaphanes Verlag, 2016). Epidemic subjectivity "spills over or migrates, in short: becomes rampant" (153). "The epidemic subject operates under the banner of the very subjective exo-expansion in which it is an expert" (155).

8. Luce Irigaray, *Speculum: Spiegel des anderen Geschlechts,* trans. Xenia Rajewsky, Gabriele Ricke, Gerburg Treusch-Dieter, and Regine Othmer (Frankfurt: Suhrkamp Verlag, 1980), 54, originally published as *Speculum de l'autre femme* (Paris: Edition de Minuit, 1974).

9. Elisabeth Grosz, *Architecture from the Outside: Essays on Virtual and Real Space,* with a foreword by Peter Eisenman (Cambridge, Mass.: MIT Press, 2001), 161.

10. This has been achieved by Peter Sloterdijk in his book *Bubbles: Spheres I; Microspherology,* trans. Weiland Hoban (Los Angeles: Semiotext(e), 2011).

11. Elisabeth Grosz, *Architecture from the Outside,* 160.

12. For a recent translation of Hölderlin's poem "Patmos," see Scott Horton *Browsings: The Harper's Blog,* July 16, 2007, https://harpers.org/blog/2007/07/patmos/.

13. See, in general, Silvia Federici, *Caliban and the Witch: Woman, the Body and Primitive Accumulation* (New York: Autonomedia, 2004).

14. Here one may even think of Quentin Meillassoux's theory of the fossil and the prehuman world in *After Finitude: An Essay on the Necessity of Contingency,* trans. Ray Brassier (London: Continuum, 2010).

15. Levi Bryant, etc.

16. Bruno Latour, *Facing Gaia: Eight Lectures on the New Climatic Regime,* trans. Catherine Porter (Medford, Mass.: Polity, 2017).

Introduction

1. The Sanskrit root is *ulka,* or fire blight, which also gave *Volcanus,* the divine smith, his name. The *electron* is the bright ray of fire blight.

2. *Electra* is the title of a large exhibition held at the Musée d'Art Moderne de la Ville de Paris in 1983–84. In the impressive catalog accompanying the exhibition, Frank Popper gives the following explanation for the choice of its title: "The name of Electra was finally chosen because of its legendary as well as its scientific connotations. In fact, Electra was the name of a Pre-Hellenic Goddess of Light, the 'Radiant,' before becoming singled out from other Electras as the daughter of Agamemnon and Clytemnestra in the tragedies of Aeschylus, Sophocles and Euripides. But a close look at the myth of Electra shows some compromising affinities between the symbolism of the name and the discoveries of electromagnetism." With that, the only and rather concise reference to the figure of Electra within the 450-page book comes to an end. *Electra: L'électricité et l'électronique dans l'art au XXe siècle,* ed. Frank Popper and Marie-Odile Briot (Paris: Friends of the Musée d'Art Moderne de la Ville de Paris, 1983), 20–22.

3. Freud writes: "What happens with a girl is almost the opposite. The castration complex prepares for the Oedipus complex instead of destroying it; the girl is driven out of her attachment to her mother through the influence of her envy for the penis and she enters the Oedipus situation as though into a haven of refuge. . . . Girls remain in it for an indeterminate length of time; they demolish it late and, even so, incompletely." Sigmund Freud, "Femininity," in *The Standard Edition of the Complete Psychological Works of Sigmund Freud,* vol. 19, trans. J. Strachey, ed. J. Strachey and A. Freud (London: Hogarth Press, 1953), 129.

4. Robert Graves, *The Greek Myths: The Complete and Definitive Edition* (London: Penguin, 2011), 425.

5. As Claude Lévi-Strauss observes: "Purity of the soul, in the Vienna School sense, is never a factor in what might more readily be called a form of abortive polygamy rather than monogamy, for, in these societies as well as in those which favorably sanction polygamous unions, and in our own, the tendency is towards a multiplicity of wives." *The Elementary Structures of Kinship,* rev. ed., trans. J. H. Bell and J. R. von Sturmer, ed. R. Needham (Boston: Beacon, 1969), 37.

6. "Rather, it is a question of being aware of the existence of machines of subjectivation which don't simply work within 'the faculties of the soul,' interpersonal relations or intra-familial complexes. Subjectivity does not only produce itself through the psychogenetic stages of psychoanalysis or the 'mathemes' of the Unconscious, but also in the large-scale social machines of language and the mass-media—which cannot be described as human." Félix Guattari, *Chaosmosis: An Ethico-aesthetic Paradigm,* trans. Paul Bains and Julian Pefanis (Sydney: Power Publications, 1995), 9.

7. Not a becoming-bride but a becoming-sacrifice.

1. Electra as Female "Oedipus"

1. "Whereas in boys the Oedipus complex is destroyed by the castration complex, in girls it is made possible and led up to by the castration complex. . . . In girls the motive for the demolition of the Oedipus complex is lacking. Castration has already had its effect." Sigmund Freud, "Some Psychical Consequences of the Anatomical Distinction between the Sexes," *SE,* vol. 29, 256, 257.

2. "I cannot evade the notion (though I hesitate to give it expression) that for women the level of what is ethically normal is different from what it is in men. Their super-ego is never so inexorable, so impersonal, so independent of its emotional origins as we require it to be in men." Freud, "Some Psychical Consequences," 257.

3. See Sigmund Freud, "Femininity," *SE,* vol. 22, 129.

4. Jean Giraudoux, *Électra* (Paris: Editions Grasset, 1987), 115.

5. Hugo von Hofmannsthal, *Electra: A Tragedy in One Act,* trans. Arthur Symons (New York: Brentano's, 1908), 70.

6. Hofmannsthal, *Electra,* 73–74, 75.

7. Hofmannsthal, 76.

8. Hofmannsthal, 84.

9. Aeschylus, *The Libation Bearers,* trans. Robert Fagles (Harmondsworth: Penguin Classics, 1966), 216.

10. Aeschylus, *Libation Bearers,* 217.

11. Aeschylus, 217.

12. Aeschylus, 217.

13. Aeschylus, 225.

14. "FIRST EUMENID: To this your pride has brought you, Electra! You are nothing more! You have nothing more!

ELECTRA: I have my conscience, I have Orestes, I have justice, I have everything!" Giraudoux, *Électra*, 131.

15. "A work of art or a mythological story is comparable to the 'primary process' of the dream; they are not reality but they present it. Symbolic events full of intensity express diverse emotions and fantasies. Electra presents the mother-daughter conflict, filled with murder and suicidal fantasies, where hate changes into masochism and sadism." Hendrika Halberstadt-Freud, *Electra versus Oedipus: The Drama of the Mother-Daughter Relationship*, trans. M. de Jager (New York: Routledge, 2010), 105. And: "In her despair Clytemnestra seeks consolation by her child, almost as if Electra was not her daughter but her mother. This moment of weakness arouses only contempt and mistrust in Electra, and she uses the opportunity to kill her mother." Halberstadt-Freud, *Electra versus Oedipus*, 109. Silvia Kronberger writes: "Electra is often interpreted as the woman who suppresses her female nature in order to perform male acts." *Die unerhörten Töchter. Fräulein Elsa und Elektra und die gesellschaftliche Funktion von Hysterie* (Innsbruck-Vienna-Munich-Bolzano: Studien Verlag, 2002), 207. But where is the "performed" male deed?

16. Giraudoux, *Électra*, 55–56.

17. Judith S. Kestenberg, "Zur weiblichen Homosexualität. Das Versagen in der Entwicklung von Mutterlichkeit," in *Stumme Liebe. Der 'lesbische Komplex' in der Psychoanalyse*, ed. Eva Maria Alves (Freiburg, Germany: Kore Edition, 1993), 47.

18. Gerburg Treusch-Dieter, *Die Heilige Hochzeit. Studien zur Totenbraut* (Herbolzheim, Germany: Centaurus, 2004), 17.

19. Euripides, *Electra*, in *Euripides V: The Complete Greek Tragedies*, trans. E. Townsend Vermeule (New York: Washington Square Press, 1969), 16.

20. In her commentary, Jenny March points out the harsh contrast between Electra's unmarried and childless state and the sexual activity of the mother and suggests that this contrast poses (postpubescent) growing up as a kind of defilement (*adultery as*

pollution). Jenny March, "Commentary," in *Sophocles: Electra* (Warminster, England: Aris and Phillips, 2001), 157.

21. Silvia Kronberger quotes Hugo Wyss: "Herein lies the tragedy of the Electra figure according to Wyss, that she achieves the opposite by becoming male, namely a femininity robbed of its sense: sexualization." *Die unerhörten Töchte*, 207.

22. As Kronberger puts it: "Electra's hatred towards the children fathered in the dirt surrounding her inhibits her own fertility." *Die unerhörten Töchte*, 203.

23. Mary Jacobus, *First Things: The Maternal Imaginary in Literature, Art and Psychoanalysis* (New York: Routledge, 1995), 18.

24. Emil Staiger, afterword to *Orestie*, by Aischylos (Stuttgart, Germany: Reclam, 1959), 127.

25. Robert Graves writes: "This ancient story has been combined with the legend of a dispute between rival dynasties in the Peloponnese: Clytaemnestra was a Spartan royal heiress; and the Spartans' claim, that their ancestor Tyndareus raised Agamemnon to the throne of Mycenae, suggests that they were victorious in a war against the Mycenaeans for the possession of Amyclae, where Agamemnon and Clytaemnestra were both honored." *The Greek Myths: The Complete and Definitive Edition* (London: Penguin, 2011), 418.

26. "Like Aeschylus, Euripides was writing religious propaganda: Orestes's absolution records the final triumph of patriarchy, and is staged at Athens, where Athene . . . connives at matricide." Graves, *Greek Myths*, 432.

27. Freud, "Femininity," 119.

28. Michael Rind comments on the connection between a rock crevice, the female genitals, and the sacrificial ax in the mountain temple of Nîl: "Inside the temple, which is not accessible to Europeans, there is a large image of the goddess, and in the most holy her yoni (vulva) is said to be represented by a cleft in the rock. Below the shrine lies a temple of Bhairavî where as late as in the last century human sacrifices were carried out. The ritual consisted in first consecrating the large axe by which the victim was to be decapitated. The person to be sacrificed was prayed to because all the gods had entered his body, and so were commemorated in this

way. Then the decapitation was carried out, the head of the victim was offered to the terrible Mother in a vessel of gold, silver, copper, raw ore, or wood. Since colonial times, goats have been sacrificed instead of humans." Michael M. Rind, *Menschenopfer. Vom Kult der Grausamkeit* (Regensburg, Germany: Universitätsverlag, 1996), 85.

29. Giordano Bruno, *Ars memoriae XI*, in *Iordano Bruno Volanti Opera latine Conscripta*, vol. 2, ed. V. Imbriani and C. M. Tallargo (Naples: D. Morano, 1886; facsimile by Frommann-Holzboog, 1962), 61.

30. Graves, *Greek Myths*, 418.

31. See Treusch-Dieter, *Die Heilige Hochzeit*, 18. Treusch-Dieter unpacks the story from the point of view of the sacrifice of the "death bride," who belongs to the sacrificial king. In my way of thinking, the two figures are not really "a pair" but come from successive generations.

32. Gunnar Heinsohn, *Die Erschaffung der Götter. Das Opfer als Ursprung der Religion* (Reinbek, Germany: Rowalt, 1997), 35–49. Especially chapter 4: "The emergence of the great sacrificial cults and the priest-kingdom at the beginning of the bronze age."

33. Sophocles has Electra say: "The murderer lying in my father's bed/ With my abandoned mother—if I must/ Call her a mother who dares sleep with him!/ She is so brazen that she lives with that/ Defiler; vengeance from the gods is not/ A thought that frightens her! As if exulting/ In what she did she noted carefully/ The day on which she treacherously killed/ My father, and each month, when that day comes,/ She holds high festivals and sacrifices/ Sheep to the Gods her Saviours." Sophocles, *Electra*, trans. H. D. F. Kitto (Oxford: Oxford University Press, 1998), III.

34. Graves, *Greek Myths*, 418.

35. Graves, *Greek Myths*, 424.

36. Graves, *Greek Myths*, 418.

37. Immanuel Velikovsky's books *Worlds in Collision* (1950) and *Earth in Upheaval* (1955) introduced this so-called catastrophism into the cultural sciences, and it has not ceased to stir controversy ever since.

38. Heinsohn, *Die Erschaffung der Götter*, 124–51.

39. Heinsohn, 382. See also Aeschylus, *Agamemnon*, lines 295–319, 114–15.

40. Initially, Frazer assumed the priority of the territorial order for totemic society, which is then followed by the genealogical one: "This theory clearly marks a transition from local hereditary totemism in the paternal line. And precisely the same theory could, mutatis mutandis, be employed to effect a change from local to hereditary totemism in the maternal line." J. G. Frazer, *Totemism and Exogamy: A Treatise on the Early Forms of Superstition and Society,* vol. 3 (Wiltshire, England: Chippenham, 1994), 157.

41. Frank Robert Vivelo, *Cultural Anthropology: A Basic Introduction* (Lanham, Md.: University Press of America, 1994), 153.

42. Vivelo, *Cultural Anthropology,* 153.

43. Vivelo, 153.

44. Claude Lévi-Strauss, *The Elementary Structures of Kinship,* rev. ed., trans. J. H. Bell and J. R. von Sturmer, ed. R. Needham (Boston: Beacon, 1969), 46.

45. Lévi-Strauss, *Elementary Structures of Kinship,* 48.

46. Lévi-Strauss, 45–46.

47. Michael M. Rind assumes the motive for sacrifice is the repetition of a "mythical event of primordial times." "Above all, in the sacrificial ritual as we know it from the Maya, this aspect is of fundamental significance. The one sacrificed is identified with a deity whose violent death, grounded in myth, has to be carried out on a deified human. For the cultic community this is a remembrance of an old myth. Here, manifold death and generation, becoming, passing and reincarnation of men, animals and plants, are the central motives. Useful plants and propagation stand in close relationship in agrarian societies, and they are the gift of a being from primordial times who had to violently experience death. The repetition of the mythical primordial event in cultic action is necessary for maintaining cosmic order as it was created. Through sacrifice the existing world retains its order, while its head as the seat of special powers plays a great role." Rind, *Menschenopfer. Vom Kult der Grausamkeit,* 18ff.

48. Claudia Jarzebowski, *Inzest. Verwandschaft und Sexualität im 18. Jahrhundert* (Vienna: Böhlau, 2006), 32–56.

49. The problems arising from this reconquering were clearly seen, for example, by Christa Rohde-Dachser in *Expeditionen in den*

dunklen Kontinent. Weiblichkeit im Diskurs der Psychoanalyse (New York: Psychosozial Verlag, 1991). In particular, see chapter 15.1, "Abstiege: Auf der Suche nach der 'anderen' Kultur," 270–73.

50. In the primitive type of totemism it is explicitly denied, according to Frazer, "that children are the fruit of the commerce of sexes. So astounding an ignorance cannot but date from a past immeasurably remote." Frazer, *Totemism and Exogamy*, vol. 3, 158. But Frazer gives a rather practical explanation for this "remote past" that we are so interested in and connects it with the interval between conception and birth. We would prefer to understand the idea of a "remote past" in the sense of a weak memory or a memory "lost" in primary consciousness. Then the "wild idea" of totemic ascendance would not be an expression of scientific ignorance but rather a satisfying symbolic solution in the face of the impossibility of an "adult" consciousness remembering adequately.

51. Gilles Deleuze and Félix Guattari, *A Thousand Plateaus: Capitalism and Schizophrenia,* trans. Brian Massumi (New York: Continuum, 2004). In particular, see chapter 10, "1730: Becoming-Intense, Becoming-Animal, Becoming-Imperceptible . . . ," 256–341.

52. Sophocles, *Electra,* 114.

53. Aeschylus, *Libation Bearers,* lines 527–37, 202. [In the German translation of the tragedy, line 530 refers to a snake but line 536 refers to a dragon (TN).]

54. George Devereux, *Dreams in Greek Tragedy: An Ethno-Psycho-Analytic Study* (Berkeley: University of California Press, 1976), 174.

55. Devereux, *Dreams in Greek Tragedy,* 172.

56. Devereux writes: "Not only is the equation: snake = phallus commonplace, but a snake's split and bloodstained skull greatly resembles the glans: the meatus is cleft-shaped and the glans is reddish and moist." Devereux, 175.

57. Devereux, 293.

58. See George Devereux, *Baubo. Die mythische Vulva,* trans. Eva Moldenhauer (Frankfurt: Syndikat, 1981), in which Devereux speaks of the "protruding" vulva in relation to the emergence of the head of a child.

59. Devereux, *Dreams in Greek Tragedy,* 173.

60. Devereux, 171.

61. Devereux, 171.

62. Jacobus de Voragine, ed., *The Golden Legend or Lives of the Saints,* trans. William Caxton, 1st ed. 1483; ed. F. S. Ellis (London: Temple Classics, 1900; reprinted 1922, 1931).

63. Medea, for example, had a chariot drawn by serpents, as did the Indian goddess Ramayana. See Graves, *Greek Myths,* 615.

64. This is a pun on *Schlange,* which also means "snake" [TN].

65. Vivelo, *Cultural Anthropology,* 153.

66. See Gerburg Treusch-Dieter on Aristotle's "On the Generation of Animals" in *Die Heilige Hochzeit,* 262.

67. "We must learn instead to think of man as what results from the incongruity of these two elements, and investigate not the metaphysical mystery of conjunction, but rather the practical and political mystery of separation. . . . It is more urgent to work on these divisions, to ask in what way—within man—has man been separated from non-man, and the animal from the human, than it is to take positions on the great issues, on so-called human rights and values. And perhaps even the most luminous sphere of our relations with the divine depends, in some way, on that darker one which separates us from the animal." Giorgio Agamben, *The Open: Man and Animal*, trans. Kevin Attell (Stanford, Calif.: Stanford University Press, 2004), 16.

68. *Shepherd and Nymph,* 1575–76, Kunsthistorisches Museum, Vienna [TN].

69. Agamben, *Open,* 86–87.

70. Agamben, 89ff.

71. There is a repeated play in this passage on *Ziege,* meaning "a female goat," but in contemporary German also meaning "witch," and similarly on *Zicke* meaning "nanny goat" but also "bitch" [TN].

72. Agamben, *Open,* 91.

73. Timarchos descends into the Trophonius cave to inquire about the daimon of Socrates. He comes across a scenario that one could rightly describe as "being worldless." He hears noises, sees colors, and witnesses the rotation of the spheres. In the end, he has the feeling of being "violently compressed," and a "violent blow to the head" brings him back to the world. See Plutarch, "De Genio

Socrates," in *Plutarch's Morals,* ed. William W. Goodwin (Boston: Little, Brown, and Company, 1874), §22, 412.

74. Peter Sloterdijk, *Bubbles — Spheres I,* trans. W. Hoban (Cambridge, Mass.: MIT Press, 2011).

75. Christene Rohde-Dachser writes: "This cave beyond the phallic discourse is a female space"; however, Rohde-Dachser defines the female "container" as a place of the "parried (negative) self of the grand patriarchal male subject." *Expeditionen in den dunklen Kontinent,* 272, 277. I do not follow this interpretation.

76. Mechtild Zeul writes: "In *Sex and Gender* Stoller postulates a symbiotic phase between the mother and the girl as well as the boy, which ends with the development of the core gender identity around the end of the second year, expressed by the clear feeling and belief of the child that she or he is a girl or a boy. Gender identity, according to Stoller, comes directly from the primary identification with the mother. The boy however, has to first differentiate himself from his primary object, from the mother. The core gender identity of the male child is therefore less secure than that of the girl, because the boy is always drawn back toward a symbiosis with the mother, and into the identification with her." "Weiblichkeit, Bild und Wirklichkeit," in *Elektra und Ödipus. Zwischen Penisneid und Kastrationsangst,* ed. Anton Szanya (Vienna: Picus, 1995), 105.

77. "Psycho-analysis has revealed that the totem animal is in reality a substitute for the father." Sigmund Freud, "Totem and Taboo," *SE,* vol. 13, 141.

78. For example, by Heide Göttner-Abedroth, *Die Göttin und ihr Heros,* 11th ed. (Munich: Frauenoffensive, 1997).

79. Freud writes: "We will now turn our interest on to the single question of what it is that brings this powerful attachment of the girl to her mother to an end. This, as we know, is its usual fate: it is destined to make room for an attachment to her father. Here we come upon a fact which is a pointer to our further advance. This step in development does not involve only a simple change of object. The turning away from the mother is accompanied by hostility; the attachment to the mother ends in hate." "Femininity," 121.

80. Freud, 133.

81. Mechtild Zeul writes: "On the basis of my material one may suggest that, in the case of the eventually heterosexual woman, the identification with the mother in the Oedipal phase is based on (or is preceded, and in a specific way, shaped by) a highly intense, colorful and developed pre-oedipal sexual relationship between the baby girl and the mother. I proceed on the assumption that this early sexual bond of the girl with the mother is an integral component of later womanhood." "Weiblichkeit. Bild und Wirklichkeit," in *Elektra und Ödipus*, 12. See also, Doris Bernstein, "The Female Superego: A Different Perspective," *International Journal for Psycho-Analysis* 64 (1983): 107–29.

82. Freud, "Femininity," 131.

83. Walter Burkert, *Homo Necans: The Anthropology of Ancient Greek Sacrificial Ritual and Myth*, trans. Peter Bing (Berkeley: University of California Press, 1983), 63.

84. [Discourse] of Hermes Trismegistus, "Poimandres," in *Hermetica: The Greek Corpus Hermeticum and the Latin Asclepius in a New English Translation with Notes and Introduction*, trans. Brian P. Copenhaver (Cambridge: Cambridge University Press, 1992), 1. In a modified form this is also what interests us in totemism and the exogamy rule. The literary ego/I encounters an "oversized figure" who reveals his name; to the question "Who are you?" he answers as the actual unknown intimus: "I am Poimandres," he says, "mind of sovereignty; I know what you want, and I am with you everywhere."

85. Arnold Gehlen writes: "Totemism—the social worship of animals— . . . is one of the few cultural forms that can justifiably be accorded a universal human significance." *Man: His Nature and Place in the World*, trans. Claire McMillan and Karl Pillemer (New York: Columbia University Press, 1987), 390. "Then, totemism would primarily be the most primitive, as yet indirect, realization of self-consciousness." Gehlen, *Man*, 391.

86. Gerhard Heard cited in Gehlen, 292.

87. As Tarde puts it: "It is a question of imitation of self; for memory or habit, its two branches, must be connected, in order to be well understood, with imitation of others, the only kind of imitation which we are concerned with here. The psychological

is explained by the social just because the social sprang from the psychological." Gabriel Tarde, *Laws of Imitation,* trans. E. C. Parsons (Gloucester, Mass.: Peter Smith, 1940), 14.

88. Aleida and Jan Assmann, in their conference volume *Verwandlungen,* suggest this strong sense of alterity. My analysis of totemism goes in the same direction both structurally and psychologically. "The discourse of identity that encompasses change excludes transformation as the other of itself. Exactly this has been our concern in this project; not only that which breaks the molds of identity, but also that which remains beyond these molds of identity." *Verwandlungen: Archäologie der literarischen Kommunikation IX* (Munich: Wilhelm Fink, 2006), 13.

89. Children have ideas about their origins that require new "clothing" if they want to "grow together" with their developing consciousness. "The development of the small child's ideas about the vagina is much affected by cultural pattern." D. W. Winnicott, *On Human Nature* (New York: Brunner/Mazel, 1988), 44.

2. Radical Totemism and Automatism

1. This is now changing; see W. J. T. Mitchell, "Migrating Images: Totemism, Fetishism, Idolatry," in *Migrating Images: Producing . . . reading . . . transporting . . . translating,* ed. Petra Stegmann and Peter B. Seel (Berlin: House of World Cultures, 2004), 14–24. On the general categorization of the relationship to "nonhumans" in totemism, see Philippe Descola, "Constructing Natures: Symbolic Ecology and Social Practice," in *Nature and Society: Anthropological Perspectives,* ed. Philippe Descola and Gisli Pàlsson (London: Routledge, 1996), 95–96. Descola's theses appear to be increasingly important for contemporary anthropological image studies.

2. Georges Bataille, *Theory of Religion,* trans. Robert Hurley (New York: Zone Books, 1989), 38.

3. Bruno Latour, *Politics of Nature: How to Bring the Sciences into Democracy,* trans. Catherine Porter (Cambridge, Mass.: Harvard University Press, 2004), 42.

4. By its "childhood" is meant the "always already past stage

of culture," which it still contains: "Totemism represents what Sir James Frazer and others regarded as the 'childhood of the human species.'" Mitchell, "Migrating Images," 21.

5. G. W. Leibniz, "The Monadology," in *Philosophical Essays,* trans. R. Ariew and D. Garber (Indianapolis: Hackett Publishing Company, 1989), § 28, 216.

6. As Sándor Ferenczi's illuminating comments point out: "In a previous work on the course of development of the reality sense in the growing child I had already reached the conclusion that the human being is dominated from the moment of birth onwards by a continuous regressive trend toward the reestablishment of the intrauterine situation, and holds fast to this unswervingly by, as it were, magical-hallucinatory means, by the aid of positive and negative hallucinations. The full development of the reality sense is attained, according to this conception, only when this regression is renounced once and for all and a substitute found for it in the world of reality." *Thalassa: A Theory of Genitality,* trans. H. A. Bunker (London: Karnac Books, 1989), 20.

7. Oliver Sacks writes about a certain Dr. P.: "How could he, on the one hand, mistake his wife for a hat and, on the other, function, as apparently he still did, as a teacher at the Music School?" *The Man Who Mistook His Wife for a Hat* (New York: Harper Perennial, 1987), 10.

8. Mario Perniola writes: "To give oneself as a thing that feels and to take a thing that feels is the new experience that asserts itself on contemporary feeling, a radical and extreme experience that has its cornerstone in the encounter between philosophy and sexuality, and constitutes the key to understanding so many disparate manifestations of present-day culture and art." *Sex Appeal of the Inorganic: Philosophies of Desire in the Modern World,* trans. Massimo Verdicchio (New York: Continuum, 2004), 1.

9. See Elisabeth von Samsonow, "Regression als totale Progression. Regulative Zuzstandsveränderungen als kulturelle 'Triebfeder,'" in *Im Garten der Philosophie. Festschrift fur Hans-Dieter Bahr,* ed. Oya Erdogan and Dietmar Koch (Munich: Wilhelm Fink, 2005), 175–84.

10. See J. G. Frazer, *Totemism and Exogamy: A Treatise on the Early Forms of Superstition and Society,* vol. 1 (Wiltshire, England: Chippenham, 1994), 4ff.

11. Lévi-Strauss cites van Gennep, who writes: "Totemism has already taxed the wisdom and ingenuity of many scholars, and there are reasons to believe that it will continue to do so for many years." Quoted in Lévi-Strauss, *Totemism,* trans. Rodney Needham (Boston: Beacon, 1963), 4.

12. Lévi-Strauss writes: "The respect and the prohibitions connected with certain animals are explained, in a complex fashion, by the triad of ideas that the group is descended from an ancestor, that the god is incarnated in an animal, and that in mythical times there existed a relation of alliance between ancestor and god." *Totemism,* 29.

13. Lévi-Strauss uses, for example, the anecdote of the American "Rainbow Division" and its rainbow emblem to prove that the semantic structure has greater significance than the more difficult to grasp cultic and religious structures (*Totemism,* 7–8). In our view, however, this "anecdote" is a brief report on contemporary Western totemism; a truly totemistic construction emerges from the subject's relation to the hypnogenic "calories" of otherness.

14. Lévi-Strauss, 4.

15. Sir William Blackstone, *Commentaries on the Laws of England* (London, 1765); quoted in Ernst H. Kantorowicz, *The King's Two Bodies: A Study in Medieval Political Theology* (Princeton, N.J.: Princeton University Press, 1997), 13.

16. Wilhelm Wundt, *Elements of Folk Psychology: Outlines of a Psychological History of the Development of Mankind,* trans. E. L. Schaub (New York: Macmillan, 1916). See, in particular, chapter 2, "The Totemic Age," 116–39. Wundt mentions two conspicuous characteristics of totemism: first, "tribal divisions and tribal organization," and second, the cult of the animal as ancestor. He writes: "Thus, totemism leads to *chieftainship* as a regular institution—one that later, of course, proves to be among the foremost factors in the dissolution of the age that gave it birth. For chieftainship gives rise to political organization; the latter culminates in the state" (119).

17. Arnold Gehlen, *Man: His Nature and Place in the World,* trans. Clare McMillan and Karl Pillimer (New York: Columbia University Press, 1988), 391–92.

18. See Elisabeth von Samsonow, "Deus sine natura. Theophanie in der Fabrica," in *Puppe. Monster. Tod. Kulturelle Transformationsprozesse der Bio- und Informationstechnologien,* ed. Johanna Riegler and Christina Lammer (Vienna: Turia + Kant, 1998), 13–17.

19. Iamblichus, *De Mysteriis* [On the Mysteries], trans. Emma C. Clarke (Atlanta: Society of Biblical Literature, 2003), 281.

20. Iamblichus, *De Mysteriis,* 283.

21. Iamblichus writes: "And indeed, if any degree of kinship or likeness, whether near or remote, is present, this is sufficient for the contact of which we are now speaking. For nothing enters, even to a minimal extent, into likeness with the gods, to which the gods are not straightaway present and united." Iamblichus, 61.

22. Wilfried Seipel, ed., *Mumien aus dem alten Ägypten. Zur Mumienforschung im Kunsthistorischen Museum* (Vienna: Kunsthistorischen Museum, 1998).

23. "Technoia" refers to the form of consciousness arising from networks but in this context can be taken to refer more generally to the "apparatus function" operating within schizosomatic consciousness [TN].

24. This "passage" is to be understood as the genesis of consciousness that, conversely, is reciprocally related to the derivation of historical consciousness in the self-appearing of absolute knowledge. Where Hegel writes in *Phenomenology of Spirit* "that the *being of the 'I' is a Thing,*" I say on the contrary that *the being of the You is a Thing.* G. W. F. Hegel, *Phenomenology of Spirit,* trans. A. V. Miller (Oxford: Oxford University Press, 1977), 480.

25. See *Multitudes* 18 (2004), "Politiques de l'individuation: penser avec Simondon," and in particular the contributions of Paolo Virno, Isabelle Stengers, Alberto Toscano, Bernard Aspe, and Muriel Combes.

26. Or also, for example, the coyote woman described by Milagros Palma: "People say that she transforms into a she-coyote without her husband noticing. Always at midnight, under the protection of darkness, she transforms into a she-coyote while her

husband quietly slept." *Mythen und Weiblichkeit. Der Karneval von Masaya Nikaragua: das fest der elftausend Jungfrauen. Die Symbolik der Mestizenkultur in Nikaragua* (Berlin: Kramer, 1994), 95. Palma only offers the usual *ready-made* explanations for the woman's animal-metamorphosis: "The image of the woman as an animal is part of the symbolism that dominates patriarchal thought, in order to deny the woman any cultural and rational competence." Palma, *Mythen und Weiblichkeit*, 87. See also Theophrastus of Hohenheim, a.k.a. Paracelsus, *Liber de nymphis, sylphis, pygmaeis et salamandris*, ed. Robert-Henri Blaser (Bern: Francke, 1960).

27. Fraser, *Totemism and Exogamy*, vol. 1, 25.

28. Fraser, *Totemism and Exogamy*, vol. 1, 24.

29. The oracle remaining silent is the subject of Plutarch's text *De defectu oraculum*, "The Obsolescence of Oracles," in *Plutarch's Moralia*, vol. 5, trans. Frank C. Babbit (Cambridge, Mass.: Harvard University Press, 1989), 371f.

30. Lynn Thorndike, *A History of Magic and Experimental Science*, vol. 5 (New York: Columbia University Press, 1941), 10f.

31. Marija Gimbutas, *The Language of the Goddess* (San Francisco: Harper, 1995).

32. Shiva said to Vishnu: "You must abandon this erotic boar form." Quoted in Wendy Doniger O'Flaherty, *Siva: The Erotic Ascetic* (Oxford: Oxford University Press, 1973), 41.

33. Fraser, *Totemism and Exogamy*, vol. 1, 82.

34. Wundt writes: "The very moment, however, that marks the passing of the sacred animal into the useful animal also signalizes the end of the totemic era and the beginning of the age of heroes and gods." *Elements of Folk Psychology*, 121. Similarly, Freud comments: "The domestication of animals and the introduction of animal breeding seems everywhere to have brought an end to the strict and unadulterated totemism of primeval days." Sigmund Freud, "Totem and Taboo," *SE*, vol. 13, 136–37.

35. Moses Maimonides, *Guide for the Perplexed*, trans. Michael Friedländer (London: Trübner & Co., 1885), 23. On Maimonides's *"remotio corporis,"* see von Samsonow, "Deus sine natura," 16–18.

36. Mike Kelley, *The Uncanny*, with essays by Mike Kelley,

John C. Welchman, and Christoph Grunenberg (Cologne, Germany: Distributed Art Pub Incorporated, 2004).

37. Here God is "Mind beyond mind, word beyond speech, it is gathered up by no discourse, by no intuition, by no name. It is and it is as no other being. Cause of all existence, and therefore itself transcending all existence." Pseudo-Dionysius, "The Divine Names," in *The Complete Works,* trans. Colm Luibheid (Mahwah, N.J.: Paulist Press, 1987), 50.

38. Tilmann Habermas, *Geliebte Objekte. Symbole und Instrumente der Identitätsbildung* (Frankfurt: Suhrkamp, 1999).

39. Frazer comments: "We must constantly bear in mind that totemism is not a consistent philosophical system, the product of exact knowledge and high intelligence, rigorous in its definitions and logical in its deductions from them. On the contrary it is a crude superstition, the offspring of underdeveloped minds, indefinite, illogical, inconsistent." *Totemism and Exogamy,* vol. 4, 4.

40. The German "*nicht dicht sein*" plays on its literal meaning of "not being dense/thick," which refers to the "porous membranes" mentioned next, but is also a colloquial phrase meaning "not right in the head" [TN].

41. Leibniz, "Monadology," 221.

42. Leibniz, "Monadology," 221.

43. See Gottfried Semper, *Style in the Technical and Tectonic Arts; or, Practical Aesthetics,* vol. 1, trans. H. F. Mallgrave and M. Robinson (Los Angeles: Getty Publications, 2004), 250.

44. As Giordano Bruno writes in his treatise "A General Account of Bonding": "Then the soul, by its own power, desires first that it be moved, redirected and captured; second, once redirected and captured, it is enlightened by a ray of the beautiful or the good or the true; third, once enlightened and illuminated, it is inflamed by sensory desire; fourth, once inflamed, it desires to be united to the thing loved; fifth, once united, it is absorbed and incorporated; sixth, once incorporated, it then loses its previous form and in a sense abandons itself and takes on an alien quality; seventh, it, itself, is transformed by the qualities of the object through which it has moved and has thus been affected." *Cause, Principle and Unity and*

Essays on Magic, trans. and ed. R. J. Blackwell and R. de Lucca (Cambridge: Cambridge University Press, 2004), 173.

45. A. Niwinski, "Once More about the Possibility of the Application of a Bath in the Mummification Process," *Bulletins et Mémoires de la Société d'Anthropologie de Paris* 13 (1981): 371.

46. Niwinski, "Once More about the Possibility," 374, illustration 1.

47. Niwinski describes the image of the lake of fire as "a lake with corpses floating in it." Niwinski, 375.

3. Totemism and Sculpture

1. Hans Belting, *Likeness and Presence: A History of the Image Before the Age of Art,* trans. E. Jephcott (Chicago: University of Chicago Press, 1997), and "Aus dem Schatten des Todes. Bild und Körper in den Anfängen," in *Der Tod in den Weltkulturen und Weltreligionen,* ed. C. von Barloewen (Munich: Diederichs, 1996), 92–136.

2. Belting, "Aus dem Schatten des Todes," 95.

3. Belting, 110.

4. Belting, 97.

5. Belting, 107.

6. Belting writes: "In this situation Vernant decided to speak of a double, a doppelganger, either a living person or a corpse, which he distinguished from an 'image' in the stricter sense." Belting, 113.

7. Belting, 117.

8. Belting writes elsewhere: "The mediality of images involves a two-fold body reference. First, we conceive of media as symbolic or virtual bodies. Second, the media inscribe themselves upon our body experience and teach us self-perception or self-oblivion: in other words, they both remind us of our body and make us forget it." *An Anthropology of Images: Picture, Medium, Body,* trans. T. Dunlap (Princeton, N.J.: Princeton University Press, 2014), 11.

9. See Jan Assmann, *Ägyptische Geheimnisse* (Munich: Wilhelm Fink Verlag, 2004), esp. ch. 8, "Das Arkanum des Leichnams: Kultgeheimnisse und Weltgeheimisse," 179–84.

10. Minucius Felix, "Octavius," in *The Ante-Nicene Fathers*, vol. 4, ed. A. Roberts and J. Donaldson, revised and chronologically arranged with brief prefaces and occasional notes by A. Cleveland Coxe (New York: Christian Literature Publishing Co., 1885), ch. 23, available at http://www.earlychristianwritings.com/text/octavius .html. Hartmut Böhme also remarks: "The silversmiths and their workers are trying to incite a revolt against the Christians, because they believe business in devotional objects, selling reproductions of the Artemis cult image, is in danger. The Christians insist that any 'gods made with hands' are not gods." *Fetishism and Culture: A Different Theory of Modernity*, trans. Anna Galt (Boston: Walter de Gruyter, 2014), 121.

11. My thanks to Jan Assmann for pointing out that the forbidden "image" is specifically a product of the sculptural arts.

12. As Böhme writes: "A deep disquiet lies buried here, one which Europe is constantly beleaguered by in its discourse on fetishism: the power of our magical relations to things is evident not just in Modern Christianity, but also in Enlightened Modernity." *Fetishism and Culture*, 132.

13. Ernst Buschor, *Frühgriechische Jünglinge* (Munich: Piper, 1950).

14. Adolf Reinle, *Das stellvertretende Bildnis. Plastiken und Gemälde von der Antike bis ins 19. Jahrhundert* (Munich: Artemis Verlag, 1984), 18.

15. Reinle, *Das stellvertretende Bildnis*.

16. Reinle, 19.

17. Hans Belting writes: "The old controversy over the relation of image and art persists up to today. If a pictorial work was not absorbed into a work of art, one could easily suspect it to be anomalous, and not worth any art historical consideration. But if it was absorbed into art, then its concept was dispensable because the concept of art was already sufficient. In this sense Arthur Schopenhauer, to whom Schlosser referred, only saw art as the creation of artistic form. The old theories of image had already withered in the Renaissance. They ceded their claims to the newly emerging art theory, which wanted to interpret all visual products aesthetically." "Repräsentation und Anti-Repräsentation. Grab und Porträt in der Frühen Neuzeit," in *Quel corps? Eine Frage der Repräsentation*, ed.

H. Belting, D. Kamper, and M. Schulz (Munich: Wilhelm Fink Verlag, 2002), 33. See also Reinle, *Das stellvertretende Bildnis,* 10.

18. D. W. Winnicott writes: "There is a no-man's land between the subject and what is objectively perceived that is natural to infancy." *Human Nature* (New York: Schocken Books, 1988), 107. This "intermediate area" is a zone densely occupied by transitional objects, which are neither subject nor object but in any case form the ground of formal religious or artistic languages. "Out of these transitional phenomena develop much of what we variously allow and greatly value under the headings of religion and art and also the little madnesses which are legitimate at the moment, according to the prevailing cultural pattern." Winnicot, *Human Nature,* 107.

19. See also François Dagognet, *Le corps multiple et un* (Le Pléssis-Robinson, France: Laboratoires Delagrange-Synthélabo, 1992), ch. 2, "Une controverse interminabel: la bataille du corps."

20. Jacqueline Lichtenstein, *The Blind Spot: An Essay on the Relations between Painting and Sculpture in the Modern Age* (Los Angeles: Getty Publications, 2008).

21. The paragone controversy concerned the merits of sculpture vs. painting [TN].

22. In his book *What Is Life?* Schrödinger writes, "Now, I think, not many more words are needed to disclose the resemblance between a clockwork and an organism," and he continues by describing the "distribution of the cogs" in a cell. Similarly, the direction of his research into the "content" of chromosomes is also clear: "They are law code and executive power—or, to use another simile, they are architect's plan and builder's craft—in one." Erwin Schrödinger, *What Is Life?: With Mind and Matter and Autobiographical Sketches* (Cambridge: Cambridge University Press, 1992), 85, 22.

23. Jacques Lacan, *The Four Fundamental Concepts of Psychoanalysis,* book 11 of *The Seminar of Jacques Lacan,* ed. J.-A. Miller, trans. A. Sheridan (New York: W. W. Norton, 1998), 106.

24. Lacan, *Four Fundamental Concepts of Psychoanalysis,* 110.

25. Lacan, 113.

26. Dagognet, *Le corps multiple et un,* 113.

27. Diane M. O'Donoghue writes: "Burials in Hebei, Liaoning

and Inner Mongolia suggest that the article identified as a 'mirror' in the archeological literature was one category of disk-shaped object created, along with others, for use in ceremonies and funerary rites." *Reflection and Reception: The Origins of the Mirror in Bronze Age China* (Stockholm: Museum of Far Eastern Antiquities, 1990), 29.

28. Roland Barthes describes how modern *plastic* is an "alchemic substance" whose concept is inscribed in the history of *plasma*. Plastic's ability of transubstantiation is "total"; it can form "buckets as well as jewels." Roland Barthes, "Plastic," in *Mythologies*, trans. A. Lavers (New York: Noonday Press, 1972), 97.

29. See Elisabeth von Samsonow, "Menschen kneten. Überlegungen zum Stofftrieb bei Schiller," *Ästhetik und Kommunikation*, "Denken mit Schiller," 128 (2005): 81–90.

30. See the section "The Continuity of Greek and Medieval Art Was Assured By the Bond between *Caelatura* or Engraving and Illumination," in Marshall McLuhan, *The Gutenberg Galaxy: The Making of Typographic Man* (Toronto: University of Toronto Press, 1962), 61. McLuhan writes: "The work of the *caelator* and engraver is much more tactile than visual and corresponds to the new bias of our electric age" (63).

31. Madonna panel from S. Maria Maggiore, Florence, Coppo di Marcovaldo. Reproduced in Belting, *Likeness and Presence*, 387.

32. Belting, 387.

33. Belting, 389. Belting continues: "The genealogy of the sculptural and the painted images of the Virgin Enthroned has not escaped scholars, but it has not yet received a convincing explanation."

34. From the satyr play "Theoroi or Isthmiasta" by Aeschylus. Quoted in Sarah P. Morris, *Daidolos and the Origins of Greek Art* (Princeton, N.J.: Princeton University Press, 1992), 218.

35. From a Platonic comedy. Quoted in Morris, *Daidolos and the Origins of Greek Art*, 222.

36. From the satyr play "Eurystheus" by Euripides. Quoted in Morris, 222.

37. Corbin writes: "The statue that is the priest of the temple of the sun is thus a living priest-statue." *Le Livre des sept Statues. Textes édités et présentés par Pierre Lory* (Paris: L'Herne, 2003), 138n.

38. Corbin, *Le Livre des sept Statues*, 77f.

39. Corbin claims: "The art of the sculptor, of the 'producer of images,' aims to connect with theurgy." Corbin, 64.

40. Grégoire Loukianoff, "Une statue parlante, ou Oracle du dieu Re-Harmakhis," *Annales du service des Antiquités de l'Égypte (ASAE)* 36 (1936): 187–93.

41. Gérard Walter, *Caesar: A Biography* (New York: Scribner, 1952), 544. Quoted in Derek J. de Solla Price, "Automata and the Origins of Mechanism and Mechanistic Philosophy," *Technology and Culture* 5, no. 1 (1965): 11.

42. Solla Price, "Automata and the Origins of Mechanism," 10.

43. Ange-Pierre Leca, *Die Mumien. Zeugen ägyptischer Vergangenheit* (Vienna: Econ, 1982), 61ff.

44. Leca, *Die Mumien*, 62.

45. I am grateful to Philipp Levar for making his research available to me. Philipp worked on the mouth opening ritual while participating in my course "Der Hang zur Unsterblichkeit. Die Technik der Verfertigung von Mumien und andere Zugänge zur Kunst des soliden Raumes" ["The Immortality Tendency: The Technique of Fabricating Mummies and Other Approaches to the Art of Solid Space"] in the winter semester 2004.

46. Giordano Bruno, *Lampas triginta staturarum*, in *Opera latine conscripta*, vol. 3, facsimile reprint of the Fiorento, Tocco et al. edition, 1879–1891 (Stuttgart, Germany: Fromann-Holzberg, 1962), 5.

47. Bruno, *Lampas triginta staturarum*, 5.

48. Bruno writes: "Sensibilia enim figuratae species et opere phantasiae et imaginationis fabrefactae, per quas subinde volumes ea, quae a sensu sunt remotiora, significari. Itaque usum atque formam antiquae philosoiae et priscorum theologorum revocabimus, qui nimirum arcane naturae eiuscemodi typis et similitudinius velare consueverunt non tantum, quantum declarere, explicare, in seriem digerere et faciliori memoriae accomodare." Bruno, 8.

49. Henry Corbin, *Spiritual Body and Celestial Earth: From Mazdean Iran to Shi'ite Iran*, trans. N. Pearson (London: I. B. Taurus, 1990).

50. Like other theologians, Joseph Pascher had difficulties accepting Spenta Armaiti was female. He described her instead as

the "compassionate god" and strips her of her celestial earthiness. He declares her to be a being with masculine power, writing that it is "Sophia whose male power shows itself in that she 'sows souls and produces theory.'" Joseph Pascher, *Der Königsweg. Zu Wiedergeburt und Vergottung bei Philon von Alexandria* (Paderborn, Germany: Ferdinand Schöningh, 1931), 213.

51. Corbin writes: "We also wish to point out that Joseph Campbell, editor of the posthumous works of Heinrich Zimmer, recently indicated how one could discover, in the Zoroastrian dualist reform, the resurgence in Iran of religious factors that belong to the pre-Aryan matriarchal world." *Spiritual Body and Celestial Earth,* 277–78.

52. Walter Burkert shares these doubts about the oriental origin of the mystery religions, of which there is no trace in Anatolia, Egypt, or Iran, nor any sign of the three stereotypes that are always talked about in relation to the mysteries. Walter Burkert, *Ancient Mystery Cults* (Cambridge, Mass.: Harvard University Press, 1987), 2ff.

53. Accordingly, there is also a heavenly botany, on which Corbin quotes J. J. Modi, *The Religious Ceremonies and Customs of the Parsees,* in *Spiritual Body and Celestial Earth,* 32, 282n73.

54. Shaikh Muhammad Karim Khan Kirmani, *Spiritual Directives for the Use of the Faithful,* quoted in Corbin, *Spiritual Body and Celestial Earth,* 224.

55. Shaikh Ahmad Ahsa'i, quoted in Corbin, *Spiritual Body and Celestial Earth,* 193.

56. Corbin explains that the first body further divides into "*jasad A*" and "*jasad B,*" the second one into "*jism A*" and "*jism B,*" and that two of them—namely, "*jasad B*" (the *caro sprituelis*) and "*jism B,*" which is the supernatural body—"will both 'return.'" Corbin, *Spiritual Body and Celestial Earth,* 193.

57. Corbin, 218.

58. Corbin, 212–13. Corbin continues: "This is what is meant when the 'headstone of the tomb's bursting' is symbolically mentioned. For then the individual arises in his imperishable Form, shaking the terrestrial dust from his head" (218).

59. Corbin, 218.

60. Corbin, ch. I, "The Mazdean Imago Terrae (Geosophy and the Feminine Angels of the Earth)," 37–38.

61. "If you are capable of feeling, you yourself will perceive, in the pages of this book and its contents, a perfume emanating from the flowers of the world of Hurqalya." Shaikh Muhamad Karim Khan Kirmani, in Corbin, *Spiritual Body and Celestial Earth*, 239. "The paradise of each one of us is absolutely proper to him. It consists of the man's works and actions, which in the other world will appear to him in the form of houris, castles, and verdant trees. *That is why the Paradise of each of us is in the Heaven of his being*" (233).

62. Shaikh Ahmad Ahsa'i describes and illustrates this "metabolism" transforming the earthly into a glass or diamond-like body in detailed diagrams. Quoted in Corbin, *Spiritual Body and Celestial Earth*, 197–210.

63. Corbin, 28.

64. Corbin quotes Shaikh Ahmad Ahsa'i: "The structure of the archetypal body of man depends on his works and on the feeling he professes about the world and about God." Also: "From the First Day, each one has been given the Last Day." Quoted in Corbin, 222, 226.

65. In the symbolism of the garden this process appears as follows: "The envoy of the light destroys the soul's five beds of darkness and the poisonous trees growing in them; the five elements of light-nature once more become visible in their purity, and in them he plants five luminous trees that bear the fruit of immortality. In this way the whole constitutes a garden in the middle of which a palace with a throne room arises for the messenger, and around it other palaces for his companions; . . . And in the garden he plants all manner of fragrant and precious plants." Richard Reitzenstein, *Das iranische Erlösungsmysterium* (Bonn, Germany: Marcus and Weber, 1921), 144.

66. See the diagrams of transformation of the two bodies *jasad* and *jism* described by Ahsa'i, in Corbin, *Spiritual Body and Celestial Earth*, 202–3.

67. Richard Reitzenstein writes: "The Manichaean designation of the Mother deity as 'Mother of the living' refers to the same idea, and the personally composed life is juxtaposed with a

similarly personally composed death." *Das iranische Erlösungsmysterium,* 137.

68. Reitzenstein, 54.

69. As Georges Didi-Huberman puts it: "This goes so far that their figurative art is largely governed by a mental and procedural structure that is entirely oriented around the replica." *Ähnlichkeit und Berührung. Archäologie, Anachronismus und die Modernität des Abdrucks* (Cologne: DuMont, 1999), 29.

70. Didi-Huberman, *Ähnlichkeit und Berührung,* 31.

71. Didier Anzieu, *The Skin Ego* (New Haven, Conn.: Yale University Press, 1989).

72. Heinrich Weinstock translates *paidagogos* as "care-giver" [*Pfleger*], which makes him the counterpart of the wet nurse and therefore inconspicuous. Sophocles, *Elektra,* in *Vollständige Dramentexte,* ed. J. Schondorff (Vienna: Langen-Müller, 1965), 33.

73. The Kitto translation refers to the market of "Apollo," but the author quotes from the Schondorff edition, Sophocles, *Elektra,* in *Vollständige Dramentexte,* 33, which instead refers to the "wolf-god" [TN].

74. The author is playing on a repetition of consonants that only exists in German: "*Mädchen-Menschen: MMenschen*" [TN].

75. Peter Dinzelbacher writes: "That animals are frequently at the center of successful films and television series (*Lassie, A Dog Named Beethoven,* etc.) is something that has happened only in the last decades, and might be explained by the increasing 'co-subjectivity' mentioned above." *Mensch und Tier in der Geschichte Europas* (Stuttgart, Germany: Alfred Kröner Verlag, 2000), xiii. Dinzelbacher understands "co-subjectivity" as the recent phenomenon of animals being able to touch human feelings: "More than 150 years have passed since Jacob Grimm outlined an attitude towards animals to which many in Europe today would probably subscribe. Over the rift of their biological and mental differences animals are not seen as distanced objects but as 'co-subjects' whose aptitudes touch us and call forth our concern" (ix).

76. Françoise Dolto writes of the stuffed animal: "In contrast, the stuffed animal plays the role of a passive ersatz-object of the child, while the child takes on the active role of the mother and the

father. For boys and girls the stuffed animal represents the symbolic mass of the dyad—stuffed animals are subjectively humanized
fetishes." *Weibliche Sexualität. Die Libido und ihr weibliches Schicksal,* trans.
W. and A. Wohnhaas (Stuttgart, Germany: Klett-Cotta, 2000),
97.

4. The Labyrinth

1. Mary Jacobus, *First Things: The Maternal Imaginary in Literature, Art
and Psychoanalysis* (New York: Routledge, 1995), 7.

2. Friedrich Nietzsche, "Ariadne's Complaint," in *Dithyrambs of
Dionysus,* bilingual edition, trans. R. J. Hollingdale (London: Anvil
Press Poetry, 2001), 65. See also Christiane Zintzen, "Die Akte
Ariadne: A Multiple Choice of a Multiple Voice," in *Ariadne im Garn.
Ria nackt. Eine Racheoper,* ed. R. Deppe, B. Hell, and O. Schmierer
(Vienna: Triton, 2002), 65–80.

3. Robert Graves, *The Greek Myths: The Complete and Definitive Edition*
(London: Penguin, 2011), 312.

4. The principles of totemism that Freud takes from Wilhelm
Wundt are found in "The Return of Totemism in Childhood":
"The members of a totem clan call themselves by the name of their
totem, and *commonly believe themselves to be actually descended from it.*" Sigmund Freud, "Totem and Taboo," SE, vol. 13, 104.

5. Claude Lévi-Strauss describes the synchrony of human
and animal grammar as the characteristic of totemism, but he
retains a structuralist conception of this, enhanced into a nom-
inalism, in his theory of *replacements* or the hypnotic exchange of
subjectivity that realizes a symbolic identity. The victim, however,
introduces an abnormality within the so-called homological relationship between the natural and "cultural" series. See Claude
Lévi-Strauss, *The Savage Mind,* trans. George Weidenfeld (New York:
Columbia University Press, 1966), 223–28.

6. Since then, the girl has been offensively displayed but no
longer seen: "Maiden-goddesses are far more typical of Greek religion than boy-gods or even, perhaps, divine youths. Divine maid-
ens are in fact so typical of this religion that it cannot be called either a 'Father religion' or a 'Mother religion,' or yet a combination

of both. It is as though the Olympian order had thrust the great Mother-Goddesses of olden time into the background for the sole purpose of throwing the divine Komi into sharper relief." Karl Kerenyi, *Science of Mythology: Essays on the Myth of the Divine Child and the Mysteries of Eleusis,* trans. R. F. C. Hull (New York: Pantheon, 1948), 148.

7. Manfred Schmeling, *Der labyrinthische Diskurs. Vom Mythos zum Erzählmodell* (Frankfurt: Athenäum, 1987), 38.

8. Gustav René Hocke, *Die Welt als Labyrinth* (Reinbek, Germany: Rowohlt, 1987), esp. 53–66; and Hermann Kern, *Labyrinthe. Erscheinungsformen und Deutungen. Gegenwart eines Urbildes* (Munich: Prestel, 1999).

9. "The hypothesis that 'Labyrinthos' was originally a dance whose movements were fixed in a graphic figure appears fully proven." Kern, *Labyrinthe,* 9.

10. See Elisabeth von Samsonow, "Projektile in Splendid Shape," in *TUMULT* 23 (1988): 24–36.

11. On the invention and meaning of the spear thrower, see André Leroi-Gourhan, *Gesture and Speech,* trans. A. Bostock Berger (Cambridge, Mass.: MIT Press, 1993).

12. Jacques Derrida and Gianni Vattimo, eds., *Religion,* trans. D. Webb et al. (Palo Alto, Calif.: Stanford University Press, 1998).

13. See Charles Mopsick, *Les grands textes de la cabale, Les rites qui font Dieu. Pratiques religieuses, efficacité théurgique dans la cabale des origins au milieu du XVIIIe siècle* (Lagrasse, France: Verdier, 1993).

14. See Helmut Jaskolski, *Das Labyrinth. Symbol der Angst, der Wiedergeburt und der Befreiung* (Stuttgart, Germany: Kreuzverlag, 1997).

15. Johann Amos Comenius, *Das Labyrinth der Welt und das Paradies des Herzens, mit einer Handzeichnung* (Jena, Germany: E. Diederichs, 1908). Hermann Kern writes of Comenius's famous drawing of the labyrinth: "The city—as an image of the world—does not have a labyrinthine shape, the title is meant metaphorically." *Labyrinthe,* 296.

16. See Graves, who writes: "In one sense the labyrinth from which Daedalus and Icarus escaped was the mosaic floor with the maze pattern, which they had to follow in the ritual partridge

dance." *Greek Myths*, 316. Furthermore, Minos "locked him [Daedalus] up for a while in the Labyrinth. . . . But Daedalus made a pair of wings for himself, and another for Icarus. . . . Then he slipped his arms into his own pair of wings and they flew off. 'Follow me closely,' he cried, 'do not set your own course!'

As they sped away from the island in a north-easterly direction, flapping their wings, the fishermen, shepherds, and ploughmen who gazed upwards mistook them for gods." *Greek Myths*, 312–13.

17. Hermann Kern's *Labyrinthe* reproduces a seventeenth-century illustration of the Christian soul in the labyrinth by Herman Hugo (300), a similar emblem of a labyrinth by Georg Thomas Hopfer from 1680 (301), and slightly later emblems by Joseph Semek (302) and Antonius Andreas von Krzesimowsky (305).

5. The Four Pre-oedipal Objects

1. S. Françoise Fontisi-Ducroux, *Dédale. Mythologie de l'artisan en grèce ancienne* (Paris: François Maspéro, 1975), ch. 2, "Statues vivantes," 96–117.

2. S. Françoise Fontesi-Ducroux, "Die technische Intelligenz des griechischen Handwerkers," trans. W. Rappl, *HEPHAISTOS, Kritische Zeitschrift zu Theorie und Praxis der Archäologie und angrenzender Gebiete* 11–12 (1992–1993): 98–100. On the flight over the labyrinth, see 98.

3. Nora and Gerhard Fischer have documented MIT's Daedalian flight experiment in their Daedalus project, *Museum vom Menschen oder wo sich Kunst und Wissenschaft wieder finden* (Vienna: Daedalus, 1996).

4. One can understand the Daedalian technique as similar to Heideggerian *Ent-fernung* [de-severance], as a contouring of *Näherung* [nearing]. See Till Platte, *Die Konstellation des Übergangs. Technik und Würde bei Heidegger* (Berlin: Duncker and Humblot, 2004), 144. The concept of technology outlined by Heidegger is absolutely central to our investigation. Heidegger did not, however, connect the Daedalian drive back to the reciprocal suppression of the symbolic orders

of the Mother and the Father and so did not see it as a motive for technical evolution.

5. "Das Ende der Menschenopfer," in *Die Konstellation des Uber-gangs. Technik un Würde bei Heidegger,* ed. F. Rottensteiner (Frankfurt: Fischer, 1989), 153.

6. "Das Ende der Menschenopfer," 155.

7. "Das Ende der Menschenopfer," 155.

8. See Gerburg Treusch-Dieter, *Die Heilige Hochzeit. Studien zur Totenbraut* (Herbolzheim, Germany: Centaurus, 2004), 186.

9. Bruce Lerro argues that cartography is the result of this devaluation, namely "the application of spatial orientation to the physical world . . . without reference to the bodily location of individuals . . . as if the land were a space not a place." *From Earth Spirits to Sky Gods: The Socioecological Origins of Monotheism, Individualism, and Hyperabstract Reasoning from the Stone Age to the Axial Iron Age* (New York: Lexington Books, 2000), 99.

10. As Apollo declares in Aeschylus's *Eumenides*: "The woman you call the mother of the child/ is not the parent, just a nurse to the seed/ the new-sown seed that grows and swells inside her." Aeschylus, *The Eumenides,* trans. R. Fagles (Harmondsworth, U.K.: Penguin Books, 1966), lines 666–68, 260.

11. Freud writes: "The oldest form of sacrifice, older than the use of fire and the knowledge of agriculture, was the sacrifice of animals." Sigmund Freud, *Totem and Taboo, SE,* vol. 13, 134.

12. Walter Burkert, *Homo Necans: The Anthropology of Ancient Greek Sacrificial Ritual and Myth,* trans. Peter Bing (Berkeley: University of California Press, 1983), 20–31.

13. Especially noteworthy in this respect is Roger Friedland, "Drag Kings at the Totem Ball: The Erotics of Collective Representation in Émile Durkheim and Sigmund Freud," in *The Cambridge Companion to Durkheim,* ed. J. C. Alexander and P. Smith (Cambridge: Cambridge University Press, 2005), 239–73.

14. Lerro, *From Earth Spirits to Sky Gods,* 108.

15. Alfred Lotka, *Elements of Physical Biology* (Baltimore: Williams and Wilkins, 1925), 16.

16. Lotka, *Elements of Physical Biology,* 17.

17. Vladimir I. Vernadsky, *The Biosphere,* revised and annotated by M. McMenamin (1926; repr. New York: Copernicus, 1997), 60.

18. Vernadsky, *The Biosphere,* 61.

19. Gilbert Simondon, *L'individuation psychice et collective* (Paris: PUF, 1999), 63, quoted in Jacques Roux, "Penser le politique avec Simondon," *Multitudes* 18 (2004): 49.

20. Jan Kott, *Gott-Essen. Interpretationen griechischer Tragödien* (Munich: Piper Verlag, 1982).

21. What doubts the Son of God to sit and eat?

These are not fruits forbidden; no interdict

Defends the touching of these viands pure;

Their taste no knowledge works, at least of evil,

But life serves, destroys life's enemy,

Hunger, with sweet restorative delight.

All these are spirits of air, and woods, and springs,

Thy gentle ministers, who come to pay

Thee homage, and acknowledge thee their Lord;

What doubt'st thou, Son of God? Sit down and eat.

John Milton, *Paradise Regained,* in *The Complete English Poems,* ed. and intro. by G. Campbell (New York: Alfred A. Knopf, 1992), book 2, lines 368–78, 468.

22. Milton, *Paradise Regained,* book 4, lines 1–6, 486.

23. Milton, book 1, lines 342–52, 453.

24. The Renaissance philosopher Pietro Pomponazzi uses the formula "the world is an animal" to describe the characteristics of the body of the Earth. Despite his immanentist premises, however, he has a tendency to depreciate it by concentrating like a child (he is "fixated" in Melanie Klein's terms) on the "excrement" hidden in the earth. See Michael Boenke, *Körper, Spiritus, Geist. Psychologie vor Descartes* (Paderborn, Germany: Wilhelm Fink, 2005), esp. ch. 3.4 "'Die Welt ist ein Tier.' Pompanazzis Anschluß an stoische Lehren in *De fato*," 57–60.

25. Jean Baudrillard, *Symbolic Exchange and Death,* trans. I. Hamilton-Grant (London: Sage Publications, 1993), esp. "The Exchange with Death in the Primitive Order," 131–32.

26. To use a concept from Thomist metaphysics, where being,

truth, and beauty are convertible. Giambattista Vico makes *verum* and *factum* convertible. In our research the bodies of the bodies producing bodies are convertible according to the logic of the ontology of the Mother.

27. See Till Platte's argument in "§13 a) The 'shock' in becoming aware of the decay of the essence of the sensible living being into a 'technologised' animal." *Die Konstellation des Übergangs*, 173–89.

28. For this reason Charles Stein asks: "Is Persephone here the goddess of that which is most forlorn?" *Persephone Unveiled: Seeing the Goddess and Freeing Your Soul* (Berkeley, Calif.: North Atlantic Books, 2006), 146.

29. On the day I wrote this sentence a girl named Natascha Kampusch, one of the most searched for persons in Austria, reappeared after eight years of "captivity." A man had kidnapped her and locked her into a pit he had prepared underneath his garage.

30. Sigmund Freud, "Referat über Obersteiner, Der Hypnotismus mit besonderer Berücksichtigung seiner klinischen und forensischen Bedeutung" (1887), translated by M. Solms as "Previously-Untranslated Review by Freud of a Monograph on Hypnotism," *International Journal of Psycho-Analysis* 70 (1989): 401.

31. François Dagognet declines this binomial through the contemporary "bi-pole 'sensory-brain.'" *Changement de perspective. Le dedans et le dehors* (Paris: La Table Ronde/Contretemps, 2002), 23–84. See also the chapter "Le renfort par l'Historie des techniques," esp. 152.

32. "Society in its entirely is becoming feminine to the extent that discrimination against women is coming to an end (as it is for madmen, children, etc., being the normal consequence of the logic of exclusion)." Baudrillard, *Symbolic Exchange and Death*, 97.

33. The main character of Fritz Lang's film *Metropolis* (1927) [TN].

34. Josef Breuer and Sigmund Freud, *Studies on Hysteria (1893–1895), SE*, vol. 2, 203.

35. As Georges Didi-Huberman points out: "This means that the uterus is endowed with the capacity of movement. This means that the woman's sort of member is *animal.*" *Invention of Hysteria: Charcot*

and the Photographic Iconography of the Salpêtrière, trans. A. Hartz (Cambridge, Mass.: MIT Press, 2003), 68.

36. Freud's expression for hysteria, quoted in Didi-Huberman, *Invention of Hysteria,* 67.

37. See the extensive analysis by Elisabeth Bronfen, *The Knotted Subject: Hysteria and Its Discontents* (Princeton, N.J.: Princeton University Press, 1998).

38. Didi-Huberman, *Invention of Hysteria,* 68.

39. "O subtle fire, soul of the world/ Benefactor electricity/ You fill the air, the earth, the waves/ The sky and its immensity." From a French newspaper from 1784, quoted by Paolo Bertulucci, "Promethean Sparks: Electricity and the Order of Nature in the Eighteenth Century," in *Variantology I: On Deep Time Relations of Arts, Sciences and Technologies,* ed. S. Zielinski and S. M. Wagnermaier (Cologne, Germany: Walther König, 2005), 41.

40. As Paolo Bertulucci writes: "Every 'electrician' was aware that the human body is a conductor of electricity, and experiments that exploited this property proliferated. With the aid of a mechanical device that acted as a source of friction (the electrical machine), many amusing experiments could be easily performed. Electricity could turn bewigged ladies into electrifying Venuses whose sparkling would not be forgotten." Bertulucci, "Promethean Sparks," 41.

ELISABETH VON SAMSONOW is an artist, writer, curator, and professor of philosophical and historical anthropology at the Academy of Fine Arts Vienna.

ANITA FRICEK is an Austrian artist based in Vienna.

STEPHEN ZEPKE is an independent researcher.